Called and Ordained

Called and Ordained

LUTHERAN PERSPECTIVES ON THE OFFICE OF THE MINISTRY

Edited by

TODD NICHOL and MARC KOLDEN

Fortress Press   Minneapolis

To Teachers and Mentors
E. CLIFFORD NELSON and HENRY E. HORN

CALLED AND ORDAINED
Lutheran Perspectives on the Office of Ministry

Scripture quotations unless otherwise noted are from the Revised Standard Version of the Bible, copyright © 1946, 1952, and 1971 by the Division of Christian Education of the National Council of Churches.

Quotations from *The Book of Concord*, copyright © 1959 Fortress Press, are used by permission of the publisher, Fortress Press.

Cover design: Jim Gerhard

Library of Congress Cataloging-in-Publication Data

Called and ordained : Lutheran perspectives on the office of the
  ministry / edited by Todd Nichol and Marc Kolden.
      p.   cm.
  ISBN 0-8006-2427-0
  1. Lutheran Church—Clergy. 2. Clergy—Office.   I. Nichol, Todd
W., 1951- . II. Kolden, Marc.
  BX8071.C34   1990
  253—dc20   89-78460
                                                                    CIP

The paper used in this publication meets the minimum requirements of American National Standard for Information Sciences—Permanence of Paper for Printed Library Materials, ANSI Z329.48-1984.   ∞™

Manufactured in the U.S.A.   AF 1-2427
  94   93   92   91   90   1   2   3   4   5   6   7   8   9   10

Contents

Preface   vii

Abbreviations   ix

Contributors   xi

PART 1
EXEGETICAL AND HISTORICAL PERSPECTIVES

1. Roy A. Harrisville • Ministry in the New Testament   3

2. James Arne Nestingen • Ministry in the Early Church   25

3. Jane E. Strohl • Ministry in the Middle Ages and the Reformation   35

4. Robert Kolb • Ministry in Martin Luther and the Lutheran
   Confessions   49

5. James H. Pragman • Ministry in Lutheran Orthodoxy and Pietism   67

6. Walter Sundberg • Ministry in Nineteenth-Century European
   Lutheranism   77

7. Todd Nichol • Ministry and Oversight in American Lutheranism   93

PART 2
THEMATIC PERSPECTIVES

8. Gerhard O. Forde • The Ordained Ministry   117

CONTENTS

9. JOSEPH A. BURGESS • An Evangelical Episcopate?   137

10. MICHAEL ROGNESS • The Office of Deacon in the Christian Church   151

11. GRACIA GRINDAL • Getting Women Ordained   161

12. ROLAND D. MARTINSON • The Pastoral Ministry   181

13. MARC KOLDEN • Ministry and Vocation for Clergy and Laity   195

AFTERWORD

TODD NICHOL and MARC KOLDEN • Perspectives in Perspective   211

Preface

It is no secret that Lutherans in the United States are in turmoil over the theology and practice of the ordained ministry. While their earlier history records comparatively little controversy over these matters, they have since the middle of the twentieth century argued intensely about the ministry, and in 1988 the newly merged Evangelical Lutheran Church in America (ELCA) commissioned an official study of the ministry as a condition of its merger. The Lutheran Church-Missouri Synod (LC-MS) is also currently engaged in official discussion of the public ministry.

High interest in the public ministry is not, however, confined to the American Lutheran churches. Indeed, Christian theologians and ecclesiastics around the world appear to be occupied and preoccupied with questions about the ministry. The inclusion of a controversial section on ministry in the widely discussed *Baptism, Eucharist, and Ministry* published by the Faith and Order Commission of the World Council of Churches is one sign of this interest. Intensive conversation about ministry in a variety of other ecumenical discussions is another.

This book, however, was written by Lutherans primarily for Lutherans. It is, in fact, specifically addressed to the people of the Lutheran churches of the United States. At the same time, because Lutheranism is by definition, even if it has not always been in practice, an expression of the larger Christian tradition, these authors write for an ecumenical audience as well. It is precisely by virtue of its Lutheran particularity that this is an ecumenical book. While the contributions of other Christian traditions and the contemporary ecumenical movement are not ignored, they are not the focus of these essays. That would require a volume of its own.

This book was conceived in the conviction that the Lutheran tradition, although plural in expression, speaks with a consistent integrity about the office of the ministry. The essayists who write here, and whose articles were all written specifically for this volume, have set themselves the task of inquiring into the sources of their tradition and developing an understanding of the public ministry of the church with reference to the fundamental Lutheran conviction and confession: that the ungodly are justified by faith alone. In mining the historical and theological resources of the Lutheran tradition, their intent has been to search out the elements of a positive, evangelical alternative to notions of the ministry not compatible with a Lutheran confession of faith. Their hope is that they can contribute to the development of a coherent notion of the public ministry of the church decisively shaped by its reference to the chief article of the evangelical faith. They understand this to be the best contribution they can make not only to their own church but to larger ecumenical circles as well. These authors do not, however, present a comprehensive statement on the ministry nor do they all agree with one another on controverted points. Readers will want to note that these writers did not read one another's essays as they worked and that in their final comments the editors write only in their own names.

All of these authors write for interested lay people of the church, pastors, and seminary students, who are asked to ponder the question of ministry from the perspective of their experiences as members of the church. Pastors particularly, from their perspectives as working ministers, are invited to consider the findings of the theologians who write from another angle of vision. In many ways church pastors know much more about these questions than these authors. Our hunch is that their experience and the theological traditions we share in common will resonate in harmony with one another. We hope that our contributions will help to deepen and enrich their understanding of their office as called and ordained ministers of the church of Christ. Moreover, we hope that our work will challenge, stimulate, and encourage these co-workers to persist in the one essential task to which the church has called them: the service of the Word of God who justifies the ungodly by faith alone.

We thank those who have written for this volume. We thank a number of other members of the faculty and staff at Luther Northwestern Theological Seminary and the staff at Fortress Press who also helped bring this book into existence. We are grateful to Dr. John A. Hollar, the late Editorial Director of Fortress Press, who died before this book appeared in print. He played an important role in putting this collection into its present form. His death is a loss to our church and to the world of theological scholarship. Finally we offer personal thanks to the two called and ordained ministers of the Lutheran church, mentors and models to many, to whom this volume is dedicated.

TODD NICHOL
MARC KOLDEN

Abbreviations

ALC	American Lutheran Church
ALCW	American Lutheran Church Women
Ap	Apology of the Augsburg Confession. In *BC*.
BC	*The Book of Concord: The Confessions of the Evangelical Lutheran Church*. Trans. and ed. by Theodore G. Tappert. Philadelphia: Fortress Press, 1959.
BEM	*Baptism, Eucharist, and Ministry*. Geneva: World Council of Churches, 1982.
CA	Augsburg Confession. In *BC*.
COCU	Consultation on Church Union
CTCR	Commission on Theology and Church Relations
DTS	Division of Theological Studies
ELC	Evangelical Lutheran Church
ELCA	Evangelical Lutheran Church in America
FC	Formula of Concord. In *BC*.
FC, SD	Formula of Concord, Solid Declaration. In *BC*.
KJV	King James Version of the Bible
LC	Large Catechism. In *BC*.
LCA	Lutheran Church in America
LC-MS	Lutheran Church–Missouri Synod
LCUSA	Lutheran Council in the USA
LCW	Lutheran Church Women
LW	*Luther's Works*. American edition. Eds. J. Pelikan and H. Lehmann. St. Louis: Concordia; Philadelphia: Fortress Press, 1955-1986.
LWF	Lutheran World Federation
RSV	Revised Standard Version of the Bible
SA	Smalcald Articles. In *BC*.

ABBREVIATIONS

SC	Small Catechism. In *BC*.
Tr	Treatise on the Power and Primacy of the Pope. In *BC*.
UCC	United Church of Christ
ULCA	United Lutheran Church in America
WA	*D. Martin Luthers Werke*. Kritische Gesamtaugabe (Weimar A.). Böhlau, 1883 to the present.
WCC	World Council of Churches

Contributors

JOSEPH A. BURGESS
Former Executive Director, Division of Theological Studies
Lutheran Council in the U.S.A.
Philadelphia, Pennsylvania

GERHARD O. FORDE
Professor of Systematic Theology
Luther Northwestern Theological Seminary
Saint Paul, Minnesota

GRACIA GRINDAL
Associate Professor of Pastoral Theology and Ministry
Luther Northwestern Theological Seminary
Saint Paul, Minnesota

ROY A. HARRISVILLE
Professor of New Testament
Luther Northwestern Theological Seminary
Saint Paul, Minnesota

ROBERT KOLB
Professor of History and Religion
Concordia College
Saint Paul, Minnesota

MARC KOLDEN
Professor of Systematic Theology
Luther Northwestern Theological Seminary
Saint Paul, Minnesota

ROLAND D. MARTINSON
Professor of Pastoral Theology and Ministry
Luther Northwestern Theological Seminary
Saint Paul, Minnesota

JAMES ARNE NESTINGEN
Associate Professor of Church History
Luther Northwestern Theological Seminary
Saint Paul, Minnesota

TODD NICHOL
Assistant Professor of Church History
Luther Northwestern Theological Seminary
Saint Paul, Minnesota

JAMES H. PRAGMAN
Pastor and Director of Ministries
Saint John Lutheran Church
Seward, Nebraska

MICHAEL ROGNESS
Associate Professor of Pastoral Theology and Ministry
Luther Northwestern Theological Seminary
Saint Paul, Minnesota

JANE E. STROHL
Assistant Professor of Church History
Luther Northwestern Theological Seminary
Saint Paul, Minnesota

WALTER SUNDBERG
Associate Professor of Church History
Luther Northwestern Theological Seminary
Saint Paul, Minnesota

EXEGETICAL AND HISTORICAL PERSPECTIVES

Part

1

Ministry
in the
New Testament

1

ROY A. HARRISVILLE

It has been stated that the topic of ministry assumes center stage when churches or fellowships that are living apart prepare for union. The reason such a topic emerges on these occasions may not be altogether or even primarily theological; whether it ever was such may be open to question. There is no doubt, however, that the persons most profoundly affected by alterations in ecclesiastical structure have been those of whom "ministry" is most often predicated, that is, the clergy and related personnel. In recent history, questions related to rank or status have assumed the order of first importance among the persons most affected by change. This need not reflect lack of interest in matters biblical or theological. It could reflect an agreement in fundamentals which makes possible attention to what is not primary. Still, primary questions are capable of using what is secondary or peripheral to call attention to themselves. This power to "manipulate" or to be evoked is what guarantees to primary questions their primacy. They cannot be stilled, which is why we call them primary. The question of the theological status of ministry is just such a primary question. This is not to say it is the first among primary questions touching Christian faith and confession, or that it is primary because it is a theological question. Not all theological questions are primary. Some may be stilled, and quite easily. The question of ministry will not die because it is linked to events in which the Christian community believes it encounters God. In the words of one Reformation confession, through the office of ministry God gives the Holy Spirit who works faith in those who hear the gospel (CA 5, *BC* 31).

Section one of this study will begin by dealing with the terms for "ministry" in the New Testament. Various uses of the terms will be noted, and conclusions drawn respecting their first, primary, or original definition. The variety of persons described as serving or ministering will be indicated, and then conclusions drawn respecting those factors that determine the type or species of ministry. Section two will deal with the use of the terms for ministry of the gospel,

3

and conclusions drawn regarding the relation between ministry and the divine activity that it serves as means. Section three will attempt an answer to the question whether certain sections of the New Testament reflect a development beyond any previously described, in sections one and two, and which would justify applying to these writings the epithet "early catholicism." Section four will treat the reflections on the variety of structure in the New Testament, and section five will set down the biblical-theological conclusions of this study.

I. USE AND DEFINITIONS OF MINISTRY

The English Term

"Ministry" derives from a Latin term (by way of the Old French?), introduced into our language amid the flood of foreign expressions sweeping England in the thirteenth century and beyond. John Wycliffe's translation of the Latin Bible (fourteenth century) may have given entree to the term in religious circles. In the Vulgate, the noun *ministerium* and its congeners are most often used (ninety-five times) to translate the Greek New Testament term *diakonia* and its relatives. Though modern English translations do not reflect that ancient practice (the RSV, for example, employs the term "ministry" only twenty-five times), adherence to it up to and within the KJV is no doubt responsible for the term's permanent home in our ecclesiastical vocabulary.

The Greek Terms and Their Uses

Together, the Greek nouns *diakonos, diakonia* and the verb *diakoneō* appear one hundred times in the New Testament: forty-three times in the letters attributed to Paul; forty-one times in the four Gospels and Acts; and sixteen times in the remainder. What is at once striking is the variety of their uses, which may be described as the (1) deipnic, (2) economic, (3) evangelic,[1] and (4) charismatic. The following passages illustrate the various types: 1) Luke 10:40 ("Martha was distracted with much *serving*"); 2) Rom. 15:25 ("I am going to Jerusalem with *aid* for the saints"); 3) Acts 20:24 ("if only I may accomplish my course and the *ministry* which I received . . . to testify to the gospel of the grace of God"); and 4) Rom. 12:6-7 ("having gifts that differ according to the grace given to us, let us use them . . . if *service*, in our serving"). As the illustrations suggest, the verb reflects the greater variety of usage. In only four instances is the term "ministry" or its relatives used in the negative sense—in Gal. 2:17 ("if, in our endeavor to be justified in Christ, we ourselves were found to be sinners, is Christ then an *agent* of sin?"), in 2 Cor. 3:7 and 9 ("the *dispensation* of death . . . the *dispensation* of condemnation"), and in the reference to Satan's servants in 2 Cor. 11:15.

4

The Common Assumption and the Lexical Challenge

Of these four dominant types in the New Testament, the evangelic (forty-nine times) and the economic (twenty-four times) have the lion's share, followed by the deipnic (nineteen times), and trailed by the charismatic (four times). An examination of the lexicons, however, would suggest that the deipnic use is earliest. H. W. Beyer's article in Kittel's *Theologisches Wörterbuch* refers to *diakoneō* as first appearing in Herodotus (fifth century B.C.E.), its original meaning to "wait at table."[2] But in the single instance in which that verb appears in Herodotus, the use is not deipnic.[3] In the three instances in which the ancient historian uses the noun (*diakonos*), it appears only once in a meal setting.[4] Bauer's lexicon cites the verb *diakoneō* as in use since Sophocles and Herodotus, sets the definition "to wait" in italics, adds in Gothic script "at table," and refers to various authors from the sixth century B.C. to the third century A.D. who employ the term within the context of a meal, allowing the reader to assume that the first or original usage of the term is deipnic.[5] In Sophocles, however, the verb *diakoneō* does not at all appear in a meal context,[6] and in only one instance can his use of the noun (*diakonos*) be termed deipnic, and that with some imagination.[7] While it is true that the deipnic use dominates in the remainder of authors cited (in Bauer ten in number), in a majority of instances the context is already that of a meal or symposium (cf. Athenaeus's *Deipnosophistes*). This would suggest discretion in the matter of assigning to our terms any first, primary, or original definition beyond the simple meaning of "to serve," a discretion observed by one old etymologist who simply penned beneath the Greek verb the words, "in general it means to serve, to minister," then added, "in whatever manner this is done."[8] Among the contemporaries of Paul, Epictetus never employs the terms in the deipnic sense. Josephus uses them at least sixty-eight times, but only six times in the context of a meal, and Philo, who uses the terms twenty-three times, uses them only twice in such a context.[9]

If the argument seems belabored, it is because of the exegetical or theological consequences of assuming that in every instance of its occurrence within the New Testament, "the original meaning of the term 'to serve at table' is never quite lost," or that "the persistent meaning indicates that the Christian office (i.e., of *diakonos*) has its origin in the common meal."[10] From this it is but a short step to identifying the term with a particular ecclesiastical office or function, such as officiating at the Eucharist.

We do not know who first insisted upon the deipnic as the original usage of the term—perhaps a Latinist who superimposed the meaning of *famulare* or *ministrare* upon the Greek—but the contention is now the common stock of exegesis and of the history of early Christianity.[11]

Further Challenge in the Variety of Subjects and Objects

Another tendency in the investigation of our terms is to ignore the great variety of their subjects, and thus to reduce the variety of services or ministries which those subjects reflect. The result of this reduction is that the subjects and their activities are rendered analogous to contemporary ecclesiastical structure. But in fact the number of those referred to as serving or ministering in the New Testament is legion. In addition to the names of persons we have come to expect to be linked to our terms—Christ, the apostles, Paul, Timothy—we encounter the names of persons and groups, whether identified or no, which suddenly appear only to disappear just as suddenly again: Archippus in Col. 4:17; Mary, the mother of James the younger and of Joses, and Salome in Mark 15:41 (cf. Matt. 27:55); Onesiphorus in 2 Tim. 1:18; Phoebe in Rom. 16:1. From this fact it is clear that the terms *diakoneō, diakonos,* and *diakonia* reflect nothing of rank or length of service.

In regard to the recipients of the activity denoted by our terms, again the list is long. Those used merely in conjunction with the term *diakoneō* include Jesus (Matt. 4:11; 27:55; Mark 1:13; 15:41; Luke 10:40; John 12:2, 26); Peter's mother-in-law (Matt. 8:15; Mark 1:31; Luke 4:39); Philemon (Philemon 13); the Twelve (Luke 8:3; 22:26); unspecified numbers such as "many," "least of these," or "all" (Matt. 20:28; Mark 10:45; Matt. 25:44; 2 Cor. 3:3); the churches in Macedonia (Acts 19:22), Jerusalem (Rom. 15:25), Ephesus (2 Tim. 1:18), or simply the church (1 Tim. 3:10, 13), or the saints (Heb. 6:10; 1 Pet. 1:12; 4:10, 11).

Results

From our study thus far three points clearly emerge. First, the verb *diakonein* means "to serve," the nouns *diakonos* and *diakonia* mean "servant" or "service," and it is the context that determines wherein such service consists. A dictionary that defined terms via their metaphorical use, or that included in those definitions the uses of terms in a multiplicity of contexts, would have room for only one word. Second, *diakoneō* and *diakonos/diakonia* allow no inferences to be drawn respecting rank or status. In light of the great variety of subjects involved in the use of these terms, the reduction of those subjects to conform to contemporary ecclesiastical structure is artificial. Finally, nothing respecting length of service or "tenure" may be inferred from our terms. In sum, the New Testament terms for service or ministry are not technical terms.

Not everything is proved by lexicography or statistical analysis. But the term *diakoneō* as it appears in the New Testament urges the conclusion that neither the subject nor the recipient of the activity denoted by the term controls its definition. Rather, the object or purpose of that activity do. The history of the interpretation of the terms for "ministry," however, points in another direction. It reflects the fairly widespread assumption that particular functions or offices correspond to the various uses of our term. To illustrate, the word *episcopos* is associated with our term's "evangelic" use by those who are anxious to draw conclusions regarding ecclesiastical structure from that association, as well as by those who are not. One author, eager to draw such conclusions, writes of the office of bishop as "the fount of ministry," that is, of the gospel of the kingdom of God.[12] Another author, however, writes that "there is further little doubt that the duties [the bishops] were to discharge closely resemble the duties carried out by the apostles," that is, spreading the gospel.[13] The point is not that the authors cited identify the office or function of bishop with that of apostle, but simply that they associate the two. This association in turn rests on a further assumption that the term *apostolos* is chiefly characterized by, if not restricted to, the founding of communities through evangelizing. But such is not always the case. In 2 Cor. 8:23, for example, the title *apostolos* is applied to Titus and others engaged in relief activity on behalf of the Jerusalem poor. In Phil. 2:25, the same title is applied to Epaphroditus, who acts as relief agent on Paul's behalf. The possibility cannot be ruled out that Paul leaned toward restricting the company of the apostles to those who had seen the risen Lord and had been commissioned by him to preach, or that the author of Acts intended to restrict the number of that company to the Twelve.[14] But as indicated above, it is also true that a certain fluidity attaches to the New Testament titles for functions or offices within the primitive church. This fact merely enforces the contention that it is not the subject or recipient but rather the object or purpose of the activity denoted by our terms which is determinative. Further, only in a most general sense does etymology render any service. To cite but one example, the way in which Acts 6:2 sets the "service of the word" (RSV: "preaching the word of God") alongside the "service of tables," the latter linked to selection (RSV: "Pick out from among you seven men . . . "), suggests that for Luke the term *episkopein* has more to do with "commission" than with the etymologically more proximate "visitation" or "inspection."

II. MINISTRY OF THE WORD

The Divine Commission and the Charism of Ministry

Epictetus, a contemporary of Paul, penned these lines:

> Did you ever hear the faculty of sight say anything about itself? Or the faculty of vision? No, but they have been appointed as servants and slaves to minister to the faculty which makes use of external impressions. . . . How, then, can any other faculty be superior to this which both uses the rest as its servants, and itself passes judgment upon each several thing and pronounces upon it?[15]

Even if the study is narrowed to the evangelic use of the terms for ministry, it is still the case that the object of the activity gives definition or integrity to the office or function. Thus, what Epictetus wrote of the "faculty of moral purpose" the New Testament affirms of the proclamation or word of God. It is the proclamation that gives definition and identity to "ministry."

This proclamation is variously defined. In the context of the use of the terms for ministry, it is called the "witness to (Jesus') resurrection" (Acts 1:25); "the word of God" (Acts 6:2; Col. 1:25), or simply "the word" (Acts 6:4); "the gospel of the grace of God" (Acts 20:24); "the message of reconciliation" (2 Cor. 5:18); "the gospel" (Eph. 3:7; Col. 1:23); "words of the faith and of the good doctrine" (1 Tim. 4:6); "the good news" (1 Pet. 1:12), and "the oracles of God" (1 Pet. 4:11). The ministry is thus a service to a word of which God is owner and source. Or again, what that word effects or brings about gives definition to "ministry." Again, in the context of the use of our terms, the effects are described as "salvation" (Rom. 11:14); "life" (2 Cor. 3:6); "reconciliation" (2 Cor. 5:18); "righteousness" (2 Cor. 11:15). The ministry is thus a service to a word through which God acts. In forty-four of the forty-nine "evangelic" uses of the terms for ministry,[16] God, Christ, or the Spirit is assumed or explicitly stated to be its efficient cause. "The idea of divine commissioning runs through the New Testament as the first essential characteristic of the Christian ministry."[17] Apart from such commissioning, service or ministry is out of the question. For this reason, the divine commissioning and "ministry"— in the Pauline correspondence symbolized by the term *charisma*—are always complementary. In 1 Cor. 12:8-10, to each "is given" a word of wisdom, of knowledge; to each "is given" faith, healing, working of miracles. In v. 28 of the same chapter, what was previously implied is flatly stated:

> God has appointed in the church first apostles, second prophets, third teachers, then workers of miracles, then healers, helpers, . . .

The same complementarity is expressed in Rom. 12:6ff.:

> Having gifts that differ according to the grace given to us, let us use them: if prophecy in proportion to our faith; if service, in our serving.

In 1 Pet. 4:10, virtually an echo of the Romans passage, the complementarity is weighted in favor of the divine commissioning by addition of the notion of stewardship: "As each has received a gift, employ it for one another, as good stewards of God's varied grace." Apart from the divine giving, not even a witness to Jesus' resurrection is qualified for ministry. The sequence of Paul's thought in 1 Cor. 9:1—"Am I not free? Am I not an apostle? Have I not seen Jesus our Lord?"—may not be reversed. That sequence includes what was perhaps the sine qua non of apostleship in the Jerusalem church, that is, a sight of the risen Lord, but ultimately Paul's apostleship rests on a "necessity," on a "being entrusted with a commission" (vv. 16-17), and of which the community at Corinth stands as validation ("you are the seal of my apostleship in the Lord," v. 2). Conversely, because the centrality lies with the commissioning, in the Hellenistic if not in the Jerusalem mission, those who have not seen the risen Jesus may act as *apostoloi* (cf. Andronicus and Junias in Rom. 16:7; Silvanus and Timothy in 1 Thess. 2:6, and, together with Paul, Barnabas in Acts 14:4, 14).

The Connection Between Ministry and the Saving Deed

But if ministry is service to a word through which God acts, so that none can serve but by divine summons, then an essential connection exists between the activity of God and the service through which it occurs, between service to the word and "salvation," "life," "reconciliation," or "righteousness." Then the ministry of proclamation is part and parcel of the redeeming activity of God, the gift of ministry or the summons to it part and parcel of the saving event. In 2 Cor. 5:18-20, Paul writes that in Jesus' death and resurrection God "has not merely instituted salvation for the world, but has also instituted the proclamation of reconciliation and the ministry of proclamation":[18]

> All this is from God, who through Christ reconciled us to himself and gave us the ministry of reconciliation; that is, in Christ God was reconciling the world to himself . . . and entrusting to us the message of reconciliation. So we are ambassadors for Christ, God making his appeal through us.

The Inevitability of the Divine Activity, and the Ministry as Conditioned

But if there is an essential connection between ministry and the saving event, in the New Testament no link is forged between that event and a ministry construed as an office or institution that abides. The circle of the apostles dies out. Subsequent service to the word is dependent upon the apostles' witness, but in the New Testament that service is not construed as the occupancy of a place left vacant by the death or retirement of its original holder.[19] An office, such as that of an apostle, may be nonrepeatable. Or an office such as that of bishop or deacon may be restricted to one particular geographical area, and the office of presbyter to still another. For this reason it is inaccurate to speak of an office or ministry as the "conditio sine qua non for ensuring that the saving act [reaches] mankind,"[20] even if that statement is not understood to mean that the persistence of the office is dependent upon human effort. Rather, as already implied in the statement concerning the complementarity of the commissioning and the charisma, there is an inevitability that attaches to the saving activity of God, an inevitability that distinguishes it from the means or instrument of its occurrence, so that those means can never be a condition, but are always conditioned. This inevitability is reflected, for example, in the sequence of four rhetorical questions in Rom. 10:14-15, in which the last and not the first member of the series serves as basis for the whole:

> How are men to call upon him in whom they have not believed? And how are they to believe in him of whom they have never heard? And how are they to hear without a preacher? And how can men preach unless they are sent?

The sending never ceases, since God wills to redeem, to save. Because the sending never ceases, there will always be believing, hearing, and preaching. For the sake of the sending, the invoking, the believing, the hearing, and the preaching abide, but only because the sending never ceases. The sending is the constant, and whatever abides of invoking, believing, hearing, and preaching is conditional upon it. The variability in the identity of the one who invokes, believes, hears, or preaches is the proof of it.

These Aspects Mirrored in the Jesus Tradition

The complementarity of the divine commission and the ministry, thus the essential link between ministry and the divine activity, and finally the inevitability of that activity which gives to ministry its character as conditioned—these material aspects of ministry in the New Testament mirror the primitive community's reminiscences of the relation between Jesus and his disciples. First, in the gospel tradition every act of service performed by a disciple is preceded by a summons. In Mark 3:14, Jesus "creates" the Twelve "to be with him, and to be sent out to preach and have authority to cast out demons." The same sequence occurs in Mark 6:7 (cf. Luke 9:1), as well as in material peculiar to Matthew and Luke (cf. Matt. 10:1, 5ff., and Luke 10:1). This relation between the creating, sending, and calling of the disciples on the one hand and their being empowered to preach and exorcise on the other is analogous to Jesus' own relation to God. In Mark 9:37 Jesus refers to "him who sent me" (cf. Luke 9:48), and in material peculiar to Luke the priority of the divine summons over Jesus' activity is made explicit in Jesus' quotation from Isaiah:

> The Spirit of the Lord is upon me, because he has anointed me to preach good news to the poor. He has sent me to proclaim release to the captives and recovering of sight to the blind, to set at liberty those who are oppressed, to proclaim the acceptable year of the Lord (Luke 4:18-19).

Second, by virtue of the preeminence of the divine summons, the activity of the disciple is identified with Jesus' own work. In Matt. 10:40a, Jesus says: "He who receives you receives me" (cf. Luke 10:16ab: "He who hears you hears me, and he who rejects you rejects me"). However, the relation between Jesus and God and that between Jesus and his disciples is not merely conceived as analogous, but as necessary. In Matt. 10:40b (cf. Luke 10:16c), Jesus continues, "and he who receives me receives him who sent me." Finally, the aspect of inevitability which gives to ministry its character as conditioned mirrors the action of Jesus which the Gospel tradition describes as a "passion," a submission to the divine willing. This submission is echoed in the so-called passion predictions with their accent on the necessity of the suffering of the Son of man (cf. Mark 8:31; 9:31; 10:33f., and parallels). As a consequence, Jesus is everywhere described in the New Testament as functionally subordinate to the Father ("not what I will, but what thou wilt," Mark 14:36).

The one apparent exception to this mirroring of the aspects of ministry in the Jesus tradition is the pericope of the "strange exorcist" in Mark 9:38-40(41).

Setting aside the usual reflections on this text, its context, its alleged situation-in-life, the religious-historical parallels and the scopus of the text, it stands the customary notion of what is constant and what variable on its head—in this instance a notion voiced by a disciple of Jesus: "Teacher, we saw a man casting out demons in your name, and we forbade him, because he was not following us." John's word assigns the constant to the disciples' activity, connoted by the phrase "following us." Because the exorcist does not share in that activity, he should be forbidden to continue what he is doing. Translated into modern idiom, John assumes that the "office" of follower is the indispensable requirement for ministry. Jesus, however, reverses the appraisal: "No one who does a mighty work in my name will be able soon after to speak evil of me," and for this reason forbids putting a stop to the stranger's activity. The reversal is further accented in the assertion that "whoever gives you a cup of water to drink in the name, because you are Christ's [not, as in the RSV: "Because you bear the name of Christ"], will by no means lose his reward." The phrase "in my name," or "in the name," does not denote a subjective conviction, but an objectively working power by which what is done is initiated and executed. This power of the name is to the alien exorcist what Jesus' call or summons is to the disciple or "follower." And, since what is done "in the name" links both disciple and stranger to Christ as source and energizer, both are ultimately related to each other. This is the force of v. 40—"he that is not against us is for us"—too facilely interpreted as Jesus' tolerance toward persons not yet summoned to decide for or against him.

The Shape of the Crucified

The purpose of this study is not to establish by means of historical research whether or not Jesus' situation-in-life, in this case his actual relation to the disciples, did in fact furnish the occasion for those material aspects of ministry in the New Testament which were just outlined.[21] What is important to note is that the New Testament authors have presented those aspects as a recapitulation of the characteristics of Jesus' earthly ministry. And the degree to which they have done so is evidence that the impulse for that presentation was scarcely merely historical. What provided the principal stimulus was the expectation that the life and activity of the minister would assume the shape of the existence of the crucified one. This expectation is voiced with reference to every office or function named in the New Testament. A few examples will suffice. Following his first passion prediction in Mark 8, Jesus addresses the disciples (*mathētai*) together with the crowd in these words:

> If any would come after me, let him deny himself and take up his cross and follow me. (Mark 8:34; in Matthew's Gospel the invitation is restricted to the disciples, cf. Matt. 16:24)

In the Fourth Gospel's substitute for the Last Supper, Jesus says:

> Truly, truly, I say to you, a servant is not greater than his master; nor is he who is sent [*apostolos*] greater than he who sent him. (John 13:16)

In Acts, identification of the one sent and the sender is made concrete in the apostles' enduring punishment and rejoicing at being "counted worthy to suffer dishonor for the name" (Acts 5:41). Again, the identification can scarcely be missed in Paul's injunction to the Ephesian elders (*presbyteroi*), set over the church by the Spirit as bishops (*episkopoi*), that they "shepherd" their charge (Acts 20:28). In 1 Tim. 6:12-13, the parallel to the confession of the "deacon" Timothy (*diakonos*, cf. 4:6), is the "good confession" of Jesus Christ before Pilate. In each of these examples, whatever the conception of the office or function named, or of the relation of that office to the life and ministry of Christ, the context of that conception is the reminiscence of the end result of that ministry in suffering and death. A disciple must take up his cross. An apostle is not greater than the one about to be "glorified," but suffers "for the name." The prototype or model of bishop or presbyter is that of "shepherd"—in the gospel tradition a self-designation of Jesus used exclusively in the context of the passion (cf. Mark 14:27; Matt. 26:31; John 10:11; cf. Heb. 13:20 and 1 Pet. 2:25). The ordination paraenesis of 1 Timothy sets the deacon's confession alongside Christ's arraignment. In a passage that appears at the midpoint of a summons to an entire community, officeholders and those without office alike, Christ before his accusers is set as example:

> For to this you have been called, because Christ also suffered for you, leaving you an example, that you should follow in his steps. He committed no sin; no guile was found on his lips. When he was reviled, he did not revile in return; when he suffered, he did not threaten; but he trusted to him who judges justly. (1 Pet. 2:21-23)

In the period following the composition of the New Testament, reference to the life of the minister or officeholder as assuming cruciform shape is absent. In a letter to the Romans, Ignatius of Antioch bids his addressees pray that he "be poured out as a libation for God while an altar is still ready."[22] The reference, with its figures from pagan sacrifice, is obviously to martyrdom, not, however, as the logical consequence of service to the gospel, but as the high point in the career of a single Syrian bishop:

> That forming yourselves into a chorus of love, you may sing to the Father in Christ Jesus, that God has vouchsafed that the bishop of Syria shall be found at the setting of the sun, having fetched him from the sun's rising.[23]

Elsewhere in Ignatius, the office of deacon is construed as a type of the service of Christ—a "trajectory," perhaps, from New Testament references to Christ as *diakonos*. For the sake of this identification, Ignatius may have reversed the relationships in the heavenly hierarchy and set the bishop, presbyter, and deacon in series with God the Father, the council of apostles, and Jesus Christ.[24]

III. DEVELOPMENT

Early Catholicism

Does the New Testament contain any other view of ministry than that just outlined? In earlier research, it was customary to draw a clear line of demarcation between the New Testament period and the period following, the latter described as reflecting "early catholicism," that is, the tendency to subordinate the present or contemporary, the living spirit of the present, to tradition or the spirit of the past. When interpreters proceed to describe the characteristics of "early catholicism," one they always cite is that of the church as repository of divine salvation with fixed ecclesiastical offices, that is, with a sacramental priesthood laying claim to apostolic succession, to authority for Scripture exposition, and to the communication of the Spirit. In newer research, it has become commonplace to trace this feature to the New Testament itself. Luke-Acts, the Pastoral Epistles, and a handful of the General or Catholic Epistles are usually referred to as reflecting this development. These writings are credited with a view of ecclesiastical office which reached its climax in the three-tiered hierarchy of bishop, deacon, and presbyter at the beginning of the second century.

Interpreters are not in agreement respecting the stimuli or occasions for this move toward "early catholicism." According to one view, the church was imperilled by enthusiasts who laid claim to pneumatic gifts and thus to authority in the church through immediate divine inspiration. In order to avoid running aground on individualism, the church was forced to reach back to forms common in Judaism or the mystery religions.[25] On a similar view, the occasion was furnished by an "authority-vacuum" created by the deaths of the apostles and by the decline of prophecy. Since, however, the first bearers of authority left behind them a tradition, that tradition could be appealed to in conflict with the pneumatics and their freedom.[26] According to another view, the persecution of leading members of the Jerusalem community and the outbreak of famine in Judea necessitated a relief fund and offices for its administration, offices that subsequently hardened into permanence.[27]

Obviously, in this historical reconstruction, the ecclesiastical office has ceased to take its definition from its purpose or object. The aspect of inevitability is now conceived as transferred from ends to means. Ministry as instrument of the divine saving activity is no longer conditioned, but a condition:

> Let all respect the deacons as Jesus Christ, even as the bishop is also a type of the Father, and the presbyters as the council of God and the college of Apostles. Without these the name of "Church" is not given.[28]

13

Thus, whether decried or celebrated, Luke-Acts, and the Pastoral and Catholic Epistles have earned the epithet "early catholicism," and thus the boundary between them and the literature of the post-apostolic age is blurred or obliterated.

Is this assessment or reconstruction correct? There are passages in the allegedly "early catholic" writings which appear to challenge it. I turn to them now.

Acts

In Acts 6, following a complaint by the Hellenists over the neglect of their widows, the Twelve call the disciples together and summon them to choose seven men to "serve tables" (*diakonein trapezais*, v. 2). The men are selected from a minority group—their names are all Greek—suggesting that the chief factor in selection is representation. The Seven are to be "of good repute, full of the Spirit and of wisdom"—qualities not restricted to "deacons" (in Acts 16:2 and 22:12, the "disciples" Timothy and Ananias are described as "of good repute"; in addition to Stephen in Acts 6:5 and 7:55, Barnabas is described in 11:24 as "full of the Spirit"; cf. 1 Tim. 3:7, where the same requirement is set for bishops). If the intention is to restrict the work of the Seven to caring for the poor, the intention is never carried out. Rather, the Seven exercise a form of ministry which the Twelve had reserved for themselves. Stephen preaches, and the content of his witness as well as the account of his death are rivalled in quantity only by the narratives of Christ's passion (the reader is actually assisted in discovering analogies to Christ's death in, for example, Acts 7:59-60 and Luke 22:34, 36). In Acts 21:8, Philip, a member of the Seven, is described as an evangelist. One author, anxious to retain the deipnic use of the verb "to serve" as primary, and to restrict it to the Seven, but whose reconstruction is rendered problematic by the curiosities noted above, suggests that Stephen's proclamation and Philip's evangelizing were in addition to their responsibilities to "serve tables":

> True, the Seven are not called deacons . . . nor is any particular diaconic work stressed. . . . Stephen proclaims the Word; Philip is called an evangelist . . . but still we ask: Didn't the men really do what they were especially and expressly appointed to do, "serve at table"? Did what was obvious need singling out . . . ? Only what was peculiar required special note, that is, that Stephen also handled the Word, and that Philip . . . was later called by God to another office.[29]

In Acts 14:4 and 14, contrary to his custom of identifying the apostolate with the Twelve, and thus describing him as brother, disciple, prophet, or teacher (cf. 9:17, 26; 13:1), Luke names Paul together with Barnabas as "apostle." The interpreters rush to the expedient of a source from which Luke is alleged (uncritically) to have gleaned the term.[30] But erecting the hypothesis of a source upon the unaccustomed usage of a single term is a hazardous affair. The style and the vocabulary are Luke's (note, for example, the characteristic *eschisthē* in

v. 4), and the account is Luke's. Luke is responsible for the scholar's irritation at his inconsistency.

In Acts 20, Paul calls the Ephesian elders together at Miletus, charging them to take heed to the flock in which the Holy Spirit has made them "overseers" (*episkopoi*, v. 28). The reference appears to support the hypothesis that the term "bishop," at least in Luke's time, applied to leaders of congregations outside Palestine—in this case, to leaders at Ephesus—whereas the term "elder" applied to leaders within the churches of Jerusalem and Palestine. Here, then, Luke is simply stating that what he or his readers customarily call "elders" were denominated "bishops" by Paul. In Acts 14, however, Paul and Barnabas are described as appointing "elders in every church" at Lystra, Iconium, and Antioch (v. 23). One explanation for this description is that Luke has committed an anachronism, trajecting the council of elders existing within his own church back into the time of Paul's first missionary journey.[31] The reader will recall that in the same chapter, and in connection with events occurring at Iconium and Lystra, Paul and Barnabas are called "apostles." Are we to assume yet another anachronism? Another explanation is that the titles "elder" or "bishop," whatever their provenance, were casually applied. The first explanation rests on the further assumption that in Luke's time the title of presbyter or elder had come to be a technical term, presumably originating in Jewish circles and restricted to leaders in the Palestinian churches, and that such was the case in the church to which Luke belonged. It is of course true that in the majority of instances in which Luke employs the term "elder" or "presbyter," he uses it in connection with decisions, commissionings, and decrees of the leaders of the Jerusalem church (cf. Acts 11:30; 15:2, 4, 6, 22, 23; 16:4; 21:18; the same is true of Luke's use of the term *apostolos*). It is also true that Paul never refers to presbyters or elders in his own epistles—provided we exclude the Pastorals from the Pauline corpus. A certain plausibility thus attaches to the hypothesis of identical offices denoted by different titles depending upon geographical location, provided the hypothesis is not used in support of the further theory of a development toward hierarchy.

The Pastoral Epistles

With one exception (1 Tim. 5:19), the title "elder" (*presbyteros*) always appears in the Pastoral Epistles in the plural (cf. 1 Tim. 5:1, 17; Titus 1:5; note the use of the term *presbyterion* in 1 Tim. 4:14), whereas the term "bishop" always appears in the singular (cf. 1 Tim. 3:1-2; Titus 1:7). This would appear to contradict the hypothesis of identical offices denoted by different titles.[32] On the other hand, in Titus 1:5, the "pastor's" summons to appoint elders "in every town" is followed by a list of requirements for bishop, urging the inference that the two terms are in fact synonymous. It has been argued that the term "elder" in Titus and 1 Timothy denotes age rather than office, so that the summons is simply to appoint bishops from among the older men.[33] But such a reading would require a double accusative for the verb "appoint" (*kathistēmi*), such as "appoint elders as bishops in every town"—in harmony with use of the verb in the active voice (without a prepositional phrase) elsewhere in the New Testament. Without the double accusative the summons lacks sense—how does one "appoint" old men? The preferred reading is to construe "elders" as an accusative of the direct object, and thus as designating office. Further, the considerable similarity between the requirements for presbyters in Titus 1:6 and those for bishop in 1 Tim. 3:1-7 urges us to regard the offices of elder and bishop as interchangeable. The elder is to be "the husband of one wife" (cf. 1 Tim. 3:2a), whose "children are believers" (cf. 1 Tim. 3:4-5), and who is free of the charge of being "profligate or insubordinate" (cf. 1 Tim. 3:2b-3).

First Timothy 4 proves yet another embarrassment to the theory of the blurring of lines between Acts, the Pastoral and General Epistles, and the post-apostolic age. Timothy, described as "deacon" (1 Tim. 4:6), or as "evangelist" (2 Tim. 4:5), is summoned to "attend to the public reading" (*tē anagnōsei*, v. 13); to "preaching" (*tē paraklēsei*, v. 13; cf. 2 Tim. 1:8; 2:15; 4:2), and to "teaching" (*tē didaskalia*, vv. 13, 16; cf. v. 11, and 6:2; in addition, cf. 2 Tim. 2:2, 24; 4:2)—all functions that the Pastorals elsewhere assign to apostles (1 Tim. 1:11; 2 Tim. 2:7), bishops (1 Tim. 3:2; Titus 1:9; 2:1, 7-8), or elders (1 Tim. 5:17). Here, at least, the activity of the deacon is not construed as rendering assistance to a superior. And, if the appellation "servant" (*doulos*, cf. 1 Tim. 4:6 and 2 Tim. 2:24), when applied to Timothy should be interpreted to reflect lesser rank, we need only recall that it makes ample appearance in apostolic self-designation.

The Catholic Epistles

If we keep strictly to the use of *diakoneō* and its congeners in the Catholic Epistles, in only three of thirteen occurrences[34] can the terms conceivably be applied to a discrete ecclesiastical office. In Eph. 6:21, Tychicus is described as "the beloved brother and faithful minister (*diakonos*) in the Lord." He is so named in Col. 4:7, a passage virtually identical to Eph. 6:21. In Col. 4:17, Archippus is admonished to "fulfill the ministry" (*diakonia*) that he has received "in the Lord." From the references to Tychicus elsewhere, it is clear that his ministry consisted of accompanying Paul (Acts 20:4), or of serving as his messenger (2 Tim. 4:12; Titus 3:12). Archippus appears a second time as an addressee together with Philemon and Apphia in Philemon 2. There Paul describes him as a "fellow soldier"—no doubt in reference to some signal ("perilous") activity on behalf or in the company of Paul. In none of these instances may we infer the exercise of a discrete office. In each case "ministry" takes its definition from its purpose or goal: service to Paul. This service is conceived of as "in the Lord," its value reflected in the adjective modifying Tychicus's ministry (*pistos* = "faithful"), or in the prefix linked to the noun used to describe Archippus (*sy-stratiotēs* = fellow soldier"; cf. Phil. 2:25, where the same expression is used of Epaphroditus, and in tandem with a cluster of nouns including "brother," "fellow worker," "messenger," and "minister").

If we restrict ourselves to the use of the terms for bishop or presbyter in the Catholic Epistles, of the seven occurrences[35] two are not applicable to ecclesiastical office.[36] In three of the five remaining passages, the term "elder" appears as self-designation or as an age-classification.[37] Only James 5:14 and 1 Pet. 5:1 refer to a specific function or activity: "Is any among you sick? Let him call for the elders of the church"; "I exhort the elders among you . . . tend the flock of God that is your charge."

Thus, the evidence for a development or alteration in the concept of ministry which would justify the term "early catholic" is slight, provided we keep to the restrictions referred to above. But again, not everything is proved by lexicography, whether or not it is in our favor. Specific terms conjuring up associations with "early catholicism" need not be present in order for the concept to be expressed. And of those passages in the Catholic Epistles in which the concept does in fact appear, 2 Pet. 1:19-21 is chief:

> And we have the prophetic word made more sure. You will do well to pay attention to this as to a lamp shining in a dark place, until the day dawns and the morning star rises in your hearts. First of all you must understand this, that no prophecy of scripture is a matter of one's own interpretation, because no prophecy ever came by the impulse of man, but men moved by the Holy Spirit spoke from God.

The epistle to which this passage belongs has been described by one who pioneered the entire discussion as "the clearest witness to early catholicism."[38] These verses make clear, so reads the argument, that the entire Old Testament construed as prophetic has replaced contemporary Christian prophecy ("we have the prophetic word made more sure"); that the dawning of the eschatological "day" has been replaced by inner illumination ("until . . . the morning star rises in your hearts"); that individual interpretation has been replaced by a teaching office ("no prophecy of scripture is a matter of one's own interpretation"), and that the Spirit as given to each has been replaced by the Spirit as bound to office ("men moved by the Holy Spirit spoke from God").[39] The argument is compelling, though questions remain. Is the author of this text concerned to establish an ecclesiastical office, or is he anxious to avoid some concrete, "clear and present danger"?[40] If the latter, then the author's concern cannot be made a universal rule, since that would require repetition of the danger. If the evaluation of this passage as "early catholic" depends upon its abstraction from its historical situation, then as long as the question concerning that situation persists, its character as "early catholic" will be equally in doubt.

These examples suffice to challenge the contention that a clear-cut "early catholic" conception of church or ministry is reflected in the New Testament itself. This is not to deny the existence of texts that mirror a different shaping of the tradition than appears in the Gospels or Paul. But such reflection cannot without further ado be dubbed "early catholic." As one advocate writes, because the restructuring of office in the church has not yet congealed into a new ecclesiology, one should rather speak of "emerging early catholicism" in the canonical writings.[41]

The absence of evidence in favor of an argument does not prove its opposite. It is true, however, that in the literature advocating early catholicism within the New Testament, references to various portions as assigning to ministry a definition other than that derived from its goal are almost always lacking in specific support. There is frequent adverting to the "stimuli" in a slackening of the eschatological relation and the identification of Christ with the church (Ephesians); in a morality fed from Old Testament-Jewish and popular philosophical tradition (James); in authoritative Scripture exposition and communication of the Spirit through the imposition of hands (2 Peter); in a concept of faith in unresolved tension with the chief witnesses of the New Testament (Jude); even in explicit argument against the pneumatic or charismatic (does Matt. 7:15-23—"on that day many will say to me, 'Lord, Lord, did we not . . . cast out demons in your name' "—furnish the reason why Matthew omits Mark's narrative of the strange exorcist?). But that these writings reflect a new ecclesiology, a new structure claiming apostolic authority is still to be proved. Until then, the epithet "early catholicism," used of writings of the New Testament which are alleged to define ecclesiastical office by something other than its purpose, should be held in abeyance.

IV. REFLECTIONS OF VARIETY OF STRUCTURE IN THE NEW TESTAMENT

If there is no evidence in the New Testament of "early" or "protocatholicism" in terms of a structure claiming apostolic authority, there is nonetheless evidence of structural variety and change. A number of texts in which our terms for "ministry" or "service" appear reflect a fellowship of itinerants. For example, in Mark 15:41 and parallels (Matt. 27:55; Luke 8:3), women are named whose ministry to Jesus consists of accompanying him throughout Galilee. The word of Jesus in Matthew 18:20—"where two or three are gathered in my name, there am I in the midst of them"—makes eminent sense as applied to a community of wanderers. And, despite its metaphorical character, the logion in John 12:26— "if any one serves me, he must follow me"—may yet reflect the surrender of stability of place as constitutive of the discipleship of Jesus (cf. Mark 8:34; Matt. 16:24, and Luke 9:23). Palestine during the years of Jesus' sojourn was a society at a critical stage. If the crisis did not touch every social stratum, it was nevertheless intense enough to affect all of society. Within this "anomie" primitive Palestinian discipleship of Jesus first flourished. As one sociologist of the New Testament has commented:

> All these people had abandoned their previously existing social world. A great religious unrest, no doubt linked to the social conflicts of that time, drove them onto the street, made them vagrant wandering preachers, outsiders and "outlaws." . . . They knew they were the "salt of the earth." And in fact they were the *cor inquietum* of a society marked by conflicts. They were the "Spirit of spiritless conditions" (K. Marx), of groups which world history usually has passed over in silence.[42]

On the other hand, it would be an error to conceive earliest Christianity as comprised solely of itinerants. In the city Jerusalem, the sedentary community became the principal bearer of the tradition. As noted earlier, Luke records of Paul, the "wandering charismatic," that together with Barnabas he appointed "elders" in the Hellenistic Christian congregation at Lystra, Iconium, and Antioch. Whether or not Paul actually installed leaders patterned and titled after the Jewish or Jewish-Christian model is moot. He is more likely to have patterned and titled them after the civil or religious models of the gentile world.[43] But that he appointed leaders who should share the settled life of their charges is beyond doubt. In fact, such sedentary fellowships and their leaders furnished the wandering charismatics their livelihood. In a letter to a congregation he had founded, Paul opens with a greeting to the "saints . . . with the bishops and deacons," and concludes with the acknowledgement of financial aid: "I have received full payment, and more; I am filled, having received . . . the gifts you sent, a fragrant offering, a sacrifice acceptable and pleasing to God" (Phil. 1:1 and 4:18). The portrait of earliest Christianity as anarchistic is a fiction. Equally fictional is the notion of the charismatic as extinguished by the legal or administrative. Beneath both these fictions lies a conception of change as marked by breaks, without gradation or overlap. If the author of 2 and 3 John was an itinerant charismatic whose authority was challenged by a local, sedentary "bishop," Diotrophes,[44] earliest "eastern" Christianity reflects competition and overlap in structure. In its instructions to the settled fellowship touching the reception of wandering "apostles," an ancient manual of church discipline reflects a similar coexistence in Syria.[45]

Prejudicial to the phenomenon of variety in earliest Christian structure is the notion of "contamination" by which the boundaries between the Pauline charismatic communities and Jewish-Christian congregations were confused. According to this theory, the contamination occurs in Acts' depiction of Paul and Barnabas as installing elders, later addressed as bishops, and which the Pastoral Epistles subsequently legitimize with the authority of Paul. Titus thus links instructions for presbyters to rules for deacons, as well as for bishops identical to presbyters salaried by the congregation, and places the installation to office in the hands of elders,[46] since the Pauline concept of a testament requires that the "charisma of God" be mediated through the apostolic laying on of hands. This attempt to mediate between the charismatic and legal or administrative is merely apparent, since the greater weight is given the administrative with the contention that early catholicism recognized in the presbyterium the shape most compatible with its ecclesiology.[47]

Equally prejudicial is the portrait of Ignatius of Antioch as concluding a development begun with a "college" of leaders in Hellenistic Christian communities and ending with the monarchical episcopal office. In his letter to the Philadelphians, the Antiochene writes:

> I cried out while I was with you, I spoke with a great voice—with God's own voice—"Give heed to the bishop, and to the presbytery and deacons."[48]

Despite the persistence of the portrait, Ignatius makes no reference to apostolic tradition as an essential element in his thought.[49] If the conception of early catholicism as already prefigured in the New Testament must give way to the phenomena of variety and overlap, then Ignatius cannot constitute the culmination of a development begun with the apostolic age. On the other hand, the variety of structure in earliest Christianity does not allow our assigning to Ignatius the rank of ecclesiastical pioneer who legitimizes his innovation by appealing to immediate, divine inspiration ("I spoke . . . with God's own voice"). Ignatius's appeal was not in the service of innovation, but of his choice of structure. And with that the Antiochene loses the status of erratic on the ecclesiastical terrain, a status often preserved to him by his interpreters.

CONCLUSION

The biblical-theological conclusion to be drawn from this study may be succinctly stated. When applied to "service of the gospel," the New Testament terms for "ministry" denote an activity dependent for its definition upon its purpose or goal. That purpose is the intention of God to save. For this reason, "ministry" cannot occur apart from the divine commissioning. Divine summons and ministry are always complementary. And since the New Testament forges no link between the saving event and a ministry construed as permanent institution, it is clear that the saving event is the constant, whereas service to it is the variable. In other words, an "inevitability" attaches to the saving activity which renders the means or instrument of its occurrence conditioned, subordinate. To assign privileged status to a particular, discrete species of ministry as condition for the divine activity is to construe as constant what the New Testament describes as variable.

On the other hand, to infer from the character of ministry as subordinate to the divine commissioning and thus as conditioned or variable that it constitutes a mere function, is to deny the complementarity of ministry and the divine commission, and thus the emphasis of the New Testament upon ministry as part and parcel of the divine saving activity.

20

The absence of "early catholicism" in favor of structural variety and overlap in the New Testament age yields further weight to the finding that ministry derives its definition from its purpose or goal. Neither the "charismatic" nor the legal-administrative may be assigned superior or inferior status, since neither is regarded as requisite to or divergent from the divine intention. Both retain their character as variable, thus subordinate.

If the intention to save is divine, so is the instrument of that intention. If there is no word of God apart from its concretion in utterance and belief, concretion is indispensable to that word.

> Do not say in your heart, "Who will ascend into heaven?" . . . or "Who will descend into the abyss?" . . . But what does it say? The word is near you, on your lips and in your heart. (Rom. 10:6-8)

The ministry of the gospel may thus be described as indispensable to the existence of the church. But what is indispensable is not on that account necessary or inevitable. As in everything else, so in the matter of structure, the New Testament attributes necessity solely to the divine intention. The reason for this attribution is clear: utterance, belief, "ministry" does not create its object. It is created by it.

NOTES

1. This use would involve such passages as Mark 10:45: "The Son of Man also came not *to be served* but *to serve*," and 1 Cor. 3:5: "What then is Apollos? What is Paul? *Servants* through whom you believed."

2. *Theologisches Wörterbuch zum Neuen Testament*, ed. Gerhard Kittel (Stuttgart: Kohlhammer, 1935), 1:81.

3. *Herodotus*, trans. A. D. Godley, *The Loeb Classical Library* (Cambridge: Harvard University Press, 1963), 3 (4.154): 356.

4. Ibid. (4.71, 72): 270; and 4 (9.82): 256.

5. *Griechisch-Deutsches Wörterbuch*, ed. Walter Bauer (Berlin: Töpelmann, 1937), 305.

6. *Sophocles*, trans. F. Storr, *The Loeb Classical Library* (Cambridge: Harvard University Press, 1967), 2 (*Philoctetes* 287 and 497): 390, 404.

7. Fragments 137.1, 150, and 1148.1.

8. Joh. Fried. Schleusner, *Novum Lexicon Graeco-Latinum in Novum Testamentum*, s. v. "Quocunque hoc fiat modo" (Glasguae: Andreas et Joannes M. Duncan, 1824), 1:462.

9. *Philo*, trans. F. H. Colson, *The Loeb Classical Library* (Cambridge: Harvard University Press, 1954), 9 (*De Vita Contemplativa* 70.1 and 71.1): 156.

10. *Theologisches Wörterbuch*, 92.

11. Cf. e.g., Eduard Meyer, *Ursprung und Anfänge des Christentums* (Darmstadt: Wissenschaftliche Buchgesellschaft, 1962), 3:251; Leon Morris, *Ministers of God* (London: Inter-Varsity Fellowship, 1964), 81; Eduard Schweizer, *Gemeinde und Gemeindeordnung im Neuen Testament* (Zurich: Zwingli Verlag, 1959), 158; John Knox, "Ministry in the Primitive Church," in *The Ministry in Historical Perspective*, ed. H. Richard Niebuhr and Daniel Day Williams (San Francisco: Harper & Row, 1983), 1. On the other hand, cf. Sanday-Headlam, *The Epistle to the Romans: The International Critical Commentary* (Edinburgh: T. & T. Clark, 1968), 357.

12. Cf. J. A. T. Robinson, "Kingdom, Church and Ministry," in *The Historic Episcopate*, ed. Kenneth M. Carey (London: Dacre Press, 1954), 21 n. 1. Robinson, however, does not describe the episcopacy as a pre-condition of the church.

13. Cf. J. K. S. Reid, *The Biblical Doctrine of the Ministry* (London: Oliver and Boyd, 1955), 26.

14. Cf. Luke 6:13; Acts 1:26; in addition, cf. Rev. 21:14.

15. *Epictetus*, trans. W. A. Oldfather, *The Loeb Classical Library* (Cambridge: Harvard University Press, 1967), 1 (2, 23): 406.

16. *Diakonia:* Acts 1:17, 25; 6:4; 20:24; 21:19; Rom. 11:13; 2 Cor. 3:8, 9; 4:1; 5:18; 6:3; Col. 4:17; 1 Tim. 1:12; 2 Tim. 4:5; Heb. 1:14. *Diakoneō:* Matt. 20:28 (2); Mark 10:45 (2); John 12:26 (2); Acts 6:2; 2 Cor. 3:3; 2 Tim. 1:18; 1 Pet. 1:12; 4:11. *Diakonos:* Matt. 20:26; John 12:26; Rom. 13:4 (2); 15:8; 16:1; 1 Cor. 3:5; 2 Cor. 3:6; 6:4; 11:15, 23; Eph. 3:7; Phil. 1:1; Col. 1:23, 25; 1 Tim. 3:8, 12; 4:6. The other occurrences include Acts 19:22; 1 Tim. 3:10, 13; Eph. 6:21, and Col. 4:7.

17. G. W. H. Lampe, *Some Aspects of the New Testament Ministry* (London: SPCK, 1949), 5.

18. Leonhard Goppelt, "The Ministry in the Lutheran Confessions and in the New Testament," *The Lutheran World* 11 (1964): 421.

19. Gerhard Krodel, "Forms and Functions of Ministries in the New Testament," *dialog* 8 (Summer 1969): 193.

20. Harding Meyer and August B. Hasler, "The Joint Lutheran/Roman Catholic Study Commission on 'The Gospel and the Church,' " *The Lutheran World* 18 (1971): 164.

21. Cf. Goppelt, "Ministry," 415; Heinrich Kraft, "Die Anfänge des geistlichen Amts," *Theologische Literaturzeitung* 100. Jahrgang, No. 2, Februar 1975, 86–88; J. Robert Nelson, "Styles of Service in the New Testament and Now," *Theology Today* 22 (April 1965): 94. Perhaps the most measured judgment appears in Jerome Quinn, "Ministry in the New Testament," in *Biblical Studies in Contemporary Thought*, ed. Miriam Ward (Somerville: Greeno, Hadden and Co., 1975), 131f.: "As the historico-critical inquiry has inched its way back from this documentation certain characteristic elements of discipleship appear to be traceable to the *Sitz im Leben Jesu* and to influence, if not control, the later developments. The first and in many respects the key historical memory concerning those most closely associated with Jesus' work was that he himself had initiated the relationship, and the invitation, indeed summons, into such an association was rooted in his expressed will."

22. *The Apostolic Fathers*, trans. Kirsopp Lake, *The Loeb Classical Library* (Cambridge: Harvard University Press, 1970), 1 (2.2): 228.

23. Ibid.

24. Cf. Ignatius to the Magnesians, 6.1, and to the Trallians, 3.1, in ibid., 200, 202, and 214.

25. Ernst Käsemann, "Paulus und der Frühkatholizismus," in *Exegetische Versuche und Besinnungen* (Göttingen: Vandenhoeck & Ruprecht, 1967), 2:250.

26. U. Luz, "Erwägungen zur Entstehung des 'Frühkatholizismus,' " *Zeitschrift für die neutestamentliche Wissenschaft* (1975): 103.

27. Cf. Quinn, "Ministry," 144, 147. According to another view, Paul's polemic against the judaizing "apostles" led to a new notion of apostleship, that is, as established upon sight of the resurrected Christ. This evolution led Luke to identify the Twelve with the apostles. Cf. Andre Lemaire, "The Ministries in the New Testament," *Biblical Theological Bulletin* 3 (June 1973): 143.

28. Ignatius to the Trallians, 3.1, in *The Apostolic Fathers* 1:214.

29. Hans Lauerer, "Die 'Diakonie' im Neuen Testament," in *Neue Kirchliche Zeitschrift* (Leipzig: A. Deichertsche Verlagsbuchhandlung, 1931), 319.

30. Cf. Hans Conzelmann, *Acts of the Apostles*, trans. James Limburg, A. Thomas Kraabel, and Donald Juel, *Hermeneia* (Philadelphia: Fortress Press, 1987), 108.

31. Cf. Krodel, "Forms and Functions," 262.

32. Cf. Philippe H. Menoud, *L'eglise et les ministres selon le Nouveau Testament* (Neuchatel: Delachaux & Niestle, 1949), 51–52.

33. Cf. Joachim Jeremias, *Die Briefe an Timotheus und Titus, Das Neue Testament Deutsch* (Göttingen: Vandenhoeck & Ruprecht, 1975), 41, 69.

34. *Diakonos:* Eph. 3:7; 6:21; Col. 1:7, 23, 24; 4:7; *diakonia:* Eph. 4:12; Col. 4:17; Heb. 1:14; *diakoneō:* Heb. 6:10; 1 Pet. 1:12; 4:10, 11.

35. *Episkopos:* 1 Pet. 2:25; *presbyteros:* Heb. 11:2; Jas. 5:14; 1 Pet. 5:1, 5; 2 John 1, 3 John 1.

36. In 1 Pet. 2:25, the term "bishop" is used of Christ, and in Heb. 11:2 the term "presbyter" or "elder" is used of the Old Testament patriarchs.

37. 2 John 1; 3 John 1, 1 Pet. 5:5.

38. Ernst Käsemann, "Eine Apologie der Urchristlichen Eschatologie," in *Exegetische Versuche und Besinnungen* 1:157.

39. Ibid., 151, 154.

40. Cf. Willi Marxsen, *Der "Frühkatholizismus" im Neuen Testament* (Neukirchen: Neukirchener Verlag, 1958), 18.

41. Luz, "Erwägungen," 90.

42. Gerd Theissen, *Studien zur Soziologie des Urchristentums* (Tübingen: J. C. B. Mohr, 1979), 230.

43. Cf. the argument on p. 14–15.

44. Cf. Hans von Campenhausen, *Kirchliches Amt und Geistliche Vollmacht* (Tübingen: J. C. B. Mohr, 1953), 132–134.

45. *The Apostolic Fathers* 1:324, 326.

46. Cf. the references on p. 15–16.

47. Carl Andresen, *Die Kirchen der alten Christenheit* (Stuttgart: Kohlhammer, 1971), 50.

48. Ignatius to the Philadelphians, 7.1, in *The Apostolic Fathers* 1:244–46.

49. Luz, "Erwägungen," 107.

Ministry
in the
Early Church

2

JAMES ARNE NESTINGEN

As Hans von Campenhausen argues in a masterful study, the doctrine of ministry in the early church developed in a tension between ecclesiastical authority and spiritual power.[1] Given the normal percentages, the results are predictable: the spiritual powers were driven underground as the ecclesiastical authorities took over, developing offices along bureaucratic and sacrificial lines that put their preeminence in church life beyond question. While over the course of time the weight of emphasis shifted, the classical tension endured. To resolve the standoff there have been repeated attempts in the various traditions of the church as well as in scholarship to reconstruct an authoritative definition of the ministry in the New Testament or the early church which resolves the standoff, but the sources themselves are irreducibly plural. They come together in their conviction that ministry of and to the Word of God and the sacraments is divinely commissioned, the action of God. But the specific form of the commissioning is something else again, and the nature of that authorization is a matter of continuing dispute.

Ministry may be authorized in the sovereign ferment of spiritual gifts or charisms bestowed by the Holy Spirit to endow individuals with various spiritual powers for ministry in the community.[2] On the other hand, authorization may also come through a succession of offices functioning to order the ferment into a more controlled form of mission.[3] Whether in actual rivalries or in apparent theological friction, neither of these two assertions of divine authorization has been able to entirely eliminate the other from its churchly standing.

Thus the story of ministry in the early church is one of shifting proportions within the controlling tension. There was never any question of divine institution—that remained a grounding assumption throughout the period. But those who spoke of ministry authorized by spiritual power—whether on the heretical fringes of Marcionism or Monatanism or in the orthodox mainline which included the approved monastic movements—generally were pushed to the peripheries.

And as the church exchanged its eschatology for a sense of permanence, the offices came to be regularized in terms of both organizational and cultic function. Thus while the tension between spiritual power and ecclesiastical office dominated the development of ministry in the early church, the crucial developments were in the offices. The office of the bishop developed hierarchically, the priesthood was subsumed in and under it, and the diaconate withered until it became merely transitional. In the meantime, the whole ministry came to be expressed in a sacrificial function.

BISHOP, PRIEST, AND DEACON

If the early bishops recognized any tension in the New Testament concerning ministry, they did not give it a hermeneutical function. They simply took the office over so that they came to represent, in George H. Williams's terms, "the fullness of the ministry." The bishop was "prophet, teacher, chief celebrant at the liturgical assembly and chairman of the board of overseers of the Christian synagogue."[4]

The letters of Ignatius of Antioch, who died around A.D. 107, demonstrate just how quickly the bishops began to take charge. The three offices of the pastorals become in his letters a threefold office, hierarchically arranged with the presbyters serving the bishops and the deacons the presbyters.[5] The laity is called to obedience to the bishop on the model of Christ's obedience to the Father. But, in fact, in Ignatius's understanding the bishop is the embodiment of the church[6]—more than that, the bishop is God-bearer, a *typos* of God among his people.[7] Yet Ignatius stands in the context of the prior New Testament definition.[8] For if the bishop is God-bearer, so are all of the other members of the congregation who have been called to holiness.[9] While believers must submit to the bishop as to Christ himself, the bishop can only claim this office in relation to Christ. It is, in von Campenhausen's terms, "a distinctive combination of pneumatic and official or ecclesiastical thinking."[10]

While Ignatius was to remain influential in the East, it was in the West, in early Roman writings like 1 Clement and the Shepherd of Hermas, that a more office-centered notion of the bishop took hold. First Clement is in a league by itself, however. The official function of the bishop is sacramental: the bishop is in charge of offering the sacrifices and prayers of the community. Thus the defining function of the office is the bishop's administration of the Lord's Supper, a characteristic definition not only for the Romans but throughout the early church. But in 1 Clement, this is not simply a communal function—it is the basis of the bishop's authority, an authority the bishop holds by design of the apostles themselves for the ordering of the community. "It will be no small sin on our part if we depose from the episcopal office those who blamelessly and in holiness have made the sacrificial offerings," 1 Clement writes.[11]

The Pastoral Epistles indicate another defining function: a bishop is to be "apt to teach" (1 Tim. 3:2). Here, too, the bishops claimed ascendancy. Ignatius himself was contemptuous of tradition, dismissing it as "the church's archives." Given attacks by the Gnostics on human tradition, early bishops were reluctant to appeal to prior teaching. But the pressure of false teaching made it all the more critical to provide an authoritative tradition and to authorize interpreters of it. The bishops, claiming a succession reaching back to the apostles themselves, became the guarantors. By the time of the Council of Nicea, early in the fourth century, this authority was so entrenched in the office of the bishops as to be beyond question.[12]

With this, then, the basic features of a hierarchical definition of ministry were already in place early in the second century: in his person or in his office, the bishop bears the authority necessary to administer the sacraments and guarantee the fidelity of the church's teaching. By the third century, the personal or sacerdotal notion already emergent in the apostolic fathers took hold across the boards without Ignatius's qualifiers. In the Eastern or Western mainline, whether in a Syrian document such as the *Didascalia Apostolorum* or in the writings of a North African like Cyprian, there was a working consensus that the bishop really was the church and that everything followed out of his office accordingly. "You ought to know that the bishop is in the church and the church is in the bishop," Cyprian wrote.[13]

Once the bishops hierarchically redefined the ministry, the rest of the patristic period was a series of small but significant developments that filled out the dimensions of this definition. One such development was the attachment of the notion of succession to the hierarchical concept of the office of bishop. It was an obscure church historian, Hegesippus of Rome, who first combined the two concepts.[14] The significance of the combination is that it shifted the source of authorization from the larger tradition to the specific succession of the office. Standing in a supposedly unbroken line, bishops could on this basis appeal to previous holders of their office as sufficient justification for their own action.[15]

Another significant development in the patristic period is the bureaucratizing of the hierarchy.[16] As long as Christianity was a minority religion subject to sporadic persecution by Roman authorities, it was difficult to consider the ministry a profession. But after the Constantinian settlement the situation changed, and with it the calling to the clergy.

The church developed in the Roman empire much as it did in the Lutheran immigration to the U.S. and Canada. Urban parishes in market towns and political centers became the mothers or fathers of developing congregations within their purview by sending witnesses, gathering people, supplying leadership, and providing organization. Cities like Alexandria and Antioch, later Constantinople, Rome, and Carthage became particularly important. But smaller centers were influential as well. With a hierarchical understanding of ministry already in place, the bureaucracy followed as a matter of course. The bishops of larger congregations in regional centers delegated presbyters or priests to the smaller congregations dependent on them, retaining supervisory powers in the sending. In this way, the title of bishop took on a regional connotation, being reserved for those in the home parishes.

The establishment of the church in the fourth century brought the church into direct parallel with the bureaucracy of the Roman empire. Set free from the occasional outbreaks of chaos which had come with persecution, the ministry could now become a profession, complete with the rank and privilege that are more typically political.[17]

The office of presbyter was upgraded somewhat by professionalization. Though they had held a distinguished place in the ministry,[18] the presbyters were in danger of becoming sacramental technicians, administering the sacraments in the bishop's absence. As the offices developed, the bishops continued to reserve for themselves confirmation and ordination, the entry-level sacraments for membership or ministry.[19] But the presbyters became priests, charged with ongoing responsibilities in the local congregations and with appropriate authority either given or taken as a result.[20] The shadowy office of deacon (previously assigned to gravediggers, singers, or people who provided some other form of service) became the novitiate for the bureaucracy. It was a transitional calling, held in preparation for moving into higher forms of service.[21] A remnant of this development is the practice common in traditional Roman Catholic seminaries of using the title "deacon" for students in their last year.

In the fourth century, then, the priesthood emerged as a vocation, an office working in parallel to local governmental officials. Having served a time as deacon, the candidate became eligible for ordination to the priesthood. Demonstrating gifts in the office, a priest could move up the scale, from smaller parishes to the larger and more important to, possibly, a regional bishopric in a metropolitan area. Progress in church offices was not, however, always so neat or sequential. It was apparently customary in at least some areas to install likely candidates into the office of bishop by force, as both Ambrose and Augustine learned from experience. And there were also instances of bishops being baptized after taking office.

The most significant development in the early church on the spiritual power side of the equation is monasticism.[22] The ascetic appeal of monasticism proved very powerful in the later patristic period. It provided a form of ministry tangential to the hierarchy in which individual gifts in their variety could express themselves. Christian monasticism began in Egypt in the third century with St. Anthony, and then moved into the West in the fourth with Athanasius-against-the-world, the great opponent of Arianism, generally receiving major credit for its movement. Although the Benedictine form, the most important in the history of monasticism, did not develop until the sixth century, earlier forms are significant because they provided alternative forms of ministry. It may be difficult to see how some of the more spectacular extremes of self-renunciation ("stylitism"—sitting on poles, for example) could be considered ministry, but leaving the world behind to seek personal sanctification, monks also left the neighbor and the possibility of service. The mid-fourth-century rule of St. Basil is an instance, an example of a monasticism ordered toward charity. It made use of the various gifts of the monks in service. The Benedictine rule, with its temperate and cordial realism, established community service, even at the edges of civilization, as a fundamental monastic standard.

Aside from monasticism, which, even when it proved troublesome was generally encouraged by the hierarchy, there were some other kinds of movements that emphasized the Spirit's endowment as basis for ministry. But whether for theological or for organizational reasons, they were considered heretical. Marcion's affinity for the Pauline epistles was a factor in undermining the Pauline witness in the early church—the Gnostics brought with them a more virulent form of some of the problems that perplexed Paul and his congregations. Another heretical movement, Monatanism, spoke of a more direct divine involvement. The Donatists also emphasized personal qualification for office over and against the office itself.

But whether it was orthodox or became heretical, the ecclesiastical offices that emerged with such defining force in the early church were not able to eliminate the spiritual power of endowed individuals who added another clause to the definition. In the calling of people such as Ambrose and Augustine, in movements such as monasticism, in theological development later considered heretical, in the congregations themselves, there were gifts manifest that salted and leavened what could not be fixed to the structures.

THE NOTION OF SACRIFICE

There is an apparent connection in the history of the church between the theology of the sacraments and the doctrine of the ministry. Some years ago, in an essay translated in *Tradition and Life in the Early Church*, von Campenhausen demonstrated this correlation. "In the West," he wrote, "to inquire into the significance of the priestly ministry is tantamount to inquiring into the relationship of the priests to the sacraments. It was the development of sacramental doctrine that determined the development of the idea of the priesthood."[23] The same correlation can be seen in the Reformation. When Luther rediscovered the theology of the cross and the New Testament's eschatology, he early in the reform—in the *Babylonian Captivity,* for example—challenged the root premise of medieval Catholicism, the sacrifice of the mass. Jaroslav Pelikan observes the fundamental character of this challenge.[24] Whatever differences it may have had with Luther at other points, here the Lutheran community was not willing to compromise, insisting on a sharp distinction between sacrament as act of God and sacrifice as act of the faithful (Ap. 24, *BC* 252).

This correlation may help to explain some of the difficulty that precipitated the study of ministry, mandated by the merging bodies that produced the ELCA.

There were some repeated assurances from officials of the merging churches, despite some strident voices in all sides, that there really were no dividing theological differences on the ministry. Even the problem of ordained parochial school teachers in one of the churches, the original sticking point in the merger talks, did not appear at all insurmountable. In the light of such considerations, an extended study of the theology of ministry hardly seemed necessary.

But when the relationship between the sacraments, particularly the Lord's Supper, and the doctrine of ministry is considered, another basis for such commission work becomes apparent. The antecedent bodies of the ELCA all brought with them the influence of strong liturgical renewal movements that have focused particular attention on the practice of the Lord's Supper. The introduction of eucharistic prayers in the *Service Book and Hymnal* of 1958 and the *Lutheran Book of Worship* of 1978 is one indication of the influence of these movements. It is also a decisive shift from the historic Lutheran confessional distinction between sacrament and sacrifice.

Given such an important theological shift and the correlation between doctrines, the division on the doctrine of ministry at the time of the merger appears to have been much more than a matter of quasi-clerical status for teachers. With the modifications in the theology of sacrament, there were some accompanying difficulties in the doctrine of the ministry as well. The real division in the ELCA at the time of its union was not between or among the merging churches. Rather, it was between parties with a particular liturgical, ecumenical agenda and the tradition they wanted to supersede. Whatever its current standing, it is critical to observe this correlation historically because of its consequence for the definition of ministry in the early church. The reappropriation of the concept of sacrifice in the first centuries shifted the cultic center of the church's life, redefining both the Lord's Supper itself and the ministry with it.

In the New Testament era, the once-and-for-all-ness of Jesus' sacrifice hit the sacrificial traditions of Judaism like a vast overcharge. The best evidence of this is the Book of Hebrews, with its deep sense of the sacrificial cultus. Crucified outside the camp (13:13), Christ "had offered for all time a single sacrifice for sin" (10:12). The whole concept of sacrifice is radically reinterpreted or better, redirected. The community no longer acts in the sacrifice to placate, appease, or satisfy; rather, God acts in the sacrifice of the Son to reclaim both creature and creation. The sacrificial system has ended, the only appropriate remainder being sacrificial service of God in relation to the neighbor. So in the Gospels Jesus repeatedly quotes the prophets concerning the priority of mercy over sacrifice. And Paul in the magnificent paranesis of Rom. 12:1 speaks of the correlate form of worship as living sacrifice, the presentation of the body, one's entire earthly existence, in all of its down-to-earth connections.

But as 2 Peter amply demonstrates, the eschatology that drives the earlier New Testament witness did not retain its ardor in the late first and early second century. Among the consequences of its cooling is the reemergence of the notion of sacrifice, particularly in relation to the Lord's Supper. What for Paul is the proclamation of the Lord's death until he comes, bearing with it the presence of the one proclaimed and all of his gifts, becomes in the church of the second century a cultic act of the community offering in the sacrament the sacrifice of its praise. Literature like 1 Clement, the Didache, and the writings of Ignatius all show evidence of the transition to a sacrificial understanding, 1 Clement identifying the sacrament as a sacrifice and making it the keystone in his doctrine of church order.

Given the extent of sacrificial language in the Old Testament and the nature of Roman religiosity, this transition is perhaps to have been expected. In fact, the only surprise is that it took the church so long to officially define what was already coming to ascendancy in the second century. It was not until the *Ego Berengarius* of the eleventh century and the fourth Lateran Council of the thirteenth that the sacrifice of the Mass was formally entrenched in the church's doctrine.

But if it took almost a whole millennium to overcome the more eschatological definition of the sacrament, the effect of the second century's shift toward a sacrificial concept is much more immediate in its understanding of ministry. George H. Williams sums it up:

> Gradually, the principal officiant at the cultual [sic] reenactment of the Supper came to be so closely identified with Christ . . . in the sacrifice of Calvary and its liturgical commemoration . . . that by contagion and by imputation the eucharistic president himself came to be looked upon as at least analogous to the high priest of the Old Covenant and the spokesman of the entire royal priesthood.[25]

With the Lord's Supper reinterpreted sacrificially, the controlling documentation for ministry shifts from the New Testament to the Old, the very sacrificial cultus that the Book of Hebrews sees as having been terminated. And in the place of the preachers of the New Testament there are now bishops who preside over the elements as well as the priests and the deacons.

From here it is just a short step to the final development in the doctrine of ministry in the early church. In the second century, the church had defined the ministry in more and more personal terms.[26] Doing so, the early church would inevitably have to face the question of what happened when particular persons proved unworthy of the trust they held. When the question did arise, it came in an especially virulent form, arising out of the persecutions in the North African church and taking hold to such a degree that it became defining of it. Donatism was the faith of North Africa so completely that Augustine finally blessed the use of coercive measures to exterminate it. The destruction of such a once vibrant church by Islam not much later may be a final consequence of this coercion.

The particular problem in Donatism was the *traditore*, the bishop who had handed over the Scripture to the authorities in times of persecution.[27] So doing, the Donatists held, the bishop had proven himself unqualified for his office. When he fell, all of his sacramental acts—from baptism to extreme unction—fell like dominoes behind him. Since the ordinations performed by the *traditores* were thereby invalid, it would follow that anyone ordained by one who had been ordained by one would also be invalidly ordained, succession having been broken. With logic like this, the North Africans must have gone to genealogy with the zeal of Mormons, here attempting to demonstrate that the validity of the sacraments administered by their pastors had not been compromised.

It was an impossible situation, as St. Augustine himself recognized.[28] To make the sacraments dependent on the sanctification of the pastors is to put the consciences of the faithful in permanent jeopardy. So Augustine offered a remedy. His solution was simple and direct: to protect the certainty of believers, it was necessary, he argued, to make the validity of the sacrament dependent on the act itself rather than the one acting as administrator.

Recognizing the pastoral import of the argument, the mainline Western tradition has with some variations followed Augustine at this point, insisting that the sacrament is valid *ex opere operato*, by virtue of the sacrament itself rather than by the virtue of the administrator.

As pastorally defensible and necessary as this development may have been, however, it is the final step into a sacerdotal understanding of ministry. If the Apostolic Fathers and the subsequent Roman tradition could identify the church by its bishop, in this new stage by ordination the priest is consecrated to represent God to the church and the church to God, mediating both ways. If earlier the ministry had come to be defined in personal terms, here in von Campenhausen's analysis, a new stage is reached: now to "the priest as such, independently of his position in the community, a definite religious capacity and quality is attributed, distinguishing him, once and for all, from the laity and making him privileged to perform his special, in fact, his priestly service."[29] A religious class composed of the ordained has emerged, set aside by the sacramental act of ordination for the sacrifice of the Mass, the Eucharist.

Though this is the final development in ministry in the patristic church, there was one more step to be taken before the decisive shape of the ministry that followed in the Middle Ages was filled out. Early in the fifth century Augustine, then the bishop in the small North African town of Hippo, near Carthage, could call his pope across the Mediterranean and instruct him concerning the findings of the Synod of Carthage. A generation later a new pope would call in his bishops and give them instructions concerning the two natures of Christ. It would take a couple of centuries and two other popes who could live up to Leo I's title, "the Great," but when Gregory I and Nicholas I finished their work the hierarchy would have its true hierarch and the sacerdotium its archtypical vicar.

But that is another story. Though the bishops of the early church could not set aside the diversity of ministries in the New Testament, they certainly overruled them in actual fact, organizing the ministry with themselves at its head and redefining the work of the church in bureaucratic, cultic, and sacrificial terms. The church that went into mission under the power of the proclaimed Word and the administered sacrament became, in its first five centuries, a sacerdotal institution, replete with bureaucrats making ultimate claims for themselves. The eschatological Word of the Creator's reclamation of creature and creation still bubbled up through the structures, as did the more free-for-all spiritual powers that salt and leaven the church. But in church life as in other institutions of God's left hand, those who organize conquer.

NOTES

1. Hans von Campenhausen, *Ecclesiastical Authority and Spiritual Power in the Church of the First Three Centuries,* trans. J. A. Baker (Stanford, Calif.: Stanford University Press, 1969).

2. See Ernst Käsemann, "Ministry and Community in the New Testament," in *Essays on New Testament Themes,* trans. W. J. Montague (London: SCM Press, 1964), 63–94.

3. Rudolf Schnackenberg, *The Church in the New Testament,* trans. W. J. O'Hara (New York: Herder & Herder, 1965), 126ff.

4. H. Richard Niebuhr and Daniel D. Williams, eds., *The Ministry in Historical Perspective* (New York: Harper & Row, 1956), 28.

5. Magnesians 13:1, 6:1 in Helmut Koester, ed., *Ignatius of Antioch* (Philadelphia: Fortress Press, 1985).

6. Smyrneans 8:1.

7. Magnesians 6:1, Smyrneans 9:1.

8. See Roy Harrisville's essay: above, chap. 1.

9. Eph. 9:2.

10. Von Campenhausen, *Ecclesiastical Authority,* 104.

11. First Clement 44:1-5. See von Campenhausen, *Ecclesiastical Authority,* 89ff.

12. Niebuhr and Williams, *The Ministry,* 63.

13. Epistle 68 in *Saint Cyprian: Letters,* trans. Rose Bernard Donna, C. S. J., *The Fathers of the Church* (Washington, D.C.: Catholic University of America Press, 1964), vol. 51.

14. Von Campenhausen, *Ecclesiastical Authority,* 163.

15. Ibid., 168.

16. A more detailed account of this development is provided by George H. Williams in Niebuhr and Williams, *The Ministry,* 51ff.

17. Ibid., 63ff.

18. Von Campenhausen, *Ecclesiastical Authority,* 84ff.

19. Niebuhr and Williams, *The Ministry,* 29.

20. Ibid., 63.

21. Ibid., 63.

22. For an account of the development of monasticism, see David Knowles, *Christian Monasticism* (New York: McGraw Hill, 1969).

23. Hans von Campenhausen, *Tradition and Life in the Early Church,* trans. A. V. Littledale (Philadelphia: Fortress Press, 1968), 217.

24. Jaroslav Pelikan, *Spirit versus Structure: Luther and the Institutions of the Church* (New York: Harper & Row, 1968), 11ff., 31ff.

25. Niebuhr and Williams, *The Ministry*, 28.

26. Von Campenhausen, *Tradition and Life*, 217, 223.

27. For a fuller account see Peter R. L. Brown, "St. Augustine's Attitude to Religious Coercion," in *Religion and Society in the Age of St. Augustine* (New York: Harper & Row, 1972), and W. H. C. Frend, *The Donatist Church: A Movement of Protest in Roman North Africa* (Oxford: Clarendon Press, 1971).

28. For a more complete account, see von Campenhausen, *Tradition and Life*, 224ff.

29. Ibid., 218.

Ministry
in the Middle Ages
and the Reformation

3

JANE E. STROHL

Western Christians, Roman Catholic and Protestant alike, are heirs of the sixteenth-century Reformation. The divisions of Christendom which marked this period resulted from a number of conflicts, not least of which was disagreement over the doctrine of the ministry. The purpose of this essay is to explore some of the competing views of ministry and ordination articulated by the Reformation churches. Attention will also be given to the paradigm emerging from the Middle Ages and ultimately codified by the Roman Catholic church at the Council of Trent, which met intermittently from 1545 to 1563. In addition, the essay will examine the position of the Eastern Orthodox tradition regarding the priesthood, as this was set forth in the late-seventeenth-century Confession of Dositheus. This document is of particular interest because it was written to counteract the Reformed sympathies of the patriarch Cyril Lucaris. Thus, it offers an Orthodox response to distinctively Protestant questions.

The goal of this survey is to identify the issues at stake and their significance for the parties to the debate, so that an appreciation of these historic differences might inform contemporary discussions of the ministry. Sixteenth-century resolutions of the problem cannot free us from the necessity of engaging the issue anew, but they can help us discuss it wisely. This study will employ select documents representative of the views of various branches of Christendom on the doctrine of ministry. It is intended to be an exercise in historical theology rather than one in social history. Thus, it will concentrate on confessional statements and theological works and the ideas expressed therein rather than on sociological data of the actual practice of ministry in these various communities.

THE DECREES OF THE COUNCIL OF TRENT

Reform was a constant concern for the church of Rome from at least the eleventh century. The struggle carried on by the Gregorian reformers to insure the church's autonomy and thus its purity focused in large part on the life of the clergy. The three major planks of their program were the abolition of clerical marriage, of simony, and of lay investiture. In addition, canons of cathedrals were encouraged to amend their life-style along monastic lines, embracing communal living and the renunciation of privately held property.

Pope Gregory VII, in his ardor to enforce his reform policies, went so far as to command the laity to reject the ministrations of priests who failed to conform to his decrees.[1] His purpose was to enforce obedience, but this measure raised again the specter of Donatism. It suggested that a priest guilty of sexual acts or simony was unable to convey sacramental grace. Indeed, in the later Middle Ages persons did become uneasy about the security of their salvation. Required to depend upon the sacramental structure of the church and its priestly hierarchy for saving grace, many Christians were repelled by the church's involvement in worldly affairs and the manifestly unsanctified life of numerous ecclesiastics. Lay people sought greater control over their spiritual lives and were unwilling to surrender them totally to the care of the institution and its ruling priestly caste. Spiritual authority had to validate itself in a life of personal worthiness. The tradition of lay piety, emphasizing purity and asceticism, went so far in some cases as to become heretical, rejecting altogether the sacraments and ministry of the institutional church. This excessive concern with the issue of priestly purity has been interpreted as the result of Gregorian reform, causing disillusioned reformers to become heretical extremists.

The cry for reform in head and members was not, therefore, something new on the scene in the late fifteenth and early sixteenth centuries. Indeed, the frustration and fury expressed by Luther and his fellow evangelicals were echoed by many Christians who did not embrace Protestant theological principles. From the great humanist Erasmus to the loyal Catholic (but hardly uncritical Romanist) Duke George of Saxony, one hears pointed critiques of the state of the church and its leadership. The papacy itself was not insensitive to the swell of popular disillusion and even recognized that it was a large part of the problem, as well as the party bearing chief responsibility for a solution. Although several decades elapsed before a church council was convened, the papacy did finally see to it that the challenge of Protestantism was met at Trent. It would be inadequate, however, to regard the proceedings as exclusively response and defense, a "counter-reformation," for Trent articulated with care the Catholic faith and gave the church sharper self-definition on its own terms, in addition to pronouncing anathemas on what lay beyond these newly clarified boundaries.

Within the first six months of its meeting the council addressed the question of preparing and providing preachers for parishes. At the fifth session regulations were laid down for the establishment of lectureships in Scripture and the liberal arts. The second chapter of the decree concerning reform from this session opens with the recognition that preaching of the Gospel is no less necessary to the church than the reading thereof and that the former is chiefly the duty of the bishops. They are enjoined to fulfill this obligation personally and, if hindered from doing so by a legitimate impediment, to appoint competent persons to take their place. Priests whose positions in parochial or other churches entailed the cure of souls are required to preach at least on Sundays and other solemn festivals or to find competent substitutes in cases of legitimate disability. The text of the decree stipulates what the substance of such preaching should be as well. Using wholesome words in proportion to their own and their hearers' mental ability, priests are to teach those things necessary for all to know in order to be saved and to impress upon the faithful "the vices that they must avoid and the virtues that they must cultivate, in order that they may escape eternal punishment and obtain the glory of heaven."[2] The decree provides for sanctions to be invoked against those prelates who neglect their pulpit duties. Finally, the council addresses the question of monastic preachers, seeking to insure that they too fulfill their charge and do so under the supervision of their superiors in the order and of the local bishop. In the past bishops had complained bitterly about these intruders in their territories, who remained exempt from episcopal authority and thus could preach what they pleased in the churches belonging to their orders (and also presumed to do so in churches that did not). The requirements set forth here seek to do justice to the legitimate claims of the bishops, who are ultimately responsible for the purity of all doctrine taught in their dioceses, while safeguarding the vocation of the preaching orders, whose influence had been so extensive in the Middle Ages.

The Sacrament of Holy Orders was taken up by the council at its twenty-third session in 1563. In four brief chapters the fathers affirm 1) the sacrificial nature of the priesthood, 2) the hierarchical orders of priesthood, 3) the distinctive sacramental grace conferred by ordination, and 4) the superiority of bishops. The Lord is understood to have instituted a new sacrifice on the night in which he was betrayed rather than a sacramental meal, and to have bestowed upon the apostles and their successors the power of consecrating, offering, and administering his body and blood. The fathers affirm that this understanding is supported by Scripture and tradition. With regard to the second point, the hierarchical organization by which one works one's way up to full priestly orders is defended as appropriate to the honor of the priesthood and as dating back to the church's infancy.[3] This tradition is understood to be instituted by divine ordinance (Canon 6). The orders enumerated include those of deacon, subdeacon, acolyte, exorcist, lector, and porter.

According to the Tridentine teaching, the Sacrament of Priestly Ordination imprints an indelible character upon the recipient which cannot be effaced or invalidated. He receives the power to confect a true sacrament, that is, to make the grace of God available to the faithful. Thus, ordination becomes the foundation of the whole sacramental system and the sacrificing priesthood the indispensable link between the church and its salvation. To assert the priesthood of all believers and thereby to reduce the ordained priesthood to the exercise of an office, possibly temporary in nature, is to derange the ecclesiastical hierarchy, which, as stated above, is understood to be established by divine warrant. Although baptism too imparts an indelible character, it does not serve as the basis for one's service in the priesthood. Ministry requires the further special grace of ordination.

Even the ordained are not endowed with an equal spiritual power among themselves. As mentioned before, there are a number of orders below the priest, and finally there is the bishop above him. Indeed, the bishops are the direct successors of the apostles and thus the preeminent possessors of the authority to celebrate the mass and to exercise the keys. The powers of the priest are derived from those of the bishop, who alone can ordain the former. In the Tridentine canons on the sacrament of order certain Protestant positions are clearly rejected. For example, denounced as "anathema" are those who 1) reduce the ministry to the office of preaching the Gospel and deny the priestly power of consecrating and offering the true body and blood of Christ; 2) reject the sacramental status of ordination, regarding it as at best a human rite for choosing ministers; 3) deny that ordination imprints a character on the recipient; 4) hold that one who has been a priest can again become a layperson; 5) dispute the distinctive powers and prerogatives of bishops which make them superior to priests by divine right.[4]

Despite the council's earlier expressed recognition of the importance of preaching, ministry is presented here chiefly as a matter of sacramental action rather than proclamation of the Word. It requires not a developed skill and human competence but a supernatural gift. Indeed, the purity of grace is guaranteed by the imposition of this permanent endowment that is in no way subject to the moral vicissitudes of the person thus set apart. The action of the Holy Spirit makes a priest, and nothing, not even his recalcitrance, can unmake him. The continuity of God's saving act is vested in a succession of persons, first and foremost in the bishops and secondarily in the priests they ordain. It is only through them that the faithful can obtain the grace necessary for their salvation, but it is also certain that through them grace is and always will be available.

The fathers at Trent emphasized the objective holiness and validity of the ministry, insured by the gift of the indelible character through the action of the Spirit. Nonetheless, they were not indifferent to the concern for personal purity and spiritual competence among the ordained. The various steps taken by the Council to upgrade priestly vocations in the church included the establishment of seminaries for clerics and provision for the continuous preparation of candidates for the ministry.[5] Training for ministry clearly involved spiritual formation and submission to discipline. Those presenting themselves as candidates for ordination were to show themselves worthy recipients before being so set apart. However, although their good works and pious demeanor might earn ordination, they are not what made it effectual. The Tridentine decree mandates that seminarians study grammar, singing, ecclesiastical computation, and other useful arts. They are to receive instruction in Scripture, the ecclesiastical books, and the homilies of the saints. Students learn the ins and outs of sacramental practice, particularly the hearing of confessions. The bishop is to insure that they attend mass daily, make confession at least once a month, commune in accordance with the counsel of their confessor, and serve in the cathedral and other churches of the diocese on festival days. The cultivation of expertise in public preaching is not emphasized, which is all the more striking, given the reforms previously enacted at the fifth session.

AN ORTHODOX VIEW

The Confession of Dositheus also upholds the hierarchy of ministry, insisting on a distinction between episcopal authority and that of priests. The episcopate is regarded as the very wellspring of the church's life.[6] God has guaranteed the indefectibility of the church through the establishment of the apostolic succession of bishops, upon whom every exercise of the priesthood depends and without whom the church could not exist. Indeed, Dositheus speaks in terms that portray the bishop as one locus of the real presence of Christ in the world. He is described as a living image of God upon the earth and a fountain of all the church's mysteries. It would seem that he does not just exercise the sacramental ministry; he is himself a sacrament.

> For since the Lord hath promised to be with us always, although He be with us by other means of grace and Divine operations, yet in a more eminent manner doth He, through the Bishop as chief functionary, make us His own and dwell with us, and through the divine Mysteries is united with us; of which the Bishop is the first minister, and chief functionary, through the Holy Spirit, and suffereth us not to fall into heresy.[7]

The bishop's and priest's responsibility and right to preach the Gospel are mentioned by Dositheus. However, in his article on the sacraments, the predominantly sacrificial nature of the priesthood is evident. Insisting that there are seven sacraments, each of them instituted in the sacred Gospel, he identifies as the dominical words of institution for the priesthood the granting of the power of the keys ("Whatsoever ye shall bind and loose upon the earth shall be bound and loosed in the heavens") and Christ's words from the last supper, "This do ye for My Memorial."[8] Thus, this latter event would be better described as the first sacrifice of the new covenant, establishing a new priesthood to offer the "true and propitiatory Sacrifice"[9] of the Eucharist on behalf of the community of believers.

THE REFORMED TRADITION

Dositheus's insistence on the distinctive character of the episcopacy was directed explicitly at the Reformed tradition's collapsing of the ecclesiastical hierarchy. In its chapter on the ministry of the church, the Second Helvetic

Confession states that the power of ministers is one and equal in all. The practice of placing one above others is accounted for as a historical development, a human innovation for the better governance of the church. Citing Jerome, the document insists that the original bishops knew that they were over "the elders rather by custom than by the prescript rule of God's truth."[10] This structure, being of human rather than divine origin, is subject to change if the well-being of the church will be better served by a different arrangement. Indeed, the adherents of the Second Helvetic Confession reserve to themselves the right to "return to the old appointment of God . . . rather . . . than the custom devised by men."[11]

The ministry as delineated in this confession is preeminently a preaching office. Qualifications for it include "sufficient learning, especially in the Scriptures, and godly eloquence."[12] The enumeration of duties of the minister in the Second Helvetic Confession contrasts sharply with the emphasis on the sacrificial powers of the Roman priesthood.[13] Ministers are to expound the Word of God, teaching the unlearned, building up the faithful, and exhorting the sluggish. They are to rebuke evildoers, rescue the wayward, comfort the fainthearted, contend with the unbelieving, and check schisms. Their pastoral responsibility includes attending to the needs of the poor and the sick. Finally, they must commend the right use of the sacraments to the faithful as well as administer them.

The confession straightforwardly denies the institution by Christ of a special priesthood of the new covenant. Priesthood is the property of all believers, who by their faith share in the kingly and priestly offices of Christ and are thus empowered to offer spiritual sacrifices to God. They require no other intermediary than the high priest Christ himself. To speak of a special priesthood endowed with the unique power to offer Christ in the mass, a power not shared by all the baptized, is denounced as detracting from Christ's honor and attributing to humans what is the prerogative of Christ alone.

The Second Helvetic Confession addresses the issue of Donatism near the end of its chapter on the church's ministry. As previously discussed, the fear existed that an immoral priest could poison the grace of the sacrament only he was empowered to celebrate. This Reformed document is concerned as much with corrupted proclamation as with debased sacraments. Although evil ministers are not to be tolerated in office without reproof, they are to be heard, for a true Word of God may issue forth from the mouth of one whose life bears not witness to the teaching he imparts.[14] God's Word remains sovereign; its only guarantee is its divine source. Yet this objective certainty is harder to discern when the means of grace are preaching/teaching rather than the sacrament. When the dominical promise is attached to the elements, then whenever those words are spoken over a cup and loaf, one may be sure that the Lord is savingly present to be met and embraced. The Catholic tradition lodges the guarantee in two places: first of all in the character impressed upon the priest which cannot be marred or destroyed, and then in the elements themselves, once the miracle of transubstantiation has been effected by the priest. When it comes to the preaching or teaching of pastors, particularly ones with spiritual or moral flaws, how is one to know whether at any given time God is using them despite themselves to speak truly? Because no indelible character is imparted to ministers, guaranteeing their constant validity as servants of saving grace, the believer must to some degree or other receive their ministrations critically.

In his discussion of ordination in Book 4, chapter 3 of the *Institutes of the Christian Religion,* Calvin acknowledges the ceremony as a rite rather than a sacrament, alleging that there is no set scriptural precept for the laying on of hands. However, the consistent use of this practice by the apostles ought, writes Calvin, to serve in lieu of a precept. Thus, the fact that ordination is not held to be a sacrament is meant in no way to diminish its importance.

> And surely it is useful for the dignity of the ministry to be commended to the people by this sort of sign, as also to warn the one ordained that he is no longer a law unto himself, but bound in servitude to God and the church. Moreover, it will be no empty sign if it is restored to its own true origin. For if the Spirit of God establishes nothing without cause in the church, we should feel that this ceremony, since it has proceeded from him, is not useless, provided it be not turned to superstitious abuse.[15]

The insistence that ordination empowers one to perform a sacrifice is a superstitious abuse, according to Calvin, but the rejection of a received indelible character is not to say that ordination is not an efficacious act. Citing Paul, he asserts that the laying on of hands imparts a particular grace. Moreover, he insists that the "whole multitude did not lay hands upon its ministers, but pastors alone did so."[16] This implies that the grace given to the special ministry is something beyond the baptismal grace possessed by the universal priesthood and is transmitted independent of the latter. At the same time, Calvin insists that the ministers are to be chosen with the consent and approval of the people, although pastors are to preside over such elections so "that the multitude may not go wrong either through fickleness, through evil intentions, or through disorder."[17] Thus, while rejecting the cleavage between clerics and laity in the Roman Catholic church and the so-called spiritual estate's hegemony over the ministry, Calvin still maintains a distinction between the people and the pastors, the latter exercising authority over the former. Pastors "have been set over the church by the doctrine of Christ to instruct the people to true godliness, to administer the sacred mysteries and to keep and exercise upright discipline."[18]

Calvin rejects the hierarchical structure of the priesthood which is characteristic of the Roman church, deliberately using the terms bishop, presbyter, pastor, and minister interchangeably. The placement of any one minister of the Word over others is a matter of human arrangement, not of divine right and superior spiritual power. Calvin recognizes four distinct offices instituted by

God for the preservation of the church: pastors and teachers, two offices engaged in the ministry of the Word; elders, charged with the censure of morals and the exercise of discipline along with the pastors; and finally deacons, to whom is entrusted the care of the poor. The various preparatory stages for the priesthood as enumerated formally by the Council of Trent are characterized by Calvin as "more the rudiments of recruits than functions to be considered as true ministries of the church."[19] Indeed, he accuses Rome of deforming the office of deacon, turning it into a lesser form of liturgical service rather than directing it to the care of the poor, just as the priesthood itself has been turned into a sacrificial office.

The fact that the holy ministry is exercised by human beings in no way detracts for Calvin from its honor. It is God's ministry that God has willed to accomplish through the agency of persons. This both ennobles and humbles us.[20] God declares regard for humankind by using some of us to represent God's person and interpret the divine will. God also thereby disciplines us in the practice of humility and obedience, for we are obliged to receive God's word from those no better than we, sometimes even from persons of lesser worth.

As a powerful manifestation of God's gracious will to save and the chief means of communicating that grace to God's children, the ministry is essential to the church. God "shows himself as though present"[21] by manifesting the power of the Spirit in the ministry, which Calvin calls God's institution. It is instrumental to the renewal of the saints and the building up of the body of Christ. To reject it is to court the destruction of the church. "For neither the light and heat of the sun, nor food and drink, are so necessary to nourish and sustain the present life as the apostolic and pastoral office is necessary to preserve the church on earth."[22] The provision of the office itself and its preservation by God's equipping persons in every generation to fill it insure the continuance of the true gospel. Moreover, although Calvin rejects the doctrine of the possession and transmission of an indelible character through the church's public priesthood, he does insist that true teaching is to be found within ecclesiastical confines. The secret call, the witness of an individual's heart to the prompting of God's summons, is not enough to validate one's taking up the ministry. One must also have the outward, solemn call of the church to be deemed trustworthy by those committed to one's charge.

THE RADICALS

As a final alternative for understanding the ministry, we shall examine two documents from radical reformers: Thomas Müntzer's 1524 sermon before the princes of Saxony and the Confession of the Anabaptist Obbe Philips from around 1560. Both reflect on the working of the Holy Spirit in the formation and validation of Christian ministers.

Müntzer is no whit behind Luther in his vehement rejection of what he deems papist idolatry, but he yokes this judgment with a denunciation of Protestant, specifically Lutheran, violation of the Spirit. The Word is implanted in many a soul, but the field remains overgrown with vices, desires, and the taste for comfort. Müntzer insists that the power of the Word of God cannot "overshadow" a person who "wants to cultivate continuously for himself a high degree of pleasure and deal [only] with the works of God and does not want to be in tribulation."[23] Yet those who are willing to brave trial and suffering, thus clearing the field, will reap the harvest and hear the inner word truly and clearly, as was the experience of the biblical patriarchs and apostles. They will come to recognize that they are dwelling places of God and the Holy Spirit and that they have been created for the sole purpose of searching out the testimonies of God in their own lives. It is, Müntzer claims, a mark of the truly apostolic, patriarchal, and prophetic spirit to attend upon visions and to receive the same in painful tribulation.[24] God's intent is for Christendom to become apostolic in the way foretold by the prophet Joel. Under these circumstances, the particular qualifications for ministry are the attainment of such visions and dreams in one's own life, the ability to distinguish between true and false inspirations, and the power to preach so as to lead others to a like experience.

Müntzer straightforwardly acknowledges that much of what passes for the work of the Holy Spirit is the deception of the devil (as, for example, among those he calls "the damnable monastic ecstatics"),[25] but the sin of those like Luther, who reject such spiritual experience out of hand, is equally damnable. These skeptics condemn the good with the bad and dismiss the truth as falsehood. Indeed, their course of action in spiritual matters betrays their own unfitness for the ministry. They prefer the good favor of their princes and personal comfort to the tribulation that alone can bring true knowledge of the inner word. Thus, they themselves have never received the visions and dreams that advance such knowledge and confirm the validity of one's call. Without this personal experience, they have no right to pass judgment on the prophecy and visions of others. After an unflattering comparison of some of his contemporaries with the seers called to interpret Nebuchadnezzar's dreams (Daniel 2), Müntzer declares:

> Such learned divines are the soothsayers who then publicly repudiate the revelation of God and thus attack the Holy Spirit at his handiwork. [They] wish to instruct the whole world and what is not according to their inexperienced understanding must right off be for them from the devil. And yet [they] are not even assured of their own salvation, which surely ought to be required (Romans 8).[26]

Müntzer turns Luther's theology of the cross against him, mocking the Wittenberg Reformer as "Brother Fattened Swine" and "Brother Soft Life."[27] He concludes his sermon by taking it upon himself to perform the bold, dangerous duty required of a minister vis-à-vis the Saxon princes, that is, to exhort them to share in the vision vouchsafed the elect and to take up the sword against the ungodly.[28]

The question of the validity of such visions remains a troublesome one. How is one to distinguish the inspiration of the Spirit from the deceits of the devil?

Müntzer does allow a role to Scripture as a norm for evaluating the significance of visions, but the ultimate source of truth is the inner word in the heart of the person. Visions and dreams propel the as yet inattentive listener along the way to full knowledge of that inner word; they are in turn tested by it. Ultimately, the authority of any minister's word depends on the clarity of his own spiritual self-knowledge, his receptiveness to the living testimony of God within his own soul, for whoever "[has not the Spirit] does not know how to say anything deeply about God, even if he had eaten through a hundred Bibles!"[29]

The issue of verifying claims to spiritual inspiration greatly troubled Obbe Philips in his involvement with radical Anabaptism. Disillusionment finally drove him from the movement, and his Confession gives us a poignant insight into the doubts that undermined his conviction of his own calling. At the outset of this document Philips writes that just as no one can believe without hearing, so no one can preach unless commissioned to do so. He asserts that those who claim such an authorization will demonstrate their commission in strength and deed.[30] Philips regards the establishment of a new ordination, office and order as a degeneration from the simplicity of service initially recovered by his community after its separation from the false hierarchy of the papacy. There arose those who were no longer content to serve God straightforwardly in the Spirit with quiet, pure hearts after the manner of the fathers and patriarchs. Rather, they presented themselves as special teachers and envoys of the Lord, "professing to have been compelled in their hearts by God to baptize, preach, and teach, and establish a new church (kercke), since the ancient church had perished."[31] Such a one was Melchior Hofmann, from whose line Philips's own credentials derived. Uncertainty shrouded the origins of Hofmann's ministry; it was not clear whether he had taken up the office on his own initiative or had been sent by someone else. Thus, although Hofmann commissioned others to preach, their claim to a valid calling was tenuous because his right so to commission them was questionable.

Philips recounts numerous cases of those who rose up on their own authority and succeeded in winning recognition as prophets, sometimes because their message was appealing and sometimes because they intimidated the doubtful. Yet for Philips, the credibility of these radical preachers following in the train of the imprisoned Hofmann was undermined by a number of factors. In addition to their dubious commissioning, the falseness of some of the commissionings they in turn imparted to others spoke against the holiness of the spirit that moved them. John Matthijs, for example, who professed to be Enoch by the power of the Holy Spirit, called John of Leyden to the office of apostle, and on the basis of this calling the latter became king of Münster by means of what Philips calls corrupt activities. Through two other such commissioned apostles, Philips received his own induction into the office of preaching, a calling that remained unconfirmed by any subjective experience.

The following day, when they were ready to go on, they summoned us along with John Scheerder, at the suggestion of other brethren, and with the laying on of hands laid upon us the office of preaching, [commissioning us] to baptize, teach, and stand before the congregation, etc. We could feel the laying on of hands and we could also hear all the words, but we neither felt nor heard the Holy Spirit, nor received any power from above, but [heard] many loose words which had neither strength nor lasting effect, as afterward we amply discovered; and after they had done these things with us, they immediately went forth the same day.[32]

For Philips, the recipient's lack of spiritual exaltation at the laying on of hands disconfirms the validity of the commissioner's ministry as well as the call being issued. In the end he rejected the authority of the radicals who first baptized and commissioned him, and he abandoned his preaching office. Moreover, he cast doubt upon the validity of the ministry of those he himself commissioned, which, according to his Confession, included his brother Dietrich, David Joris, and Menno Simons.

The welter of visions, prophecies, and inspirations among his fellow believers undermined Philips's originally naive confidence. He writes that at first "[w]e supposed in our simplicity that if we guarded ourselves against the papists, Lutherans, and Zwinglians, then all was well and we need have no cares."[33] Yet as teachers proliferated, so did their doctrines. With each claiming the inspiration of the Spirit and a valid commissioning, the only way to test the spirits was to see whose prophecies were confirmed by events. The rise and fall of the kingdom at Münster revealed the hypocrisy and falseness of the radical movement to Philips, who from the outset was troubled by its descent into violence and intolerance. Hofmann and Matthijs died discredited and dishonored, their celebrated prophecies unfulfilled. Indeed, the fate they had foretold for the godless fell upon themselves, and those who gave up patient suffering to take arms against the alleged unbelievers were themselves slaughtered. For Philips, the final and most painful proof of the falseness of his community's preachers and their message was the quality of life they produced among their hearers. No sooner was a believer baptized than he began attacking those who were not part of his particular community. The congregations were constantly wrangling with one another over issues of theology and practice. Their life was marked, laments Philips, by backbiting, blasphemy, slander, and condemnations of their fellow believers as heretical and godless.

Thus it is that a reasonable, impartial Christian may truly say that it is no Christian congregation but a desolate abomination, that it can be no temple of God but a cave of murderers, full of hate, envy, jealousy, spiritual pride, pseudo piety, hypocrisy, contempt, defamation. They could suffer neither the love nor benefit of another who was not of their belief, sect, opinion, and who did not say yea and amen to all their enterprises and onslaughts.[34]

At the end of his painful experience among the Anabaptists, Philips concludes that the essential measure of ministry's validity is its commitment to and success in establishing and preserving Christian charity. Where there is not love, neither is there truth.

CONCLUSION

Each view described has manifested the conviction that ministry is established and maintained by divine action, whether the hand of God is seen in the impressing of an indelible mark, the clothing of the Word in human words of proclamation, or the imparting of Spirit-filled prophecies and visions. These views reveal also the inevitable tension between the need for certainty and the structures that can provide it, and the sovereignty of God, whose ways of acting remain, to some degree or other, inscrutable. I remember sitting in a graduate seminar on comparative confessions one afternoon. The topic for the day was ministry. In the course of the discussion, which ranged from the parish to the papacy, a Roman Catholic colleague, by no means indifferent to the controversy sparked by some of the present pontiff's positions, commented that ultimately God would not allow the Holy Father to lead the church into ways that were harmful to our salvation. The Protestants in the room were caught off guard by both her candor and her confidence. We are heirs to a core religious experience that leaves a legacy of suspicion and requires a formidable degree of personal responsibility for the purity of the faith. One could describe the magisterial reformers' work as bringing a lifelong suit of pastoral malpractice against the ministry, from priest to pope, of the medieval church. Fearing the normless vagaries of the kind of radical spiritism mourned by Obbe Philips, they never divorced the call to ministry from the structures of the church. Yet their experience with the Roman hierarchy did not allow them to make a straightforward identification of authoritative ecclesiastical action and divine inspiration. God wills to work through the ministry, founded by God's Word for the Gospel's sake. Yet at times God preserves the Gospel in, with, and despite the ministry rather than through it.

NOTES

1. "Those who obtain churches by the gift of money must forfeit them completely, and no one henceforth shall be permitted to buy or sell them. Also, those who fall into the crime of fornication may not celebrate masses or serve at the altar in minor orders. We have further decreed that, if they disobey our statutes, or rather those of the holy fathers, the people shall in no way accept their ministrations, so that those who are not corrected by the love of God or the honor of their office may be brought to their senses by the shame of the world and the rebuke of the people." Letter of Gregory to Otto, bishop of Constance in *The Crisis of Church and State 1050–1300*, ed. Brian Tierney (Englewood Cliffs, N.J.: Prentice-Hall, Inc., 1964), 52.

2. *Canons and Decrees of the Council of Trent*, trans. Rev. J. H. Schroeder, O.P. (St. Louis: B. Herder, 1941), 26.

3. "But since the ministry of so holy a priesthood is something divine, that it might be exercised in a more worthy manner and with greater veneration, it was consistent

that in the most well-ordered arrangement of the Church there should be several distinct orders of ministers, who by virtue of their office should minister to the priesthood, so distributed that those already having the clerical tonsure should ascend through the minor to the major orders." Ibid., 160–61.

4. Ibid., 162–63. See especially canons 1, 3, 4, and 7.

5. Ibid., 175–76.

6. "The Confession of Dositheus," in *Creeds of the Churches*, ed. John H. Leith, 3d ed. (Atlanta: John Knox Press, 1982), 492–93.

7. Ibid., 493.

8. Ibid., 498.

9. Ibid., 504.

10. "The Second Helvetic Confession," in Leith, ed., *Creeds*, 158.

11. Ibid.

12. Ibid., 153.

13. Ibid., 158-59.

14. "For we know that the voice of Christ is to be heard, though it be out of the mouths of evil ministers; forasmuch as the Lord himself said, 'Practice and observe whatever they tell you, but not what they do' (Matt. 23:3). "We know that the sacraments are sanctified by the institution, and through the word of Christ; and that they are effectual to the godly, although they be administered by ungodly ministers." Ibid., 160.

15. John Calvin, *Institutes of the Christian Religion*, ed. John T. McNeill (Philadelphia: Westminster Press, 1960), 2:1067.

16. Ibid.

17. Ibid., 1066.

18. Ibid., 1059.

19. Ibid., 1077.

20. Ibid., 1053–54.

21. Ibid., 1055.

22. Ibid.

23. Thomas Müntzer, "Sermon Before the Princes" in *Spiritual and Anabaptist Writers*, ed. George H. Williams and Angel M. Mergal (Philadelphia: Westminster Press, 1957), 60.

24. Ibid., 59-60.

25. Ibid., 56.

26. Ibid., 55-56.

27. Ibid., 61.

28. "If you could only as clearly recognize the harm being [done] to Christendom and rightly consider it, you would acquire just the same zeal as Jehu the king (2 Kings 9—10); and the same as that which the whole book of Revelation proclaims. And I know for a certainty that you would thereupon hold yourselves back only with great effort from [letting] the sword exert its power. For the pitiable corruption of holy Christendom has become so great that at the present time no tongue can tell it all. Therefore a new Daniel must arise and interpret for you your vision and this [prophet], as Moses teaches (Deut. 20:2), must go in front of the army. He must reconcile the anger of the princes and the enraged people. For if you will rightly experience the corruption of Christendom and the deception of the false clerics and the vicious reprobates, you will become so enraged at them that no one can think it through. Without doubt it will vex you and go right to your heart that you have been so kindly after they, with the very sweetest words,

misled you into the most shameful conceptions (Prov. 6:1ff.) against all established truth."
Ibid., 64–65.

29. Ibid., 58.

30. Obbe Philips, "A Confession," in Williams and Mergal, eds., *Spiritual and Anabaptist Writers*, 206.

31. Ibid., 207–8.

32. Ibid., 217.

33. Ibid., 213.

34. Ibid., 224–25.

The Doctrine of Ministry
in Martin Luther
and the Lutheran Confessions

4

ROBERT KOLB

The fundamental appeal of Luther's Reformation sprang from its effective address of the crisis in pastoral care which plagued the Western church at the end of the Middle Ages. During the fifteenth century European Christians had become increasingly active in expressing their piety in traditional ways. At the same time many had found increasing frustration because the old system of caring for Christian "souls" did not seem to be working. Priests had failed to be good pastors.[1] Luther was propelled to center stage in the Western church by events that arose out of his deep personal concern for what the abuse of the indulgence trade was doing to the piety of the parishioners of Wittenberg. His was a Reformation, a revolution, of pastoral care.

THE PASTORAL OFFICE, THE PRIESTHOOD OF ALL BELIEVERS, AND LUTHER'S EVANGELICAL BREAKTHROUGH

As Luther had grown up, he had been taught that the sacrament of ordination bestowed upon the priest the power to dictate and to dominate in God's church, both over God's dealing with believers and over the life of the believers themselves. Like the pagan shaman who was his ideological ancestor, such a priest was given a special quality that enabled him to do things no others could do. His standing before God gave him special standing over his parishioners; his power to dispense God's grace gave him special power over them. It was little wonder then that a sensitive spirit like Luther's was terrified at the thought of assuming such power in his first celebration of the mass.[2] During the course of the development of his own understanding of the way God works in the world, in the late 1510s, Luther came to see that the power of God is expressed through the Word, not through priests who had attained a special spiritual status. By 1520 Luther had come to see that God's Word places in believers' mouths a power to serve one another, a power that has nothing to do with dictating or dominating.[3]

In order to understand the way Luther defined this power to serve up the Word of God to fellow believers and to serve one another through the Word, we must recognize that his teaching regarding the public ministry of the Word rested on two presuppositions. The first is that the believer lives in two distinct but inseparable relationships, one with God, the other with other human creatures. In 1535 Luther called attention to the importance of this distinction of the two kinds of righteousness by labelling it "our theology."[4] The "vertical" relationship—with God—is fundamentally a relationship that God establishes through the Word of God's promise, to which believers react with trust. The "horizontal" relationship—with other human creatures—is fundamentally a relationship defined by the design that God has written into the human nature, a design that demands conformity with certain external standards of performance if human life is to be experienced as God wills it to be experienced. God's Word of gospel establishes the first relationship; God's Word of law regulates the second. All believers are equal in God's sight: there is no "respect of persons" (Acts 10:34, KJV), no Jew nor Greek, no slave nor free, no male nor female (Gal. 3:28). But, Luther taught, in the horizontal sphere God has structured the human life to be lived in three situations: home (family and economic activities), the political realm, and the church. All people are given "offices" or responsibilities in each of these situations, and Christians recognize that these responsibilities are actually callings or vocations from God.

In so describing God's design for human life Luther broke through the medieval understanding of the relationship of the sacred and profane. Therefore he taught that, even though the offices of spouse or parent or public official do not have the same eternal impact as does the office of pastor, the pastor's calling to the office and responsibility of preaching the Word possesses no spiritual superiority or special holiness. This means that the activities of the pastoral office contribute nothing to its holder's standing before God (the vertical dimension of life). The pastor exercises the same office that Christ exercised as his occupational vocation on earth, but that does not confer on the pastor a more godly nature or status; like all sinners pastors stand worthy before God only because of the forgiveness of sins bestowed through Jesus Christ.[5]

The second presupposition that Luther bequeathed to his followers served as a basis for their understanding of the pastoral office: that God accomplishes the restoration of the vertical relationship in the believer's life, the relationship of faith or trust in God, through God's Word of promise. Luther presupposed that God works his saving will through this Word, which takes form in or is conveyed by selected elements of the created order: through the human flesh of Jesus of Nazareth, the incarnate second person of the Trinity; through human language, fundamentally in the Scriptures and derivatively in every written and oral address of the biblical message to human hearers; through elements of water and of bread-body and wine-blood, which are joined to the Word of forgiveness and life; through believers, who apply the Word to the lives of other human creatures. That Word, Luther presumed, comes to believers in preaching, in baptism, in absolution, in the Lord's Supper, and in the mutual conversation and consolation of Christians with one another (SA 3:4, *BC* 310). God created all reality by saying, "Let there be . . . ," and God re-creates sinners into faithful children through the Word of forgiveness. God's Word of law always confronts the sinner with accusation and condemnation, in addition to whatever else it may do; the Word of gospel bestows forgiveness and new life.

Luther combatted both a magical kind of understanding of the way God works with human creatures, so prominent in popular late medieval Christianity, and the dismissal of external instruments of God's power, in Word and Sacrament, as promoted by spiritualists and Anabaptists, the heirs of the schismatic medieval tradition. Instead, Luther insisted that God acts in and through the Word in its various forms.[6] The papal party insisted on an ontological view of the ministry and a defense of the established system of doing things; both gutted the dynamic power of a ministry set to alter people's lives through the energy of the gospel. The "radical" reformers' neoplatonic world view refused to permit the possibility that God, who is spirit, could design a world in which selected elements of the created order could effectively convey God's love and power. Luther dismissed both views, and in doing so formulated an understanding of the pastoral office to match.

Nineteenth- and twentieth-century discussions of Luther's understanding of the ministry have often been framed by questions about power in the church which Luther was not answering. Since the French Revolution Western Christians have shared the general cultural concern about personal "rights." Thus they have wanted to determine where the line between clerical and lay rights and power lies. That question indeed commanded the attention of the medieval church although the context for posing it changed with the coming of the modern era. Luther conceived of the entire relationship between clergy and laity differently. He ignored questions related to dominance and dictation by one or the other, questions of who controlled whom and what in the church. Instead, he pursued the definition of the power to serve, both God and one another, within the assembly of God's people, through God's Word.

> We neither can nor ought to give the name of priest to those who are in charge of Word and sacrament among the people. The reason they have been called priests is either because of the custom of the heathen people or as a vestige of the Jewish nation. The result is greatly injurious to the church. According to the New Testament Scriptures better names would be ministers, deacons, bishops, stewards, presbyters. . . . Paul's frequent use of the word "stewardship" or "household," "ministry," "minister," "servant," "one serving with the gospel," etc. emphasizes that it is not the estate, or order, or any authority or dignity that he wants to uphold, but only the office and the function.[7]

It is indeed true that there are "ambiguities in Luther's terms priest, estate, office/offices, public/private" and "ministry, Gemeinde, and person" which make more difficult the task of assessing Luther's doctrine of the pastoral office.[8] But it is indeed clear that he, like his colleague Philip Melanchthon, understood "ministry" as a "verbal noun"[9] (a term borrowed from Peter Fraenkel). Melanchthon—and Luther—regarded the medieval term for the office of the ministry, "ministerium," as a word that describes both the thing and the action that constitutes the thing and gives it its purpose—in the case of ministerium, serving. The Reformers in no way denied that God had instituted a specific office for conveying the power of the Word into the lives of sinners, but they emphasized that the pastor who filled that office did so by serving in a specific way, as the agent of God's forgiving and re-creating Word. Luther regarded the office without such serving as an empty shell and husk, a shadow of God's design, consumed by its holder's lust for personal power to replace the emptiness that comes when service no longer fills the framework of office. Thus, Luther believed, pastors truly maintain and defend their office not by insisting on their prerogatives as officeholders but simply by practicing and exercising their office with genuine care for and willing service to their people through exercising the power of God's Word as God had designed its use among the people.

For Luther this office of the pastoral ministry was simply designed to serve. It was designed to serve by loosing the power of God's Word, the power to forgive sins and give new life. It was designed to serve the church, which is the priesthood of all believers. The concept of the universal priesthood, which appeared in Luther's writings very early in his public career, is often played off against his concept of the public ministry, but such games misunderstand Luther's distinction of the two spheres of relationship and his concept of mutual service in and through God's Word. These misunderstandings often fail to recognize the different agendas or questions that Luther addressed with each concept.

In his treatises of 1520, which issued his program for reform, Luther attacked the medieval conception of papal and priestly power. In his *To the Christian Nobility of the German Nation,* he condemned the papal use of "three walls" to keep Christendom in subjection to itself. Those three walls consisted of the papal claims to temporal power over earthly rulers, to the sole right to interpret Scripture, and to the sole right to call a council.[10] In *The Babylonian Captivity of the Church* he criticized the abuse of the Lord's Supper which made it an instrument of priestly tyranny over God's people. The priests had used the sacrament "to set up a seed bed of implacable discord, by which clergy and laymen should be separated from each other farther than heaven from earth, to the incredible injury of the grace of baptism and to the confusion of our fellowship in the gospel." He continued by defining the proper office of the ministry: "The duty of a priest is to preach, and if he does not preach, he is as much a priest as a picture of a man is a man. . . . It is the ministry of the Word that makes the priest and the bishop."[11] Hellmut Lieberg has summarized three distortions that lay beneath this medieval conception of the priesthood, as Luther set them forth. First, it made the priests into agents who could render satisfaction to God, and thus control God's grace, through their role in the mass. Second, it made them agents of works-righteousness as they enforced God's law and attained grace through regulating the performance of its demands. Third, it made the priests superior to the laity by virtue of their priestly place in a hierarchy.[12] Each of these three distortions betrayed the oppressive nature of the medieval priesthood, which tried to dominate and dictate to both God and believers. It manipulated God's grace through the sacrifice of the mass and through the works performed and prescribed by the priestly caste. It exacted obedience beyond the demands of God's law. It exacted obeisance and obsequiousness beyond human propriety from God's people.

Luther addressed this perversion of the biblical concept of the ministry of the Word by responding to two questions. The first asked how God had designed the means by which to restore the vertical relationship through the Word, in the horizontal sphere; the answer was through the ministry of Word. The second asked whether service as "priests" gave some believers a higher status before God, in the vertical sphere; the answer announced that all believers are equally priests before God. In *To the Christian Nobility of the German Nation* Luther stated, "All Christians truly are of the spiritual estate, and there is no difference among them except of office. Paul says in 1 Cor. 12:[12-13] that we are all one body, yet every member has its own work by which it serves the others."[13] In his *The Freedom of a Christian*, written the same year, Luther commented on 1 Pet. 2:9,

> Hence all of us who believe in Christ are priests and kings. . . . Not only are we the freest of kings, we are also priests forever which is far more excellent than being kings, for as priests we are worthy to appear before God to pray for others and to teach one another divine things. These are the functions of priests, and they cannot be granted to any unbeliever. Thus Christ has made it possible for us, provided we believe in him, to be not only his brethren, co-heirs, and fellow-kings, but also his fellow priests. Therefore we may boldly come into the presence of God in the spirit of faith [Heb. 10:19, 22] and cry "Abba Father!" pray for one another, and do all things which we see done foreshadowed in the outer and visible works of priests.[14]

At the same time, however, Luther was also ready to answer the question regarding how God uses the Word to establish a saving relationship with humankind. The answer to that question entails not only how the Word itself functions but through whom it functions publicly: "Although we are all equally priests, we cannot all publicly minister and teach." In rejecting "so great a display of power and so terrible a tyranny that no heathen empire or other earthly power can be compared with it,"[15] the tyranny of the papally dominated and directed sacerdotal system of the medieval church, Luther did not reject the office of the public ministry. For he viewed it as a gift from God in the horizontal sphere of human relationships, a special position to which some are called to make possible the formal and public use of God's saving Word. "A Priest is not identical with Presbyter or Minister—for one is born to be priest, one becomes a minister," he could write three years later. Although, in words that demonstrate the ambiguity of his use of these terms, Luther could write, "the first office [that is, function], that of the ministry of the Word, therefore, is common to all Christians," he insisted that the formal exercise of any sharing of the Word be invested in those who are called to such a public ministry through the election by a congregation.[16]

For Luther did indeed believe that the entire church had been given the Word to proclaim. But for the sake of good order, and because God's design for the structure of the church includes leadership, and because God had given the people a variety of gifts, some were to be designated and called by the rest to exercise this formal position as first servants of the church, pastors for the flock.[17] There can be no doubt where Luther saw the focus of all the activities of these called pastors. He listed their functions:

> to teach, to preach and proclaim the Word of God, to baptize, to consecrate or administer the Eucharist, to bind and loose sins, to pray for others, to sacrifice, and to judge all doctrine and spirits. Certainly these are splendid and royal duties. But the first and foremost of all on which everything else depends, is the teaching of the Word of God. For we teach with the Word, we baptize with the Word, we sacrifice with the Word, we judge all things by the Word.[18]

Because for Luther the pastoral ministry was so completely focused on care for God's people through the Word, he could reject the medieval view of an indelible character that was bestowed for life upon the recipient of ordination. God called pastors to serve, and when they no longer served, by serving up the Word, they should no longer occupy the office of the Word. "In this view of ministry, the so-called 'indelible character' vanishes and the perpetuity of the office is shown to be fictitious. A minister may be deposed if he proves unfaithful."[19]

For no magical power was attached to this office or position. God had created it to serve the whole body of believers, of the priests of God. Those priests, Luther believed, should call—or at least have a part in calling—those who would serve God by serving them through the stewardship of the Word in their midst and for their sake. The power of the priesthood over the pastor did not exist for Luther; priests have only the power to support the ministry of the Word through encouragement and prayer. The power of the ministry over the priesthood did not exist for Luther. Pastors have only the power to bring death to sinners and life to God's children through the Word. Luther's chief concern in his understanding of both the public ministry and the priesthood of all believers was the same as the chief concern of every aspect of his teaching: that sinners might be brought to repentance and life in and through the gospel of Jesus Christ.

THE OFFICE OF THE MINISTRY IN *THE BOOK OF CONCORD*

Luther's followers caught that central concern, and so it is no wonder that the defining documents of the Lutheran church, the Lutheran confessions, can be viewed not only as confessions of the faith or as introductions to the Christian life, but also as guidelines for the effective pastoral care of believers. Only with a very narrow definition of the pastoral office can it be said that "there is surprisingly little about the office of the ministry in the Confessions, and where they do treat of it, the discussion of the subject is almost always incidental to the main theme."[20] Indeed, any Lutheran discussion of the pastoral office must be a part of the larger treatment of the plan of God to save the people through the action of the means of grace. But with that in mind we can read the *BC* as a handbook for that office.

The Book of Concord reiterates Luther's critique of the abuses of the office of the public ministry in the medieval church. His own preface to the Smalcald Articles voiced the complaint that "neither the bishops nor the canons care how the poor people live or die. . . . Those people cannot hear Christ speak to them as the true shepherd speaking to his sheep" (SA preface, *BC* 290). Likewise, Melanchthon not only attacked public offenses against morality among the clergy, such as performing the Mass for money (Ap 12.15–16, *BC* 184) or living licentiously (Ap 23.44, *BC* 245); he also criticized the abuse of the confessional, where the priest should have been comforting consciences and exercising the most significant power of God, the forgiveness of sins. Instead, clergy too often were making "tragic spectacles" by fighting with one another over jurisdiction to conduct confession and were also subjecting the laity to a legalistic checkpoint system as they exacted penance from their parishioners (Ap 11. 8 *BC* 181). The Wittenberg movement intended to do things differently. In responding to the papal party's criticism of the CA treatment of confession and absolution, Melanchthon rejoiced that "we have so explained and extolled the blessing of absolution and the power of the keys that many troubled consciences have received consolation from our teaching." Such pastoral care had encouraged many devout people and had brought Luther the praise of all good people "since it discloses a sure and firm consolation for the conscience," in contrast to previous pastoral practice (Ap 11.2, *BC* 181).

That pastoral practice tied public ministry inextricably to the Word. When titles were applied to the first seven articles of the CA, the title "the office of the ministry" (German) or "the ministry of the church" (Latin) was chosen for its fifth article, which followed and flowed from the central teaching of the document, as expressed in its fourth article, its treatment of justification through faith in Christ. This title was accurate in one sense and yet, at least at first glance, seems deceptive. For the article indeed begins by stating "to obtain such faith God instituted the office of the ministry," but it defines the "office of the ministry" with the phrase "that is, [through it God] provided the Gospel and the sacraments," the means or instruments by which he bestows the Holy Spirit, who effects faith "when and where he pleases, in those who hear the Gospel" (CA 5.1, 2, *BC* 31). The public ministry of the church is inextricably linked with God's tools for creating faith, for re-creating human creatures as God's children—the means of grace, Word, and sacrament. The pastoral office is the Holy Spirit's instrument by which the power of God's gospel is conveyed to people; the means of grace are the instruments that the pastor uses to apply God's power to his chosen children. Pastor and Word are like horse and carriage: the church does not have one without the other.

The pastor is the servant of God's command and of God's people's needs, according to Melanchthon. He believed that in the exercise of their calling to preach the Word and administer the sacraments pastors "do not represent their own persons but the person of Christ, because of the church's call. . . . When they offer the Word of Christ or the sacraments, they do so in Christ's place and stead" (Ap 7.28, *BC* 173; cf. Ap 7.47, *BC* 177). They should not confuse themselves with their Lord, but they should understand that they function because the Lord has called and commissioned them to do the task of conveying the benefits of his incarnation. Servants both of their congregations and of the congregations' Lord, pastors do not find themselves, however, caught between the two; for they serve God's purposes by obeying God, and they serve their people's requirements by bringing the divine help of God's Word to them. God's purposes are always congruent with the people's need, but the people's demands are not always congruent with God's command. The pastor serves them first and foremost by serving up the bitter pill of repentance and then the banquet of God's feast of forgiveness.

As for Luther, so also for Melanchthon and the authors of the Formula of Concord (FC), the pastoral ministry exists as the channel through which the Word does its work in the public arena; it exists to lead, guide, and serve the entire congregation of God's people in exercising God's callings to live in the Word and out of its power. Melanchthon defined the basic functions of the minister of the Word thus: "The gospel requires of those who preside over the churches that they preach the gospel, remit sins, administer the sacraments, and in addition, exercise jurisdiction, that is, excommunicate those who are guilty of notorious crimes, and absolve those who repent" (Tr 60, *BC* 330). In the CA he had used a similar definition of the functions of the pastoral office in discussing "the power of bishops" (CA 28, *BC* 81–94). "Our teachers assert that according to the Gospel the power of the keys or the power of bishops is a power and command of God to preach the Gospel, to forgive and retain sins, and to administer and distribute the sacraments" (CA 28.5, *BC* 81; German), Melanchthon wrote, and he supported that simple definition by citing John 20:21-23. He believed that God had ordained the public ministry, "the office of the bishop, to preach the Gospel, forgive sins, judge doctrine and condemn doctrine that is contrary to the Gospel, and exclude from the Christian community the ungodly whose wicked conduct is manifest. All this is to be done not by human power but by God's Word alone" (CA 28.21, *BC* 84; German). The pastoral ministry, from which Melanchthon refused to distinguish any special role for the bishop, is the means by which God gives "eternal righteousness, the Holy Spirit, and eternal life" (CA 28.8–9, *BC* 82; German). This meant a rejection of the medieval model of clerical leadership, which Melanchthon understood to be that of a priest who presided over the sacrifice of the Mass in order to obtain grace for Christian people. The Wittenbergers taught, in contrast, that pastors deliver what God has already established through the death and resurrection of Jesus, the forgiveness that the Word and sacraments convey (Ap 13.7–10, *BC* 212).

Melanchthon was delighted to report that this model was working. With joy he cited the example of the evangelical churches that he had represented at Augsburg, writing in the Apology that the Lord's Supper was used by "many in our circles" every Lord's day, after the people had been instructed, examined, and absolved. In the same circles pastors had been instructing and examining the youth publicly, and the preaching of the gospel, which is "the chief worship of God," was heard regularly (Ap 15.40–42, *BC* 220).

The prime responsibility of the evangelical pastor, according to Melanchthon, is to convey the gospel of forgiveness in Jesus Christ to his people. Pastors are not responsible for converting anyone. They are not responsible for maintaining anyone's faith. The Holy Spirit does that through the Word. The pastor's task is to apply God's Word faithfully and aptly to God's people. David Chytraeus, Melanchthon's disciple, drove that point home when, in preparing the FC's article on the human will, he wrote, "On the one hand, it is true that both the preacher's planting and watering and the hearer's running and willing would be in vain, and no conversion would follow if there were not added the power and operation of the Holy Spirit, who through the Word preached and heard illuminates and converts hearts so that men believe this Word and give their assent to it. On the other hand, neither the preacher nor the hearer should question this grace and operation of the Holy Spirit." At that point Chytraeus picked up the words of his colleague, Jacob Andreae:

> [The preacher and hearer] should be certain that, when the Word of God is preached, pure and unalloyed according to God's command and will, and when the people diligently and earnestly listen to it and meditate on it, God is certainly present with his grace and gives what man is unable by his own powers to take or to give. We should not and cannot pass judgment on the Holy Spirit's presence,

operations, and gifts merely on the basis of our feeling, how and when we perceive it in our hearts. On the contrary, because the Holy Spirit's activity often is hidden, and happens under cover of great weakness, we should be certain, because of and on the basis of his promise, that the Word which is heard and preached in an office and work of the Holy Spirit, whereby he assuredly is potent and active in our hearts (2 Cor. 2:14ff.). (FC, SD 2.55–56, *BC* 531–32)

Chytraeus and Andreae were giving their readers in the pastoral office both a message of law and of gospel in this passage. They were reminding the pastors of their obligation to work hard to present God's Word accurately and aptly, effectively and clearly. At the same time they were reassuring these pastors that their work serves as the Spirit's instrument, and that the Spirit is both in control of the course of the Word and ready to forgive the preacher who errs in applying it.

The prime responsibility of the evangelical pastor is to convey the gospel of forgiveness in Jesus Christ to Christ's people. Many other tasks have fallen to pastors throughout the history of the church, and pastors continually face the possibility of distraction from their prime task by important but secondary activities. Onto the pastor's desk in a modern congregation fall all sorts of administrative tasks and requests for services related to the entire range of human living. Furthermore, the preaching of the gospel presumes the proclamation of God's accusing law, and it presumes instruction in the practice of Christian piety, as Melanchthon indicated in offering a list of the subjects on which evangelical pastors should preach: 1) "penitence and the fear of God"—the accusing force of the law; 2) "faith in Christ, the righteousness of faith, comfort for the conscience through faith"—the means God uses to justify, the gospel; 3) and the goal of such preaching, the exercise of the forgiven life, restored to truly human living—"the exercise of faith, prayer and our assurance that it is efficacious and is heard, the cross, respect for rulers and for all civil ordinances, the distinction between the kingdom of Christ (or the spiritual kingdom) and political affairs, marriage, the education and instruction of children, chastity, and all the works of love" (Ap 15.43, *BC* 221).

Nonetheless, pastors must always confront and reject the temptation to subvert their ministries by confusing the task to which the pastoral office commits them with other duties and responsibilities foisted on them by their own desire to "be more than just a preacher of forgiveness" or by the desires of others to have the pastor "do something practical, too." In their day Melanchthon and Luther were forced to evaluate the way in which the German bishops conducted their public duties. In the time of Charlemagne, when good lieutenants were hard for an emperor to find, secular powers and duties had been appended to the spiritual responsibilities of the office of bishop. The prince-bishops of the Holy Roman Empire had become more prince than bishop, to the great detriment of their episcopal functions.

Therefore, in Art. 28 of the CA Melanchthon dwelt at great length not only on the definition of the bishop's calling but also on the confusion and the damage done to his pastoral function by his having to fill a formal political role in secular society. Melanchthon followed up his fundamental definition of the office of the Word as the instrument of God's forgiveness, mediated through Word and sacrament, by observing, "the two authorities, the spiritual and the temporal, are not to be mingled or confused, for the spiritual power has its commission to preach the Gospel and administer the sacraments. Hence it should not invade the function of the other, should not set up and depose kings, should not annul temporal laws or undermine obedience to government, should not make or prescribe to the temporal power laws concerning worldly matters" (CA 28.12–14, *BC* 83). Melanchthon was willing to grant the bishops of the church the exercise of such a secular role in theory: "In cases where bishops possess temporal authority and the sword, they possess it not as bishops by divine right, but by human, imperial right, bestowed by Roman emperors and kings for the temporal administration of their lands. Such authority has nothing at all to do with the office of the Gospel" (CA 28.19–20, *BC* 83-84; German) [in the Latin: "This, however, is a function other than the ministry of the Gospel"]. As a matter of fact, the adherents of the CA found unworkable Melanchthon's theoretical granting of the possibility that the ministers of the gospel could also function as officers of the state. In the places where they replaced medieval bishops with evangelical holders of the office, they entrusted the former bishops' political responsibilities to secular administrators. In our day and age the absence of a cultural sense of the sacred tempts church and society alike to want to summon preachers of the gospel to secular tasks of all sorts. For every culture needs to have some sense of the sacred and transcendent, of the moral and ethical, even if it strives for a valueless public square. Pastors cannot avoid the necessity of addressing cultural questions to which the law of God speaks, and they cannot avoid having the world hear what they say. But they should beware of the maelstrom of society's swirling surges, of the tar baby of cultural involvement for its own sake or on its own terms. For the gospel of which they are servant stands as a rock of offense to every cultural system and every religion which a society devises for itself. Pastors stand as the confessors of the church, demarcating its existence from that of the state and society that surround it. Chytraeus was writing against the background of the controversy over the decision of Melanchthon and his colleagues at the University of Wittenberg to try to save the evangelical faith through compromise in the face of political persecution (after the imperial victory of the armies of Charles V over the Lutheran princes in 1548), as he urged, "especially the ministers of the Word, as leaders of the community of God, are obligated to confess openly, not only by words but also through their deeds and actions, the true doctrine and all that pertains to it, according to the Word of God" (FC, SD 10.10, *BC* 612).

"NOT BY HUMAN POWER BUT BY GOD'S WORD ALONE"

Such confession is a part of their call, of their calling, of their office. The prime function of the evangelical pastor is to convey the gospel of forgiveness in Jesus Christ to Christ's people. But "ministry" denotes not only a function but also an official position, an institution, which God designed to give leadership to the community of his people. Melanchthon presumed that Christ had established an office that would serve believers by carrying out the functions of absolving and of proclaiming the love of God in Christ. In his confessional writings he did not attempt to define the relationship between the priesthood of all believers and the pastoral office. He presumed that God calls all believers to be priests in their baptisms and that God has designed the public ministry and the leadership that is supplied through the pastoral office as a sine qua non of the church's life.[21] It is not true that in a congregation where pastoral leadership is strong, the exercise of the priesthood of all believers will probably be weak, or that strong exercise of the royal priesthood will weaken the pastor. Good priests and good pastors reinforce each other in the tasks that God has assigned to each. Speaking of the universal priesthood and the office of preaching Norman Nagel comments, "Each is the peculiar gift it is, and as gift for each other. They are the gifts of the Lord Jesus, and this is called in question when they are played off against each other. To do that we have to take them into our hands, to adjust or improve them according to some notion of ours."[22]

Although some of Luther's followers over the centuries have fallen into bitter disputes over the forms of the ministry and the governance of the church, by comparison with other confessional traditions Lutherans have been notoriously indifferent to questions of church polity. The silence of the Lutheran confessions on specific forms for the exercise of the public ministry may have contributed to the ambiguity and even indifference of many of Luther's heirs to such questions.

Nonetheless, there is no question that the Reformers were convinced that it was God's will that there be an office that bears God-given responsibility for the public exercise of absolution and the public proclamation of the gospel. The observation that "the office of the ministry is the process of the gospel" is not false,[23] but neither is it the entire truth. God knows fallen human nature too well simply to entrust the gospel to going with the flow. Therefore, he has structured the responsibility and constituted the function of public proclamation in the office of the pastoral ministry. No external form—no bishops or consistories or vows or regulations—can ensure the proper proclamation of the gospel. Nothing can preserve the gospel but its faithful proclamation; only the gospel itself can guarantee the gospel. But by ordaining the public ministry, the Wittenbergers believed, God had left less to chance the conduct of the functions of the gospel, preaching forgiveness, administering the sacraments, pronouncing absolution. Therefore, Melanchthon insisted that pastors be "properly called"

(CA 14, *BC* 36); "the church has the command to appoint ministers: to this we must subscribe wholeheartedly, for we know that God approves this ministry and is present in it" (Ap 13.12, *BC* 211). (It is precisely for this reason that Melanchthon could label ordination into the pastoral office a sacrament—because "the ministry of the Word has God's command and glorious promises: 'The Gospel is the power of God for salvation to everyone who has faith [Rom. 1:16]' again, 'My Word that goes forth from my mouth shall not return to me empty, but it shall accomplish that which I purpose, and prosper in the thing for which I sent it' [Isa. 55:11]" (Ap 13.11–13, *BC* 212–13). Although Melanchthon used the term "sacrament" more freely than his successors felt comfortable doing, his point must still be noted.) But he did not offer specific details regarding the shape of the institution of the pastoral office.

Hermann Sasse caught the spirit of the Wittenbergers when he observed that "the church is correctly ordered in the sense of Lutheran teaching when it is so constituted as to offer the office of the ministry a maximum of possibilities to accomplish its service of the proclamation of the pure gospel and of the proper administration of the sacraments in the name and according to the commission of the Lord of the church and when it preserves a maximum of possibilities for the congregation which Jesus Christ himself has called through the Word and the sacraments to live its life in the world and to carry out its service for human creatures. . . ."[24] Edmund Schlink concludes on the basis of Sasse's judgment that the confessional position on the public ministry therefore means that, "liberated by the Gospel for service to the Gospel, 'man' establishes ordinances in the church for examinations, ordinations, and installations, for the relationship of congregation, pastor and church administration for the unfolding of the functions of the *one* spiritual office in various offices arranged by the church, for the cooperation of the voice of the universal priesthood of believers in the activities of church administration, etc."[25]

The call to the pastoral office was certainly no matter of indifference to Luther. Rather, he took great comfort in the fact that God had called him through the church to teach God's Word. For by virtue of the call pastors can know that they have not established themselves in office: they neither need nor can depend on themselves or directly themselves in the conduct of the office. Wilhelm Maurer has observed in commenting on CA Art. 14, "Because God himself is at work in the ministry of the Word, no one can be self-called; only God—even if through human means—can call to this service."[26] Pastors themselves need to know that they do not stand alone, that they have not entered into this activity of preaching the gospel on their own or by their own volition. That means then that they do not decide whether—but only how—to proclaim the Word of the Lord. "To fear no one and to set forth the truth freely and openly is not a test of the pastor's courage; it is a matter of office and command. Those who preach should not wear out and let themselves be chased into a corner, nor should they become impatient and creep away to the wilderness."[27] Pastors may also rely on the fact that God has designated them to be his servants in those moments when they must overcome doubt about their capacity to stand against the cultural forces that want to gut or silence their message. They must take comfort in their calls when their exercise of the public ministry is questioned and mocked. And when the criticism has the ring of the truth about it, and refuge is available only in the gospel that forgives also the pastor's failure to exercise God's calling well, then they must also stand firmly upon God's expressed desire that even such a sinner as this serve his gospel, too. As Christians, pastors, too, experience that the whole of their lives is the life of repentance.

Not only pastors need to know that they carry out the functions of their office because God has called them to do so. Their people need to know that, too. Maurer quotes Luther that "the office of comfort," as he calls it, "is weak if not authorized and is not pleasing and satisfying to God above all."

> It is Luther's personal interest in salvation that lies behind his great concern with the saving activity of the office; his insistence on proper calling cannot be based solely on his opposition to the Anabaptists and spiritualists. Clearly, personal possession of the Spirit is not what constitutes a call; the office is not personal but is based on the Spirit and on Christ. . . . In comforting and teaching, the pastor does not own the Spirit; the pastor is merely a steward. "If that were not so, everything would be up in the air. I would have to be rebaptized tomorrow, because I would not know whether the person who baptized me was trustworthy. . . . But that is what you must know for sure—that he has the authority to baptize, to preach, and to absolve." As soon as he moves from office to person he becomes unreliable.[28]

In addition to their concern that the public ministry of the church be defined as a ministry of forgiveness through Word and sacrament, Luther and Melanchthon were concerned to define it in such a way that no minister of the Word exercise tyrannous power over other ministers of the Word. To that end Melanchthon began his argument in the Tr by insisting that the papacy erred by claiming primacy over other bishops by divine right. God had not so instituted and shaped the public ministry, and the papacy's arrogation of such power to itself was a mark of its Antichristian nature (Tr 39–59, *BC* 327-30). "In Luke 22:24-27 Christ expressly forbids lordship among the apostles. . . . Christ . . . taught [the apostles] that no one should have lordship or superiority among them but that the apostles should be sent forth as equals and exercise the ministry of the Gospel in common." To exercise power within the church in the manner of secular rulers was expressly forbidden by Christ, who had sent out his disciples "as equals, without discrimination" (John 20:21), Melanchthon argued. Paul, too, "makes ministers equal and teaches that the church is above the ministers. Therefore he does not attribute to Peter superiority or authority over the church or the other ministers" (1 Cor. 3:4-8, 1 Cor. 3:21, 22). Melanchthon continued, "This is to say that neither Peter nor the other ministers should assume lordship or authority over the church, nor burden the church with traditions, nor let anybody's authority count for more than the Word, nor set the authority of Cephas over against the authority of other apostles" (Tr 7–9, 11, *BC* 320–21). This does not mean that Luther and Melanchthon rejected any role for overseers among the pastors of the church, nor did they reject the possibility of those who would serve as preachers or deacons alongside the pastors. From occasional statements of Luther's, Maurer concludes that the reformer regarded both the office of bishop and the office of deacon as "derived from the pastoral office" and thus designed to "serve the truth and effectiveness of the gospel."[29] That gospel united overseers and assistants with the pastors in one office, in which some had different tasks but all had one assignment, as Melanchthon summarized it: "Christ gave the apostles only spiritual power, that is, the command to preach the Gospel, proclaim the forgiveness of sins, administer the sacraments, and excommunicate the godless without physical violence" (Tr 31, *BC* 325).

To carry out this ministry of the Word pastors must use the Word themselves, the Reformers believed. Luther admonished the readers of his Large Catechism, focusing on pastors who would pick up the book, "Now that pastors are free from the useless, bothersome babbling of the [canonical] Seven Hours [the prescribed communal devotional program of the cloister], it would be fine if every morning, noon, and evening they would read, instead, at least a page or two from the Catechism, the Prayer Book, the New Testament, or something else from the Bible, and would pray the Lord's Prayer for themselves and their parishioners. In this way they might show honor and gratitude to the Gospel" (LC Preface, 3, *BC* 358). For, as he stated a bit later, "Not only do we need God's Word daily as we need our daily bread; we also must use it daily against the daily, incessant attacks and ambushes of the devil with his thousand arts" (LC Preface, 13, *BC* 360). Luther did not merely study God's Word for a lecture or a sermon; he lived with it, used it, imbibed it, immersed his entire thinking and planning in it. This review of the Word for Luther was based upon the summary of the Scriptures in the catechism, which the believer should read and teach, learn, meditate upon, and ponder (LC Preface, 19, *BC* 361; cf. SC, Preface, 6, *BC* 359).

In the Table of Responsibilities Luther laid out his expectations of those who hold the pastoral office with the words of 1 Tim. 3:2-6: the pastor should be "temperate, sensible, dignified, hospitable, an apt teacher, no drunkard, not violent but gentle, not quarrelsome, and no lover of money." That prescription holds the mirror of the law up to ministers of the Word in every generation of the church's history.

As the same time the Lutheran confessions apply the gospel to pastors as well. Melanchthon reacted to the criticism exchanged between pastors and people by observing, "Perfection (that is, the integrity of the church) is preserved when the strong bear with the weak, when the people put the best construction on the faults of their clergy, when the bishops take into account the weakness of the people" (Ap 4.233, *BC* 140). Luther's admonition to all Christians to seek the peace that Christ offers in absolution applies to pastors as well as lay people. The highest art of the confessor is to know the passages of Scripture with which to comfort and to strengthen the faith of those whose consciences are heavily burdened or who are distressed and sorely tried (SC 5:29). But often confessors cannot apply their own medicine to themselves and must flee to another to hear the peace of Christ. "If you are poor and miserable, then go and make use of the healing medicine" (LC, Confession, 26, *BC* 460) is advice that Luther would give to pastors, too.

Lutheran pastors are called to be ready always to apply the salve of Christ's blood to aching consciences and distressed minds. They are called and given the responsibility of applying the healing and life-restoring power of the gospel of Jesus Christ to lives broken by the proclamation and impact of God's law. Temptations stand on every hand inviting pastors at the end of the twentieth century to abandon the model for ministry set forth by the authors of the *BC*. The world tempts us to play its games and to serve as business managers, as social directors, as the "cheapest shrinks" in town. Within the church arise temptations to organize and to institute and use power in the world's way. Inevitably the law must govern the relationships of people within the institutional life of the church. But pastors must remember that their call has to do with the gospel. Whatever other duties they must or may assume, their people count on them to do what God has designed their calling to do, "preach the Gospel, forgive sins, judge doctrine and condemn doctrine that is contrary to the Gospel, and exclude from the Christian community the ungodly whose wicked conduct is manifest . . . not by human power but by God's Word alone" (CA 28.21, *BC* 84; German).

NOTES

1. On late medieval piety, see Bernd Moeller, "Piety in Germany Around 1500," in *The Reformation in Medieval Perspective*, ed. Steven E. Ozment (Chicago: Quadrangle, 1971), 50–75. Ozment depicts the crisis of pastoral care (without using the term) in his *The Reformation in the Cities: The Appeal of Protestantism to Sixteenth-Century Germany and Switzerland* (New Haven: Yale University Press, 1975).

2. James M. Kittelson, *Luther the Reformer: The Story of the Man and His Career* (Minneapolis: Augsburg, 1986), 53–55; Martin Brecht, *Martin Luther: His Road to Reformation, 1483–1521,* trans. James L. Schaaf (Philadelphia: Fortress Press, 1985), 70–76.

3. Treatments of Luther's doctrine of the pastoral office and related topics include Jan Aarts, *Die Lehre Martin Luthers über das Amt in der Kirche, Eine genetisch-systematische Untersuchung seiner Schriften von 1512 bis 1525* (Helsinki: Luther-Agricola-Gesellschaft, 1972); Wilhelm Brunotte, *Das geistliche Amt bei Luther* (Berlin: Lutherisches Verlagshaus, 1959); Hellmut Lieberg, *Amt und Ordination bei Luther und Melanchthon* (Göttingen: Vandenhoeck & Ruprecht, 1962). See also Paul Althaus, *The Theology of Martin Luther,*

trans. Robert C. Schultz (Philadelphia: Fortress Press, 1966), 323–32; B. A. Gerrish, "Priesthood and Ministry in the Theology of Luther," *Church History* 34 (1965): 404–22; Lowell C. Green, "Change in Luther's Doctrine of the Ministry," *The Lutheran Quarterly* 18 (1966): 173–83; Robert H. Fischer, "Another Look at Luther's Doctrine of the Ministry," *The Lutheran Quarterly* 18 (1966): 260–71; David P. Daniel, "A Spiritual Condominium: Luther's Views on Priesthood and Ministry with Some Structural Implications," *Concordia Journal* 14 (1988): 266-82.

4. *Lectures on Galatians* (1535), *LW* 26:7, chaps. 1–4 with a summary of the distinction on 4–12. It shapes the entire commentary on Galatians which was given in lecture, 1531–32, and published in 1535. His earliest statement of what he called the "two kinds of righteousness" was presented in two tracts issued in 1519, one of which is available in English: "Two Kind of Righteousness, 1519," in *LW* 31: 293–306.

5. The best overview of Luther's thought in this regard is found in Gustaf Wingren, *Luther on Vocation*, trans. Carl C. Rasmussen (Philadelphia: Muhlenberg Press, 1957). See Luther's "Confession concerning Christ's Supper, 1528," in *LW* 37: esp. 364–65, which served as background for the writing of the CA. On the use of Luther's concept of the two governments and the three estates in the CA and the Ap, see Robert Kolb, "God Calling, 'Take Care of My People': Luther's Concept of Vocation in the Augsburg Confession and Its Apology," *Concordia Journal* 8, no. 1 (1982): 4–11, and Wilhelm Maurer, *Historical Commentary on the Augsburg Confession*, trans. H. George Anderson (Philadelphia: Fortress Press, 1986), 85–97. See also Edmund Schlinck, *Theology of the Lutheran Confessions*, trans. Paul F. Koehneke and Herbert J. A. Bouman (Philadelphia: Muhlenberg Press, 1961), 230; Willard D. Allbeck, *Studies in the Lutheran Confessions* (Philadelphia: Fortress Press, 1968), 71; and Daniel, "Spiritual Condominium."

6. Leif Grane, *The Augsburg Confession: A Commentary*, trans. John H. Rasmussen (Minneapolis: Augsburg Publishing House, 1987), 72–73.

7. "Concerning the Ministry" (1523) vol. 40 (*Church and Ministry II*), vol. 40 of *LW*, ed. Conrad Bergendoff (Philadelphia: Muhlenberg Press, 1958), 35.

8. Fischer, "Luther's Doctrine of the Ministry," 268; he refers to a wider discussion of some of the problems involved with these terms in Gerrish, "Priesthood and Ministry," 416–20. The problems lie not so much in Luther's own ambiguousness, though that is not to be denied, but more in the rich meaning of the German word *Amt*, which embraces both functions of service to the people appropriate to each of society's many offices, and the official positions that take shape in institutional form to ensure the proper carrying out of those functions; see *Deutsches Wörterbuch*, ed. Jacob Grimm and Wilhelm Grimm, (Leipzig: Hirzel, 1854), 1:280–81.

9. According to this interpretation, words such as "doctrine," "tradition," and also "confession" involved not only the content of what was taught, handed down, or confessed, but also the action involved in the respective process. See Peter Fraenkel, "Revelation and Tradition: Notes on Some Aspects of Doctrinal Continuity in the Theology of Philip Melanchthon," *Studia Theologica* 13 (1959): 97–133, esp. 116–18.

10. *LW* 44:126–36.

11. *LW* 36:112, 115.

12. Lieberg, *Amt und Ordination*, 24–39.

13. *LW* 44:127.

14. *LW* 31:354–55. On the individualistic interpretation of Luther's understanding of the priesthood of all believers, see B. A. Gerrish's necessary rejoinder, "Priesthood and Ministry," 410–11.

15. Ibid., 356.

16. *LW* 40:18–22, 40–44. On the importance of the distinction between public and private exercise of the power of the Word for Luther, see Brunotte, *Das geistliche Amt*, 56–59.

17. Lieberg, *Amt und Ordination*, 69–103, treats these concepts in detail.

18. *LW* 40:21.

19. Ibid., 35.

20. Edgar M. Carlson, "The Doctrine of the Ministry in the Confessions," *The Lutheran Quarterly* 15 (1963): 118.

21. See the discussions of these issues in Schlink, *Lutheran Confessions*, 243–54, and Holsten Fagerberg, *A New Look at the Lutheran Confessions, 1529–1537*, trans. Gene J. Lund (St. Louis: Concordia Publishing House, 1972), 226–36.

22. Norman E. Nagel, "The Office of the Holy Ministry in the Confessions," *Concordia Journal* 14 (1988): 285 (283–99).

23. Friedrich Mildenberger, *Theology of the Lutheran Confessions*, trans. Erwin L. Lueker, ed. Robert C. Schultz (Philadelphia: Fortress Press, 1986), 119.

24. Hermann Sasse, *Kirchenregiment und weltliche Obrigkeit nach lutherischer Lehre* (Munich: Kaiser, 1935), 60, cited partially in Schlink, *Lutheran Confessions*, 252.

25. Ibid.

26. Maurer, *Augsburg Confession*, 190–91.

27. Ibid., 199.

28. Ibid., 191–92.

29. Ibid., 195.

Ministry
in Lutheran Orthodoxy
and Pietism

5

JAMES H. PRAGMAN

Yoking Lutheran Orthodoxy and Lutheran Pietism together in the same chapter will seem unusual, if not dangerous and impossible, to students of the history of the Lutheran churches.[1] Lutheran Orthodoxy marked a level of new maturation for the Lutheran churches. Serious and industrious Lutheran scholars expended their creative energies in studying, analyzing, applying, and structuring the theological heritage of Martin Luther, Philip Melanchthon, and the Lutheran Confessors so that the heritage might be protected and preserved in the dangerous decades of theological conflict and war following the Reformation century. The Lutheran Orthodox mentality was shaped by many factors, not the least of which was the series of religious wars that ravaged Europe during the late sixteenth century and the first half of the seventeenth century. Germany, in particular, experienced the horror of the Thirty Years War; exhaustion led to the acceptance of the Peace of Westphalia (1648), and the dividing lines between Catholic and Lutheran and Calvinist solidified as part of the theological landscape. The Lutheran Orthodox theologians rendered a positive service to their contemporaries as they pored over the theological tradition begun by Martin Luther and then passed it on to their successors. They buttressed, defended, and explicated that tradition so that the evangelical verities of the past could remain the living reality of another generation.

Toward the end of the seventeenth century, however, some theologians and pastors were beginning to notice that the spirit of the evangelical churches was formal and arid, that Christianity in those churches seemed to be ritualistic and formal, organized but not personal. A reaction developed, and that reaction is Lutheran Pietism. The theologians of this movement did not intend to challenge the central truths espoused by the Lutheran Orthodox theologians, but they did want to revitalize the spirit of the churches as well as the personal Christianity of the churches' members. The Pietists did not believe that they were doing anything but continuing Martin Luther's reformation. The Pietists believed that

67

the churches were losing their grasp of the true spirit of Christianity and that revitalization was needed within the churches. These views, of course, seemed to challenge and criticize the Lutheran Orthodox theologians; consequently, the relationship between the Orthodox and the Pietists was often neither positive nor happy. While the Orthodox focused on the correct presentation and apprehension of the Christian faith in all of its articles, the Pietists focused on the personal application of the truths of Christianity in the lives of God's people: the focus was shifting from the "head" to the "heart," and some were fearful that such a focus would lead to the destruction of the truth of the gospel.

Yet, nevertheless, both movements within the evangelical churches saw the church's ministry as essential for the well-being of the churches. In the Lutheran theological tradition, the ministry is the divine institution in the church by which the Word of God is preached and proclaimed and the holy sacraments are administered. We turn now to review the thought of both the Lutheran Orthodox theologians and Lutheran Pietism on the office of the public ministry.

THE ORTHODOX VISION OF THE CHURCH'S MINISTRY

The Orthodox period in the history of the Lutheran churches begins in the last quarter of the sixteenth century and continues into the first quarter of the eighteenth century. During that period of time, Luther's theology and the theology of the Lutheran Confessions was explored in great detail by exacting scholars. While that intellectual effort is part of the creative heritage of the Lutheran churches today, evaluations of that effort vary from theologian to theologian. Some see that period as a very helpful, necessary, and productive part of the Lutheran heritage; others characterize the period as one of a dead, pedestrian approach to the church's theological task. Be that as it may, those theologians who spoke of the church's ministry were precise in their understanding of that "locus" in their monumental tomes.

John Gerhard (1582–1637) spoke for many of his colleagues when he set forth this definition of the church's ministry:

> We conclude that the ministry of the church is a sacred and public office, divinely instituted and committed to certain men through a legitimate calling that they, equipped as they are with special power, teach the Word of God, administer the sacraments and preserve discipline in the church to promote the conversion and salvation of men and to spread the glory of God.[2]

This definition is similar to the definitions offered by many Orthodox theologians who preceded and followed Gerhard. The definition reflects wide unanimity in the way the Orthodox theologians understood the ministry. There is a clear understanding that the ministry of the church is an office that is divinely instituted. The office is not a human arrangement, but a divine one given to the church to accomplish some explicit results: teaching the Word of God, administering the sacraments, and preserving discipline in the church. And, of course, all of those functions are to be carried forward by the public office of the ministry so that human beings can be saved and God can be glorified.

There is, however, no emphasis on a particular structure for the public office of the ministry, that is, on the need to structure ministry according to the pattern of bishop/presbyter/deacon. That focus is absent from the discussions of the Orthodox theologians—nor should we expect them to set forth such a view. The seventeenth century was a century of strident theological and religious polemics. The difference between the Lutheran churches and the church at Rome was clearly delineated.

The Orthodox theologians insisted that the office of the public ministry is necessary in the church because God had instituted that office. However, that office is not absolutely necessary because the Lord of the church could accomplish the purposes of the ministry in other ways. Nevertheless, since God had instituted the office of the public ministry, the church must have it.

The divine call is the means by which the ministry is established in the church. The Orthodox theologians analyzed the component parts of that call with great thoroughness. One of the emphases of their approach was to insist that individuals could not put themselves forward to serve in the church's ministry unless the church had acted through the calling process to place them in that office. Occasionally, because of unique circumstances, a layman might step forward to function as a minister in the church, but such an emergency did not establish a general principle for the exercise of the ministry in a local congregation.

The Orthodox theologians distinguished between mediate and immediate calls. The immediate call is one in which God directly and "immediately" called an individual such as Paul or Isaiah to exercise a ministry among the people of God. The mediate call is a call in which God works through a third party (for example, a congregation) to bring an individual into the church's ministry. While these calls can be distinguished from each other, they possess the same authority and can have the same results. Thus, contemporary pastors in the church can speak with the same confidence that St. Peter demonstrated when he spoke the Word to the people who heard his sermons.

The Orthodox theologians also insisted that the whole church, that is, the magistrates, the church authorities, and the laity (the *Ordo Politicus*, the *Ordo Ecclesiasticus*, and the *Ordo Oeconomicus*, respectively) must be actively involved in the calling of pastors and ministers in the church because God has given the whole church—not just selected parts of the church—the authority to call and fill the office of the public ministry.

In general, the Orthodox theologians wanted contemporary practice in their churches to conform to apostolic practice, particularly as that practice could be known on the basis of the New Testament. Of course, those theologians recognized that the New Testament did not provide an exact "procedures manual" or "blueprint" for the calling process. For example, the members of the *Ordo*

Politicus in the first century A.D. were usually not members of the Christian church. Consequently, the insistence that this *ordo* must function as a full participant in the calling process could not be demonstrated conclusively as an essential part of apostolic practice. Nevertheless, the Orthodox theologians insisted that the principle, that is, that all members and parts of the church must participate in the calling of pastors, still applied: the overriding principle that all things must be done decently and in order assumed that all members of the church participated fully in the calling of a pastor.

The Orthodox theologians set high standards for those who would serve in the church as its pastors and teachers. St. Paul's comments in 1 Timothy 3 and Titus 1, along with other sections of Scripture, were thoroughly studied and analyzed by the Orthodox theologians. It was also clear to them that all pastors and teachers in the church must be male: in the views of these theologians St. Paul's statements in 1 Corinthians 14 and 1 Timothy 2 absolutely forbade the service of women as pastors in the church.

A man who is properly qualified for the office of the public ministry and who has been called to fill that office must be ordained before the call can be exercised. But what is the meaning or the necessity of ordination? The Orthodox theologians assumed that ordination to the pastoral office was necessary if for no other reason than that all things must be done decently and in order in the church. Many of the Orthodox theologians taught that ordination related to the capacity of the one called to assume the responsibilities and duties of the pastoral ministry, but not to the essence of the ministry or the call to the ministry. Thus, ordination is ecclesiastical attestation of the ability of the candidate to accept and exercise the call extended by the church. Some of the theologians taught simply that ordination is public testimony that the call being extended to the pastoral candidate was legitimate and that the one called possessed the necessary aptitude for the office.

Of course, the Orthodox theologians roundly rejected any notion that ordination conferred some sort of "indelible character" on the ordinand. Nevertheless, no one could be ordained without being examined to determine his fitness for the office and the thoroughness of his theological preparation for ministry. Ordination is "necessary" in the church, but its necessity is not absolute. Furthermore, ordination should not be conferred if an individual does not possess a legitimate call to function in the church as the pastor of a specific congregation.

When the Orthodox theologians discussed the various duties and responsibilities of the pastoral office, a clear picture of the pastor's work emerged. The pastor must preach the Word of God. The second duty, according to one reckoning, is the administration of the sacraments. Third, the pastor should pray for those committed to his spiritual care and keeping. The next duty was that the pastor provide a proper example for the living of the Christian life. The fifth duty is the exercise of church discipline among the members of the flock. The sixth duty is the maintenance of the church's rites. And, finally, the pastor must care for the poor and visit the sick.[3]

While other theologians might alter the listing and perhaps arrange these duties in a different order or priority, all of them demonstrated a clear grasp of what a pastor in the church should do in response to the call he received as a pastor in the church. Furthermore, these theologians shared a common assumption: the pastor is the minister in the church. The office of the public ministry is the pastoral office. The pastoral office is the legitimate heir to all the forms of ministry noted in the New Testament's record of apostolic practice.

Nevertheless, the Orthodox theologians also recognized that pastors and ministers in the church could be distinguished from one another and ranked variously. Moreover, their study of the Scriptures demonstrated that the ministers in the church of the apostolic age exercised different aspects of the one office of the public ministry. Thus, the New Testament spoke of bishops and deacons, of presbyters and teachers, of evangelists and prophets. At the same time, the Orthodox theologians concluded that the biblical material did not provide a clear picture of the structural and/or subordinate relationships among ministers bearing different names or titles. Even if a more or less clear pattern of the relationship between various ministers in the early church (pastor, prophet, evangelist, teacher, presbyter, bishop, deacon, and so on) could be determined, the Orthodox theologians did not believe that the church must adhere strictly to such a pattern in successive ages of the church. In other words, as the church assesses its needs and requirements from time to time, the church has the freedom to arrange its ministry in response to those needs and requirements. These conclusions were reached only after extensive and exhaustive studies of the material in 1 Cor. 12:28-31 and Eph. 4:11-13. As a matter of fact, the Orthodox theologians displayed some ingenuity in their efforts to distinguish, for example, a prophet from an evangelist and an apostle from a pastor.

While various titles and offices could be distinguished from one another on various grounds, the Orthodox theologians nevertheless insisted that the church possesses only one ministry, performed by various ministers with differing titles and responsibilities and ranks. These theologians recognized that the various ministers of the church had been blessed with different gifts for ministry: some could teach while others were more suited as "table waiters." The evidence of different gifts had led to the establishment of different positions in the one office of the public ministry. Thus, the Orthodox theologians did not accept the notion that a "bishop," for example, had a different ministry than did a "pastor" or "presbyter" in the church because Christ gave the church only one ministry and authorized the church to fill that one ministry with qualified men who were capable of preaching the Word and administering the sacraments for the eternal salvation of people and for the glory of God.

Because the church has been granted one ministry and the power for the exercise of that one ministry, it is absurd for those who occupy the one office of the public ministry to struggle among themselves for authority or the privileges of rank. Both the church and the ministry—in all of its forms—belong to God alone! The center of both the church and its ministry is the gospel proclaimed in the church's ministry. Everything in the understanding of the church and its ministry focuses on that center: the gospel of God's righteousness in Christ which justifies by faith alone.

THE PIETIST VISION OF THE CHURCH'S MINISTRY

In the late seventeenth century, as the theologians of Lutheran Orthodoxy rehearsed their systems of theology, other theologians were beginning to look in different directions for the church's renewal. Philip Jacob Spener, a student of the Orthodox theologian John Conrad Dannhauer, was asked to write a preface for a new printing of John Arndt's *True Christianity*. That preface, later printed as a separate volume, marked the birth of Pietism in Lutheran circles. *Pia Desideria*[4] eloquently expresses the frustration Pastor Spener knew so well as he attempted to exercise his ministry as a Lutheran pastor as well as his determination to inject new life into the Lutheran churches. Spener's *Pia Desideria* analyzed the situation he discovered in the churches and also set forth a series of proposals to rectify the situation.

Spener believed that the church was suffering because the Word of God was not receiving the use God intended it to receive in the church. He also believed the church was suffering because the focus for ministry in the church had been narrowly set on the public ministry of the church and the universal priesthood of believers had been ignored. Furthermore, Spener insisted that the essence of true Christianity consisted in practice, not in a rather intellectual knowledge of the truth. He lamented the polemical character of theological discourse in the church: pastor and professor argued over doctrinal minutiae in most unedifying ways. Spener believed also that theological education, particularly the preparation of pastors at German universities, needed radical reform. Theological preparation at the universities had become in general a series of intellectual exercises. The spiritual formation of future pastors was being neglected in the quest for theological orthodoxy and *reine Lehre* at the universities. And Spener considered the pastors' style of preaching to be a continuing problem. The church needed preachers who could preach truly edifying sermons, full of proper content delivered in a positive style. Preaching in the church had become irrelevant to the life of the people.

These assessments of the church's life at the end of the seventeenth century include the germ of Spener's proposals for change. A close study of Spener's analysis reveals that he viewed the public ministry of the church as the key to the achievement of the reform he wanted for the church. However, Spener was unwilling to accept the notion that only the ordained clergy of the church was the key to reforming the spirituality of the church. He believed that the ministry is a gift to the whole church and that all the members of the church as spiritual priests before God must exercise the ministry they had received.

Spener, and those who worked with him in developing the Pietist movement, wanted to revitalize the church by revitalizing its members as well as its clergy. One of the devices Spener advocated was the *collegia pietatis*, gatherings of lay people for the purpose of Bible study, prayer, and hymn singing. These gatherings took place apart from the direction of the clergy, although pastors were seen as a resource for the study and prayer taking place in those gatherings. The *collegia* were not to be in opposition to the clergy: they were intended to extend the ministry of preaching carried on by the clergy. Spener's critics, however, saw this emphasis on the ministry of the laity as a threat to the privileged office of the ministry in the church. Pietism, however, did emphasize the role of the laity in ministry, and that is one of the distinguishing marks of the Lutheran Pietist movement.

These observations, however, should not be interpreted to mean that Lutheran Pietists rejected the unique role of the public ministry in the life of the church. The Pietists insisted that the church's pastoral office had been divinely established and instituted and that it was necessary for the church's life and being. This office was essential for the edification of the people of God.

The Pietists also emphasized the unique qualifications and characteristics of the church's public ministers. Focusing on St. Paul's discussion of qualifications in 1 Timothy 3 and Titus 1, Spener expressed the fond hope that pastors in the church would exemplify those qualifications more and more. Furthermore, echoing the Lutheran Orthodox theologians, Spener insisted that only men could occupy the pastoral office in the church.

The Pietists believed that better pastors would produce better Christians: that philosophy animated their critique of the contemporary church at the beginning of the eighteenth century. A full-scale reformation of theological education was an integral part of the Pietist approach to ministry. The heart and core of a proper theological curriculum for pastors was the study of God's Word: an exegetical, rather than a philosophical/systematic, approach to pastoral ministry exemplified the Pietist position. The Pietists wanted their pastors to be pious, God-fearing, converted individuals who loved the Lord above all things even as they served the laity of the church. Pietists did not understand how people could be godly if the clergy was not godly.

The Pietists, much like the Lutheran Orthodox theologians, insisted that no one could serve as a pastor in the church without having received and accepted a legitimate call to serve as a pastor. Moreover, all parts of the church—the magistracy, the clergy, and the laity—must participate in the calling of pastors. But, in character with the direction of the movement, Spener also developed practical guidelines to help pastors evaluate the calls they might receive to serve in the church's ministry. The focus on decency and good order in the structure of the pastoral ministry which we saw among the Orthodox theologians also characterized the Pietists. The call bound all parties—the pastor, the congregation, and society—together in a holy relationship.

Ordination is a part of the call to the pastoral ministry, and the Pietists placed a value on ordination. Ordination was ratification and confirmation of the call that a pastor had received. Spener insisted that ordination is public testimony or ratification of the pastoral call. At the same time, then, ordination confers no special gift or grace on the ordinand, even though ordination must be observed for the sake of good order in the church. When Pietist Lutheran preachers arrived in North America in the eighteenth century, they soon came to recognize the need for additional clergy and the need to provide ordination for them. Some Pietists, in a kind of emergency situation, would not insist on ordination, but the general practice of the church, that is, ordination of candidates for the pastoral ministry of the church, was for them the normal rule.

The Pietists discussed the tasks of the public ministry in the church with great thoroughness. The role of the sermon in building up the church's members was underscored heavily in Pietist writings. The sermon was a means for edifying the congregation. And sermons should speak directly from the pastor's heart to the human condition. Moreover, pastors were urged to make use of the *collegia pietatis* as a help in edifying the people of God. Then, after a pastor had preached on a Sunday, members of a *collegium* could gather on Monday or Thursday to review the sermon and make direct application of the sermon's lessons to the Christian's life.

Spener and the other Pietists also stressed the importance of confirmation and the confessional as aids in the pastor's ministry. Confirmation had to be more than a "coming of age" rite: confirmation must assist in deepening and strengthening the spiritual life of the church. Furthermore, the confessional can be used to help Christians prepare for the reception of the Lord's Supper so that they receive it worthily. The pastor must work diligently to build up the members of the church so that they grow and develop in their life of faith.

The Pietists recognized that ministers in the church could be and were ranked. They studied the rankings in 1 Cor. 12:28-31 and Eph. 4:11-13 and recognized the distinctions between an apostle and an evangelist and a pastor/teacher. Nevertheless, the Pietists in general also concluded that all pastors and teachers are also bishops in the church. Thus, bishops are pastors and preachers; they are *Seel-sorger* and *Seel-hirten* in the church. But such titles and identities are secondary to the real issue of ministry. That issue is the doing of it: ministry is the building up of the people of God—that is, edification—and other elements are clearly secondary. Furthermore, Spener and other Pietists recognized that the exercise of ministry in the practical existence of the church does not conform easily to rigid distinctions of rank and title. The Pietists focused on the goal and outcome of ministry, rather than on ranking or on structure for ministry. The practical outcome of edification must be the primary goal for the conduct of the church's ministry.

ORTHODOXY AND PIETISM: THE CONNECTION

Although Orthodoxy and Pietism are often perceived as antagonistic movements, both share a common heritage. Both movements focus on the preaching of the Word of God and on the administration of the sacraments as the essence of the office of the public ministry. In other words, the church has been given the ministry of pastors and teachers and other ministers in the church so that the Word of God can be preached and the sacraments administered.

Nevertheless, both groups view the public ministry differently from each other. For the Orthodox theologians, the ministry is the divine institution entrusted with the preservation and continuity of divine truth in the church. The Word is the treasure that must be protected and preserved in fidelity to the tradition handed down from the fathers to the present generation; it is the ministry's solitary and wonderful burden, and faithfulness to it is the mark of the church's ministry.

For the Pietists, the Word is the great treasure of the church, but it must be shared and ministered in such a way that the laity is transformed and edified and the Reformation is continued. Moreover, the Pietists tended to dissolve the clear distinction between the clergy and the laity: the clergy works to develop the spirituality of the laity, and the laity is capable of exercising spiritual responsibility for itself. And yet the Pietists did not intend in any way to suggest that the public ministry of the church was unimportant or unnecessary: the public ministry is God's institution and gift to the church.

In spite of these differences and others, both the Orthodox theologians and the Pietists seem to be unimpressed with the need to conform their views on ministry to the traditional patterns of the pre-Reformation church. The titles given to ministers in the church—for example, Pfarrer, Superintendent, Rector, Pastor—were secondary. However, the Pietists did inaugurate the use of the title "Pastor" for those who filled the office of the public ministry. In their view, the ministers of the church are shepherds of the flock who pastor the people of God and edify them in the faith. For the Orthodox theologians, the ministers of the church are guardians, defenders, and proclaimers who set forth the truth of God for the people's welfare in response to the call and commission of Almighty God. Each movement, in its own way, focused on the ministry of Word and sacrament in such a way that the inherent connection between church and Word and ministry was maintained.

NOTES

1. A much more extensive review of the Orthodox and Pietist understandings of the office of the public ministry is available in my *Traditions of Ministry: A History of the Doctrine of the Ministry in Lutheran Theology* (St. Louis: Concordia Publishing House, 1983), 58–126; notes, 191–99. The interested reader is referred to that resource for additional explication and bibliographical information.

2. John Gerhard, *Loci Theologici cum Pro Adstruenda Veritate tum Pro Destruenda Quorumvis Contradicentium Falsitate per Theses Nervose Solide et Copiose Explicati*, ed. Fr. Frank (Leipzig: J. C. Hinrichs, 1885), 6:10 (Locus 23, par. 24, p. 10). The translation was made by Richard Dinda; his translation is available on microfiche from Concordia Publishing House, St. Louis, Missouri.

3. Ibid., 6:177–96 (Locus 23, par. 265–89, pp. 177–96).

4. Philip Jacob Spener, *Pia Desideria*, trans. and ed. Theodore G. Tappert (Philadelphia: Fortress Press, 1964).

6

Ministry
in Nineteenth-Century
European Lutheranism

WALTER SUNDBERG

The most significant European Lutheran interpretations of the office of the ministry in the nineteenth century were forged in German lands, especially in Prussia, in the debate between liberal Protestantism and a powerful, conservative confessional movement.[1] This debate was not confined to a single issue. Theological consideration of ministry was intertwined with reflections on the church, sacraments, and the meaning of the Reformation. It also involved consideration of the status of Lutheranism in relation to the Reformed and Roman Catholic traditions. That is, the debate led to a nascent consciousness of the problems of ecumenism and ecumenical strategy as we understand these problems today. Finally, it was a highly politicized theological debate, for it entailed a controversial assessment of Christianity as a cultural and legal authority under state control that yet was under threat in an increasingly secularized society.

In the last two decades, Lutheran theology has taken up the same issues that captured the attention of its nineteenth-century forebears: ministry, church, sacraments, politics, and an ecumenical strategy that pits a Catholic identity against a Protestant identity. It is fair to say that the way these contemporary concerns are conceived is more deeply rooted in the nineteenth century than it is in the Reformation itself. So it is to the nineteenth century that we must turn to illuminate our present.

THE POLITICAL SITUATION OF THE CHURCH

Various forces of enormous cultural import were at work in Prussia at the beginning of the nineteenth century. It was a time of critical transition for a state that would eventually become the cornerstone of modern German nationality. Ideals of the French Enlightenment, dominant at the court of Friedrich II ("the Great," 1740–86), came under sharp attack because of the failure of the French Revolution and the ascendancy of Napoleon. Napoleon's defeat of the Prussian army at Jena and Auerstädt (October 1806) and the humiliating Treaty of Tilsit (July 1807) encouraged a fierce, anti-Gallic nationalism in the subjects of Friedrich the Great's successor, Friedrich Wilhelm III (1797–1840).

These events also politicized the Protestant clergy in a way not seen before as church leaders began to relate theological convictions to nationalist sentiment.[2] While the independence of the Prussian state and the sovereignty of German culture were objectives shared by virtually all in ecclesiastical authority, important segments of the clergy divided into "liberal" and "conservative" camps over the question of how these objectives could be reached. The liberals believed that German political and cultural sovereignty did not require the rejection of the critical and democratic agenda of the Enlightenment. Indeed, this agenda was interpreted as part of the broad heritage of the Reformation. In the Enlightenment, the liberals asserted, the Protestant tradition was reaffirmed. The conservatives opposed the Enlightenment, judging it to be the cause of a dangerous revolutionary spirit that was contrary to the will of God and that needed to be resisted for the sake of church and state. Indeed, the meaning of the Reformation became a matter of interpretative conflict among conservatives. Protestant identity itself became problematical in a way that it had not been before because of disagreement about the Reformation heritage. Further, the Roman Catholic church, so long considered an enemy of the gospel, was looked upon with new eyes by conservative theologians and Prussian church bureaucrats as a political ally in the struggle against the forces of modernity.

After Prussian independence was secured, the liberal and conservative camps remained in place. Their conflicting assessments of the Enlightenment (and therefore modernity), the Reformation, and Protestant versus Catholic identity continued to divide them as new issues arose which demanded theological and ecclesiastical response.

LIBERAL PROTESTANTISM

The Liberal Protestant position found its preeminent advocate in Friedrich Ernst Daniel Schleiermacher (1768–1834). This great theologian—aptly called the church father of the nineteenth century[3]—believed that while the French Revolution had certainly led to the political chaos of the Terror and the tyranny of Napoleon, the return to the political arrangements of the old regime—that is, the return to the strict separation of authority between the nobility and the common folk—was not the answer to Prussia's future. Schleiermacher, as one historian has put it, made "no secret of his belief that not the will and command of the ruler, but only the efforts of the whole people could, eventually, liberate Prussia."[4] The impact of Schleiermacher's preaching was particularly significant. He was acknowledged to be the "first great political preacher since Luther."[5] No doubt adding to this reputation was Schleiermacher's willingness to speak out publicly against those in authority with whom he disagreed. He remained fiercely independent of those in political power throughout his career.

Schleiermacher grounded his politics in a theological position, centering in ecclesiology, that was self-consciously Protestant.[6] In his opinion a key principle of the Reformation is the assertion that the individual enjoys the privilege of an immediate relationship to Christ through the Spirit. The individual Christian is an able discerner of truth. He or she is not dependent on mediating individuals or institutions in order to be a responsible self in the world. As Schleiermacher puts it in his "utopia of church order,"[7] the fourth of the *Speeches* (1799):

> When one stands out before the others he is neither justified by office nor by compact; nor is it pride or ignorance that inspires him with assurance. It is the free impulse of his spirit, the feeling of heart-felt unanimity and completest equality, the common abolition of all first and last, of all earthly order.[8]

The center of the church's attention are those elements in human experience which disclose "divine things." This center required, above all, the spoken word: "On the highest subject with which language has to deal, it is fitting that the fulness and splendour of human speech be expended."[9] This notion Schleiermacher argues he has learned from Luther.[10]

According to Schleiermacher, to be evangelical is to have this conception of the church: a community of believers, joined in the Spirit by explicit faith, dedicated not to ritual, custom, or inherited privilege, but to the search for and the exposition of the truth. This conception reflects an enormously flexible and tolerant view of church order, yet one with limits. It is a conception that, in the first instance, is vigorously Protestant in its suspicion of all formal claims to authority that interfere with the individual's relationship to Christ. Schleiermacher declares that hierarchism, clericalism, and uncritical appeals to doctrinal orthodoxy are barriers to the creation of an authentic spiritual community. In this regard the Roman Catholic church comes under especially harsh judgment. Its organizing principle is a "priestly government" that falsely makes its "foundation stone . . . the higher personal religious worth of the priests." Its "first principle" is that the laity require priestly mediation in order to "enjoy their share in the blessings of the church."[11] The Catholic church denies freedom to the Christian. Against the Catholic church, Schleiermacher argues, the Protestant must take a stand.

Schleiermacher never retreats from this uncompromising position. It has to do with the very core of his understanding of ecclesiology. The Holy Spirit envelopes the whole body of believers; no privileged group can claim Christ for itself. As Schleiermacher expresses his position in the masterpiece of his maturity, *The Christian Faith*:

> No individual or small group can represent Christ: all the more must we regard this transference of offices as deriving solely from the whole body, and the formation of the clergy into a self-contained and self-propagating corporation has no Scriptural basis of any kind.[12]

A second important limit to Schleiermacher's conception of the church is related to the first: worldly authorities are not to interfere in church affairs. "Evangelical faith rejects princely rule in the church in the same way as priestly rule."[13] Schleiermacher is forthright in his statement of this position. In the *Speeches* he defends it as a lesson of history by making this blanket assertion about all the "Constantinian settlements" that the church has endured: "As soon as a prince declared a church to be a community with special privileges, a distinguished member of the civil world, the corruption of that church was begun and almost irrevocably decided."[14]

Schleiermacher tested his convictions about political authority in the church in his lengthy debate with King Friedrich Wilhelm III in the so-called Agenda Controversy (1822–29). The situation was as follows: the king declared the Prussian Church of the Evangelical Union by royal decree in 1817. The king, a member of the Reformed church, found it intolerable that he could not receive the Lord's Supper with his Lutheran wife. He judged the reasons for this to be the dogmatic and ecclesiastical differences that had lessened in importance under the impact of Pietism and the Enlightenment. The king, however, was no rationalist. In his reform he desired a return to the roots of the Reformation in order to combat the "ideas of 1789." On the basis of his personal interest, but also out of a sincere desire to advance the cause of the church against a secular, revolutionary world, the king prepared his own liturgy and regulations and sought to impose these on all churches in his territories. The legal basis for this was at hand. Since 1794 the Prussian law code made canon law part of the administrative law of the state. The church was, in effect, a dependent corporation of the state.[15]

Schleiermacher supported the Union church as a member of the Reformed clergy. He believed that it would advance the noble cause of evangelical freedom by creating a united community dedicated to the principles of the Reformation. He hoped that evangelical doctrine would be tested and affirmed in such a union, not by the forms of the past, but by the process of translation and theological reflection for the present age. The king's imposition of a new liturgy, however, attacked the essence of evangelical identity by threatening the freedom of the congregation to determine its own worship under the power of the Spirit. The church through its synods and theological leadership, Schleiermacher believed, must be allowed to make its own decisions.

During the course of this controversy, Schleiermacher made enduring contributions to the development of Protestant thinking on church and ministry. First, he gave vital expression to what would later come to be known as the Protestant principle. In his famous definition, Paul Tillich describes this principle as, "the divine and human protest against any absolute claim made for a relative reality, even if this claim is made by a Protestant church. The Protestant principle is the judge of every religious and cultural reality."[16] It is Schleiermacher, above all, who enunciated this idea in an arresting way at the beginning of the nineteenth century in the particular struggles of the Prussian Union church. The principle has remained a pillar of liberal Protestant tradition to the present day.

Second, Schleiermacher defined the essential difference between Protestantism and Catholicism in a way that, as Avery Dulles asserts, "is not doctrinal but rather metadoctrinal, not material but formal."[17] Catholicism and Protestantism are "distinctive forms" of Christianity. They are in "antithesis." What is distinctive about Catholicism is that it "makes the individual's relation to Christ dependent on his relation to the Church." What is distinctive about Protestantism is that it "makes the individual's relation to the Church dependent on his relation to Christ."[18] As we have seen, Schleiermacher is particularly harsh in his judgment of the Roman church. It goes against the grain of his evangelical consciousness. But the distinction he makes between the two Christian communions should not therefore be dismissed as an unenlightened prejudice. It is, rather, an informed, radical, and immensely important distinction.

Schleiermacher focused his attention on the crucial theological subjects of ecclesiology and authority. In his view, the central determining factors of division between Catholics and Protestants are the nature of the church and the question of that to which the individual Christian pledges allegiance. The political ramifications of Schleiermacher's analysis of Catholic/Protestant differences are important to note. The question of the individual's relation to Christ and to the church, the tension between these loyalties, the problems of authority and freedom, are all fundamental political issues of great importance for modern Christian culture. And these are precisely the issues that Schleiermacher's distinction between Catholicism and Protestantism addresses. Investigated in a deliberate and critical way, Schleiermacher's typology will enable contemporary Christians to reconceive the ecumenical problem at a deep and profound level. As Dulles correctly observes of Schleiermacher's typological division of the two churches: "Even if the two communities achieved total agreement on the controverted doctrines, said Schleiermacher, this would not bring about a reunion, for the two churches are governed by different spirits. They approach questions with different orientations."[19] Recent ecumenical "agreements," it should be observed, have borne out this troubling, but inescapable fact.

Third, there is the matter of ministry itself. Schleiermacher's work is a reaffirmation of the controversial Reformation principle of the priesthood of all believers restated for a new age. The ministry of Christ is not an exclusive privilege. While there must be an "ordered public ministry and the constitution of the churches that goes along with it" so that the church's presence in the world is not "isolated and sporadic in character," no particular form of organization is theologically required. Indeed, "a Church fellowship can be quite in the evangelical spirit" even if it "concedes to every Christian the right of leadership."[20] This conviction is the heart of Schleiermacher's democratic liberalism. It also calls to mind the revolutionary claims asserted by Luther in his battle against pope and emperor, church and state. When Luther, for example, defines the church as "a high, deep, hidden thing which one may neither perceive nor see, but must grasp only by faith. . . . Naked children, men, women, farmers, citizens who possess no tonsures, miters, or priestly vestments . . . belong to the church,"[21] one sees at least one source of Schleiermacher's inspiration.

This is not to say that Schleiermacher's theology is without its difficulties. In his eagerness to defend the individual Christian and the congregation against the abuses of institutional power, Schleiermacher courts the danger of hypostatizing the priesthood of all believers. Perceived as agents of the Spirit's work, contemporary believers become, in his theology, the measure of Christian truth. The doctrinal tradition and the gospel are redefined by the demands of the present. In this connection, it may also be said that Schleiermacher's evangelical consciousness seems to be more of an attitude than a set of specific beliefs. He seeks to represent the "spirit" of the Reformation rather than its theological loci. But calling upon the Spirit's presence in the church to justify this approach is not enough of a rationale to legitimate his theological stance. As one of the most acute critics of Schleiermacher has said:

> The calling on the Holy Spirit is theologically legitimate only if, at the same time, a discerning of the spirits is carried out; but the criterion for the discerning of the spirits, the objective word of the Gospel, finds no fundamental consideration in Schleiermacher's theology.[22]

This is serious criticism and has been, since the pioneering work of Karl Barth beginning in the 1920s, the focus of scholarship on Schleiermacher. This criticism, however, should not blind us to the genuine contribution of this nineteenth-century giant to the issues of church and ministry in modern culture from the perspective of Protestant identity.

LUTHERAN CONFESSIONALISM

Finding a place for the "objective word" was not a problem for the Lutheran Confessionalism of the nineteenth century. The objective word is the *raison d'etre* of the movement. But that said, other generalizations are more difficult to make. Lutheran Confessionalism is a complex phenomenon that includes a broad variety of theologians whose work spans most of the century, roughly from 1800 to 1870. It is clear from the literature that the movement is not easy to organize and assess, and it has been subject to widely varying interpretations.[23] Hermann Sasse, for example, a strict confessional theologian, has admiringly described the movement as, "renovation . . . simply the rediscovery of the living content of scripture, of the Gospel of the Crucified and Risen One, the living experience of justification."[24] By contrast Emmanuel Hirsch makes this contemptuous appraisal:

> In contrast to Neoprotestantism [i.e., Liberal Protestantism], there is lacking here, according to purely intellectual standards, outstanding, truly creative personalities.

> One has, in part, the impression that the idea of the church must have been written in popular church magazines rather than in theological books.[25]

This controversy over assessment has to do with the movement's origins at the turn of the nineteenth century. The same cultural and political forces that shaped the "creative personality" of Schleiermacher also shaped the confessional movement. Its response to the challenge of these forces was different, however. Whereas the cumulative effect of the Enlightenment, the French Revolution, the Prussian reforms, and the War of Liberation caused Schleiermacher to reaffirm the Protestant impulse toward freedom and individualism, the confessionalists "seemed to be strengthened in their belief that throne and altar must oppose the revolutionary ideas of the time."[26] Hierarchism, clericalism, and uncritical appeals to doctrinal orthodoxy were anathema to Schleiermacher; to the confessionalists, they were the marks of truth. To Schleiermacher a pluralistic culture was evidence of the Spirit's work abroad in the world; to the confessionalists it was the enemy of God.

The confessionalists' political stance is well illustrated in the work of Friedrich Julius Stahl (1802–61). Born a Jew, Stahl converted to Christianity in 1819. Four years later his entire family followed him into the faith. At Würzburg, Erlangen, and, finally, Berlin, he served as professor of political and ecclesiastical law. A prominent jurist, Stahl also became a preeminent statesman and churchman. He was among the inner circle of advisors to Friedrich Wilhelm IV (1840–61) in that sovereign's effort, after his father's death, to continue the quest to make Prussia a "Christian state." Stahl came into his own as a political power during the period of reaction (1848–58) as one of the founding members of the Conservative Party.

For Stahl, "the valid principle in the church, as in the civil community, was the *Legitimitätsprinzip* [principle of legitimacy]. The priesthood of all believers was not a *constitutional* principle."[27] Equality before God as members of the Kingdom of Heaven is one thing; life on this earth, including life in the church, is another. On this earth there must be hierarchy, that is, distinction between king and subject, ministry and laity. The dangerous alternative Stahl found frightening to contemplate. "Since 1789," he asserted, there has been the social philosophy of revolution: "revolution is the establishment of the entire public condition on the will of man instead of on God's order and working."[28] The demands of the revolution are the sovereignty of the people and unrestricted freedom of such things as "domicile and occupation . . . public teaching . . . sectarian institutions . . . divorce." Revolution further means "equality" and "separation of church and state."[29] These political arrangements are contrary to the divine will:

> The revolution is, therefore, the most serious sin in the political sphere. If one considers other wrongs, even those as serious as usurpation, tyranny, and the repression of conscience, which are indeed transgressions against God's order, they

are not the fundamental abolition of God's order, for the purpose of substituting the authority of a human arrangement.[30]

The threat of revolution requires the church to establish its order on a proper basis. A collegial system of church government (which Stahl identifies with Reformed theology and "free" Protestantism) distorts God's intention that the human community be hierarchically structured. Hence Stahl asserts that only an episcopal system can insure the integrity of the church's obligation to proclaim the divine will.[31] Ministry is grounded in the teaching office *(Lehramt)*, established by Christ and passed on through the apostles. The teaching office stands apart from the congregation in its ability to represent the Word of God. It mediates between Christ and the individual in all areas of Christian life. The office is the prerogative of a particular class of officeholders who exercise priority in biblical interpretation and in the performance of sacramental ritual: "In preaching and prayer, the pastor is the representative of the truly gathered community in Spirit and faith, the 'first-born' before many brethren . . . the 'father over the sons'."[32]

While Stahl maintains that the offices of bishop and pastor are human institutions without claim to infallibility, he nevertheless offers an understanding of the church which otherwise bears a remarkable resemblance to Roman Catholic church order. Indeed, Stahl's Catholic sympathies are undisguised. The appeal of the Roman church is the appeal of a stable institution able to withstand the forces of revolution. That is, the Roman church is politically attractive, so much that one can easily find in Stahl's work the most strongly expressed ecumenical sentiments. He repeatedly argues, for example, for the need for visible unity between the Lutheran and Roman churches in order to enhance the church's struggling witness in the secular, modern world.

> At this time when the entire church is struggling for its existence, when opposition to the revolution has made clear the importance of the unbroken, historical connection between the two churches [i.e., Lutheran and Roman Catholic], we desire to cultivate the bonds of recognition and communion, and attend to *the longing for unity and universality* [my emphasis], which human aspirations and arrangements certainly cannot effect, but which only God's intervention can.[33]

Similar statements can be found in the work of other confessionalists such as Theodor Kliefoth (1810–95), August Vilmar (1800–1868), and Wilhelm Löhe (1808–72). Even officials in the government were open to such arguments insofar as they sensed a common interest between conservative and authoritarian Prussian policy and the negative stance of Rome toward the Enlightenment and revolution. For example, jurist Ernst Ludwig von Gerlach (1795–1872), a major figure in the government, supported the expansion of Roman Catholic influence in Prussia and asserted that he was closer to the Jesuits than to Protestant liberals. He hoped for reunion with Rome and, for a time, the common opinion was that he himself would convert. Von Gerlach employed the term "evangelical catholicity" to define his position as a conservative Lutheran. To this day the term has retained its polemical and programmatic associations as it signals strong Roman sympathies among Lutherans who employ it.[34]

The revolutionary upheavals of 1848, in which student and worker demonstrations disrupted government in the capitals of Europe, prompted terrible fears among those in authority. It was widely believed that the ferment of the French Revolution had continued its destructive force unchecked in European society.[35] Renewed fear of revolution further encouraged the confessional reaction of Lutheran theologians. In this regard, the doctrine of the ministry became a particular focus of attention.[36]

The strong tendency, apparent in Stahl, to identify a specific historical community of faith as divinely established according to dogma and an episcopal system of order—that is, the tendency to equate the invisible church with a visible church—undergirds the theology of the influential Bavarian pastor and teacher Wilhelm Löhe, whose "Aphorisms concerning New Testament Offices" appeared in 1849.[37] Löhe asserts that the gospel of Word and sacrament depends on the apostolic ministry established by Christ. The office of ministry stands over against the congregation. It is nothing less than the source of the congregation: "Not the office originates from the congregation, but it is more accurate to say, the congregation originates from the office."[38] Without the ministry, the congregation is only indirectly linked to its Lord. Any collegial church order that gives congregations the right to vote on ecclesiastical affairs is "not only unapostolic, but highly dangerous."[39] The idea that congregations can choose their own ministers is out of the question. The clergy must be seen as the "strong princes of the church":[40] like princes they cannot be elected by the people; rather, the ministry arises by succession to the ministerial office, "from person to person, by reason of God."[41]

Like Schleiermacher, Löhe is highly suspicious of the interference of the government in church affairs. The prince should not be *summus episcopus*. But unlike Schleiermacher, Löhe does not affirm the freedom of individual Christians and congregations. Rather, it is the clergy, representing their people in synods, who are responsible for the life of the church. If exclusive clerical control cannot be allowed—that is, if there must be leadership in the church directly from the laity—then it is better that the prince rules and not the members of the church: "a tyrant is easier to endure, if indeed one there must be, than the many."[42] Löhe conceives the office of ministry not only as the center of authority in church order, but also as itself a means of grace. Ordination, by the laying on of hands, is nothing less than a consecration. Ordination provides "capability," "privilege," "charism" for ministry; it is entirely other than "a naked ceremony."[43] Just how far Löhe can take this notion is apparent in his "New Aphorisms" (1851) where he declares that there is an essential difference between the word of forgiveness spoken by one Christian to another and the word of forgiveness spoken by the office of ministry: only the latter provides absolution.[44] As Gerhard Müller observes, even Löhe's staunchest defenders have to acknowledge that he oversteps the boundaries of any recognizable Reformation position in this claim.[45]

THE ERLANGEN THEOLOGIANS

This conservative extremism concerning church order and ministry did not go unchallenged at the time. Johann Christian Konrad von Hofmann (1810–77), a professor at Erlangen, responded to Löhe quickly. "After a long time fighting against those who made the office dependent on the congregation," Hofmann wrote in 1849, "those who make the church dependent on the office" must now be debated.[46] According to Hofmann, Löhe confuses gifts given to the entire church with the institution of a particular office. It is an open question whether such an office is an authentic teaching of the New Testament. In any event, the hearing of the gospel and service to the gospel do not require the office of the ministry in order to happen in the church. Further, Löhe's understanding of ordination as "a communication of powers" is a Roman Catholic idea. It is certainly neither a New Testament teaching nor a Protestant teaching. To conceive of the gospel as ecclesiastically bound is to go against the heart of the Reformation. To be sure, the ministry must be guaranteed in its independence from "individual congregations." But it cannot be placed over the church.[47]

Johann Wilhelm Friedrich Höfling (1802–53) and Gottlieb Christoph Adolph von Harless (1806–79) followed Hofmann's lead. Höfling insists that the ministry belongs *iure divino* to the entire Christian community. In his reaction to the extreme confessionalist position, he tends toward an entirely opposite view, combining "the professional ministry with the universal priesthood."[48] Harless asserts that "visible unity and purity" cannot be claimed to be "marks of the true church." The church is, as Luther says, hidden; it is grasped only by faith, and it is not seen by our eyes. The church is broken, sinful, unfaithful in itself, and yet Christ remains present in it, calling it his own.[49] While the office of ministry has "fullness of power"—that is, while it represents the Lord Jesus Christ independently of congregational control—this independence, says Harless, is, nevertheless, the result of the call of the church. Therefore, the authority of the clergy cannot be properly understood as being caused by a particular, individualized power or grace that resides within the office itself. Power and grace belong to the Word, rooted in the living Christ. Christ alone is the foundation of the Word and he establishes the office of ministry.[50] The promise of Christ is bestowed on the entire congregation. It does not require an elite for mediation.

THE LUTHERAN DOCTRINE OF MINISTRY IN LIGHT OF REFORMED CRITICISM

The nineteenth-century conflict among Lutherans over church and ministry has often been portrayed as a conflict between a "high church" position (Stahl,

Löhe, et. al.) and a "low church" position (Liberal Protestants, the Erlangen theologians—especially Höfling). The former teaches that ministry is a "divine institution": the latter interprets ministry "functionally" as a privilege transferred by the congregation. The standard response to this interpretation of the conflict has been to consider these two sides as "false alternatives" and to assert that the church "as Body of Christ and as *creatura verbi*" must be measured by the Word alone: "A genuine alternative," proposes Gerhard Müller, "would rather be the opposition and at the same time the *union of gospel and congregation.*"[51] Of the nineteenth-century figures we have considered, Harless seems to come the closest to this understanding.

These observations are quite to the point. But there is much more at stake here than a question of "false alternatives." It is particularly important in today's ecclesiastical climate that this be realized.

A clue to this deeper level of the nineteenth-century Lutheran conflict is provided by Karl Barth. Early in his theological career, Barth warned his Reformed brothers and sisters against the tendency to try to contain God within the bounds of a specific creed and a specific church. He pointed to the Lutherans as especially vulnerable to this distortion, quoting a nineteenth-century Lutheran hymn to support his case:

> Secure Church, our Church!
> Her wall, her safety and defence
> Is Augsburg's conquering creed,
> A mighty rampart around her.

"So wrote a Lutheran eighty years ago," Barth commented. "No Reformed creed could be so hymned. The Reformed church has never been in that sense 'a secure church.' "[52]

In another essay, recalling Luther's polemical retort to Zwingli at Marburg, Barth questioned what he called the Lutheran *est:* that is, the tendency to define God's presence unambiguously in human reality through guaranteed channels. Against this position Barth declares: "when the *last* word falls, the Lutheran *Yes* [i.e., the *est*] may be crossed with the Reformed *But*—not with *No.* . . . The point *from which* Luther began is again reached; the point where identity again becomes likeness, where the critical question must again arise so that the divine answer may be and may remain the truth."[53]

Lutherans may find it difficult to hear any word of truth in an argument such as this from a Reformed theologian. Such an argument is usually interpreted as an indication of Reformed "deficiency" in the doctrines of the sacraments, Christology, church, and ministry. It has also usually been seen as a Reformed assault upon the Lutheran "sacramental principle"[54] or, more generally, as an assault upon the incarnational principle of *finitum capax infiniti.*[55] However, while Lutherans might properly respond to the Reformed in defense of Lutheran doctrine concerning the Lord's Supper and Christology, the fact remains that the Reformed have good reason for suspicion when they consider the broad course of Lutheran theological and ecclesiastical history, particularly that of the nineteenth century. That is, Reformed criticism is especially telling with regard to a certain strand of confessional Lutheran teaching concerning church and ministry.

The nineteenth century is a period when the incarnational principle of Lutheran theological method was directed by influential Lutheran figures toward the creation of a theological position seeking to insure a "secure church" and an invulnerable ministry. The basic motivation of these theologians, who often allied themselves with established yet endangered elites, sought to protect the Lutheran church from a changing world. In this contest, the "Lutheran *est*" was illegitimately generalized for political purposes and became identified with a particular regime. Lutherans naively, and wrongly, judged that a visible, united church structure and a formalized doctrine of ministry would stem the tide of modernity. Indeed, they even found the Roman church, in one of its most reactionary phases, appealing. But just as the Syllabus of Errors (1864) and Vatican I (1870) failed to protect Catholicism from secular culture, so too the extremes of confessional Lutheranism failed.

Fortunately, Lutheranism had sufficient resources within its own tradition to develop a capacity for self-criticism. The Erlangen theologians, particularly Harless, drew upon these resources to counter the unwarranted extension of the incarnational principle into ecclesiology and ministry.

LESSONS FOR LUTHERAN IDENTITY

And what are these resources that were drawn upon by Harless and others? They are the resources of fundamental Reformation teaching concerning the nature of the church. The church is indeed "a high deep hidden thing" as Luther said. That is, Lutheranism teaches the hiddenness of the church. It experiences this as part of the hiddenness of God in the world. Human limitations, human finitude, the inevitable human tragedies of life are the unrelenting facts with which we live. The Lutheran claim is, however, that precisely in this finitude human beings can be released from the illusion and also the burden of trying to be gods. In this fallen world much is unclear. God's word, however, proclaims that human beings are accepted in Jesus Christ and that we will not be abandoned. Christians are called forth as the priesthood of all believers to undergo a transformation: to stop being turned in upon themselves and to stand before the God who saves and the neighbor who is in need. Christians are called into this world, a world that is affirmed in its secularity and independence (the two kingdoms). Christians are called as the church: the democracy of the justified.

In this fundamental teaching Lutherans, along with the Protestant tradition generally, stand opposed to the strong emphasis in Catholic doctrine that identifies the church as a guaranteed visible structure in the world by means of ecclesiastical hierarchy in general and the episcopal office in particular. Against such a tendency, fundamental Reformation teaching asserts that whenever the church has proclaimed its structural visibility as a redeemed community and whenever it has defined its ministry as the prerogative of an elite class, it has usually sinned both by thinking that it is somehow morally superior to the rest of the world and by treating its theology as a guaranteed ideology. The true church is hidden in the world because it is made up of the people of the world—sinners all. It is God's church because God has declared it to be so, not because of any quality inhering in it.

Lutherans need to recall these fundamental Reformation insights today. Ours is a time when, like the nineteenth century, ecclesiology and ministry are increasingly subject to the intense use of the incarnational principle of theological reflection based on disturbing political assumptions. This is most apparent in recent arguments supporting Lutheran-Catholic ecumenical relations. When the Catholic theologians Karl Rahner and Heinrich Fries suggest to Protestants that church unity is "a matter of life or death for Christendom" in a time of "worldwide militant atheism" and "relativistic skepticism," or when Wolfhart Pannenberg argues for the visible unity of the church on the basis that "the division of the church" has led to the development of "a world free from all religious ties, a world in which the theory of the state, in union with changing political ideologies, established its independence, and economic forces were allowed to follow their own laws," or when the culminating document of the international Lutheran-Catholic dialogue, *Facing Unity*, proposes the unity of the church on the basis of the unity of the clergy by means of ordination under the authority and discipline of the Bishop of Rome,[56] we find ourselves in a thought-world strange to the Reformation, but familiar to Friedrich Julius Stahl. It is a world in which modernity is feared and "Christendom" and an elite priesthood are objects of great longing.

If reflection on the nineteenth-century debate on church and ministry teaches us anything, it should teach us these simple truths: First, the disunity of the church did not cause the modern world and the visible unity of the church under a ministry "legitimated" by Rome will not make it less of a modern world than it is. Second, God's Word alone is "a matter of life and death" for the church, not the romantic traditionalist dream of a visible, hierarchical, and episcopal structure. And finally, if anything is endangered by the quest for the visible unity of the church under the worldly, political structure of one or another form of episcopacy, it is the church itself and the integrity of its gospel ministry.

NOTES

1. Basic orientation to this subject may be found in: Claude Welch, *Protestant Thought in the Nineteenth Century* (New Haven: Yale University Press, 1972), 1:59–85, 190–240; Emanuel Hirsch, *Geschichte der neuern evangelischen Theologie*, 4th ed. (Gütersloh: Gütersloher Verlaghaus Gerd Mohn, 1968), 5:145–231; Holsten Fagerberg, *Bekenntnis,*

Kirche und Amt (Uppsala: Almquist & Boktryckeri, 1952). Helpful background is given in John Stroup, *The Struggle for Identity in the Clerical Estate* (Leiden: E. J. Brill, 1984), 26–42.

2. See Robert M. Bigler, *The Politics of German Protestantism: The Rise of the Protestant Church Elite in Prussia, 1815–1848* (Berkeley: University of California Press, 1972), 3–50.

3. The title originates with Christian Lülmann, *Schleiermacher der Kirchenvater des 19. Jahrhunderts*, Sammlung gemeinverständlicher Vortraege und Schriften, no. 48 (Tübingen, 1907). What does it mean to be a church father? Essentially, I think, it means to be an unavoidable figure in theology. This Schleiermacher certainly is. For example, consider the judgment of Karl Barth, who fought Schleiermacher's theology throughout his entire career: "Nobody can say today whether we have really overcome his influence, or whether we are still at heart children of his age, for all the protest against him, which now, admittedly, has increased in volume and is carried out according to basic principles." *Protestant Theology in the Nineteenth Century: Its Background and History* (Valley Forge, Pa.: Judson Press, 1973), 426.

4. Bigler, *German Protestantism*, 27.

5. So the judgment of Rublemann Friedrich Eylert (d. 1852), court preacher and later bishop, quoted in ibid., 29.

6. On the following see esp., Hirsch, *Geschichte*, 148–64; also: B. A. Gerrish, "Schleiermacher and the Reformation: A Question of Doctrinal Development," in *The Old Protestantism and the New* (Chicago: University of Chicago Press, 1982), 179–95.

7. Martin Honecker, *Schleiermacher und das Kirchenrecht*, Theologische Existenz heute, no. 148, ed. Karl Gerhard Steck and Georg Eichholz (Munich: Chr. Kaiser Verlag, 1968), 8.

8. Friedrich Schleiermacher, *On Religion: Speeches to Its Cultured Despisers*, trans. John Oman (New York: Harper & Brothers, 1958), 151.

9. Ibid.

10. "For this is the kernel and spirit of all Luther's orders of worship: that everything must so proceed that the Word may prevail; that where God's Word is not preached, it is better neither to sing, nor to read, nor to come together; that order is an outward thing, and, be it as good as you please, it can fall into abuse." This from *Gespräch zweier selbst überlegender evangelischer Christen über die Schrift LUTHER IN BEZUG AUF DIE NEUE PREUSSISCHE AGENDE; Ein letztes Wort oder ein erstes* (1827), translated in Gerrish, "Schleiermacher and Reformation," 193.

11. Schleiermacher, *Speeches*, 206.

12. *The Christian Faith*, trans. and ed. H. R. Mackintosh and J. S. Stewart (Edinburgh: T. & T. Clark, 1928), 615.

13. Hirsch, *Geschichte*, 163.

14. *Speeches*, 167.

15. Bigler, *German Protestantism*, 6.

16. Paul Tillich, *The Protestant Era*, trans. James Luther Adams (Chicago: University of Chicago Press, 1948), 163.

17. Avery Dulles, "The Catholicity of the Augsburg Confession," *Journal of Religion* 63 (1983): 340.

18. Schleiermacher, *The Christian Faith*, 103.

19. Dulles, "Augsburg Confession," 340. On the influence of Schleiermacher's typology in the nineteenth century, see Dulles's entire argument, 339–45.

20. *The Christian Faith*, 616f.

21. *LW* 41:211.

22. Honecker, *Schleiermacher und das Kirchenrecht*, 43.

23. In addition to the above cited works by Welch, Hirsch, Fagerberg, and Bigler, mention should be made of the studies of Friedrich Wilhelm Kantzenbach: *Die Erlanger Theologie* (Munich: Evangelische Pressverband für Bayern, 1960); *Gestalten und Typen des Neuluthertums* (Gütersloh: Gütersloher Verlagshaus Gerd Mohn, 1968); *Evangelium und Dogma* (Stuttgart: Evangelisches Verlagswerk, 1959). See also: Wilhelm Schnee-melcher, "Conf. Aug. VII im Luthertum des 19. Jahrhunderts," *Evangelishe Theologie* 9 (1949–50): 308–33; Gerhard Müller, "Das neulutherische Amtsverständnis in refor-matorischer Sicht," *Kerygma und Dogma* 17 (1971): 46-74.

See also analyses of the movement in: Barth, *Protestant Theology*, 607–15, 625–33 (On J. C. K. Hofmann and August Vilmar); Theodore G. Tappert, *Lutheran Confessional Theology in America, 1840–1880* (New York and London: Oxford University Press, 1972). Older accounts of the movement still of value include: F. Lichtenberger, *History of German Theology in the Nineteenth Century*, trans. W. Hastie (Edinburgh: T. & T. Clark, 1889), 206–20, 421–66; Martin Kähler, *Geschichte des protestantishe Dogmatik im 19. Jahrhundert* (Munich: Chr. Kaiser Verlag, 1962), 167–92; Werner Elert, *Der Kampf um das Christentum* (Munich: C. H. Beck, 1921), esp. 285–91; Horst Stephan, *Geschichte der deutschen evangelischen Theologie*, 2d rev. ed., ed. Martin Schmidt (Berlin: A. Tö-pelmann, 1960), 166–89.

24. Hermann Sasse, "The Confessional Problem in Today's World," *The Lutheran Layman* 27 (1957): 20.

25. Hirsch, *Geschichte*, 171.

26. Bigler, *German Protestantism*, 33.

27. Welch, *Protestant Thought* 1:197.

28. Friederich Julius Stahl, *What Is Revolution? with The Reformation and Revolution*, trans. Timothy David Taylor (State College, Pa.: Bleinheim, 1977), 2.

29. Ibid., 3.

30. Ibid., 8.

31. See Friedrich Julius Stahl, *Die Kirchenverfassung nach Lehre und Recht der Protes-tanten* (Erlangen: Theodor Blaesing, 1840).

32. Hirsch, *Geschichte*, 182.

33. *What Is the Revolution?* 20.

34. On von Gerlach and the concept of "evangelical catholicity" see: Sven-Erik Brodd, *Evangelisk Katolicitet: Ett studium av innehåll och funktion under 1800-och 1900-talen* (Lund, Swed.: C. W. K. Gleerup, 1982); James Hastings Nichols, *Romanticism in Amer-ican Theology* (Chicago: University of Chicago Press, 1961), 71-74.

35. One of the finest studies of this intense period remains the fascinating, detailed narrative of Priscilla Robertson, *Revolutions of 1848: A Social History* (New York: Harper & Brothers, 1960).

36. "The immediate reason for discussion over the office [of ministry] was the February revolution 1848." Fagerberg, *Bekenntnis*, 101.

37. Wilhelm Löhe, *Gesammelte Werke*, ed. Klaus Ganzert (Neuendettelsau: Fremund-Verlag, 1954), 5:255–330.

38. Ibid., 262.

39. Ibid., 287f.

40. Ibid., 274.

41. Ibid., 294.
42. Ibid., 325.
43. Ibid., 296.
44. Ibid., 549.
45. Müller, "Die neulutherische Amtsverständnis," 58.
46. "Das Amt und die Ämter in der apostolischen Kirche," *Zeitschrift für Protestantismus und Kirche* 18 (1849): 129. Cited in Müller, "Die neulutherische Amtsverständnis," 61.
47. Quotations in Müller, ibid., 63f.
48. Holsten Fagerberg, *A New Look at the Lutheran Confessions*, trans. Gene J. Lund (St. Louis: Concordia Publishing House, 1972), 226.
49. G. Chr. Adolph Harless, *Kirche und Amt nach lutherischer Lehre* (Stuttgart: Samuel Gottlieb Liesching, 1853), 11f. On Hoefling, see Müller, "Die neulutherische Amtsverständnis," 64–68; Fagerberg, *Bekenntnis*, 225–39.
50. Harless, *Kirche und Amt*, 25.
51. Müller, "Die neulutherische Amtsverständnis," 74.
52. Karl Barth, *Theology and Church: Shorter Writings 1920–1928*, trans. Louise Pettibone Smith (London: SCM Press, 1962), 115.
53. Ibid., 110f.
54. See Carl Braaten, *Principles of Lutheran Theology* (Philadelphia: Fortress, 1983), 87–105.
55. See Hermann Sasse, *Here We Stand*, trans. Theodore G. Tappert (New York: Harper & Brothers), 118–60.
56. Heinrich Fries and Karl Rahner, *Unity of the Churches: An Actual Possibility*, trans. Ruth and Eric Gritsch (Philadelphia: Fortress Press; New York: Paulist Press, 1985), 1; Wolfhart Pannenberg, *The Church*, trans. Keith Crim (Philadelphia: Westminster Press, 1983), 84; *Facing Unity* (Lutheran World Federation, 1985).

Ministry
and Oversight
in American Lutheranism

7

TODD NICHOL

Although much given to theological controversy, American Lutherans have only rarely debated the doctrine of the ministry. As a rule they have turned to the topic of the ordained ministry and its oversight in periods of passage or in moments when the complexities of institutional life have required that they attend to the place of the clergy in the life of the church.[1] Infrequent polemical exchanges over the ministry between Lutheran bodies have, for example, usually taken place in the context of early struggles to constitute synodical bodies and supply pastors for far-flung, quickly multiplying congregations. Similarly, discussion of the ministry within the churches has generally occurred during pioneering periods or times of profound historical change.[2] Patching up these quarrels quickly, the American Lutheran churches have generally rejected extreme answers to theological and practical questions concerning the ordained ministry and the office of oversight. In contrast to European Lutherans of the nineteenth century, who debated the ministry at length, American Lutherans of the period were relatively little occupied with the topic and not favorably inclined toward the extreme positions taken by the principal antagonists in the European controversy.[3] Neither the sacramental, authoritarian view of the ordained ministry favored by Friedrich Julius Stahl nor the strictly functional conception of ministry urged by Johann Wilhelm Friedrich Höfling, for example, found many adherents in North America. American Lutherans by and large simply discarded the nineteenth-century European typology pitting *Stand* against *Amt*, divine institution against ecclesiastical convention, ontology against function, authority against majority.

Free of the political entanglements and other cultural factors that influenced their European counterparts, Lutheran theologians in the United States abandoned the antinomies that governed the European debate over the ministry, pursued a creative course of their own, and established a considerable consensus on the essential elements of a doctrine of the ministry and oversight. By the

93

end of the nineteenth century, indeed, most American Lutheran theologians agreed that: the public ministry of the church is divinely instituted; there is one such office; the tasks of the ministers of the church are the preaching of the Word and the administration of the sacraments; the call to the public ministry normally originates in the Christian congregation; ordination to the ministry of the church is a ratification of the call including the laying on of hands and intercessory prayer for the new pastor; the office of oversight is a practically necessary ordinance the arrangement of which is left to the discretion of the church. These matters agreed to, there was diverse opinion on a number of questions related to ministry, polity, and oversight as well as considerable pluralism in practice, although from a distance these Lutherans appear to have been remarkably alike in practical as well as theological matters.

Four mentors of the American Lutheran tradition—representing a diversity of ethnic backgrounds and pieties as well as a denominational variety ranging from the Missouri Synod, on the one hand, to the Lutheran Free Church, on the other—can epitomize the formation of this consensus: Carl Ferdinand Wilhelm Walther, Charles Porterfield Krauth, Matthias Loy, and Georg Sverdrup.[4]

CARL FERDINAND WILHELM WALTHER

C. F. W. Walther (1811–87) was the first of these theologians to elaborate a doctrine of ministry. The occasion of Walther's efforts was a crisis in the colony of Saxon Lutherans which arrived in Missouri in 1839 under the leadership of the Dresden pastor, Martin Stephan. Stephan had persuaded the colonists to invest him with the rank of archbishop and they had granted him sweeping powers over their communal life. His authority over the colony was such, as one historian put it, that he "had convinced his followers that he was their only means of grace. They believed that outside Stephan there was no salvation."[5] Stephan's fall from power was, however, swift. Charged by three women with sexual impropriety, he was deposed from office and sent into exile across the Mississippi not long after the Saxons arrived in America.

Betrayed by a bishop who had become for them the guarantor of ecclesial identity and stranded in the American West, the leaderless colony plunged into chaos. In this trying situation the young pastor C. F. W. Walther emerged as the architect of a new church order, proposing a theology of the ordained ministry and a polity that acknowledged a large role for both lay and clerical members in the life of the church. Later, in controversy with J. A. A. Grabau of the Buffalo Synod, Walther refined his position in a small volume of immense influence, *The Voice of Our Church on the Question of the Church and the Ministry.*[6]

The armature of Walther's book is a series of theses supported by quotations from the Scripture, the Lutheran confessions, Luther, and the Lutheran scholastics.[7] With the help of these witnesses, Walther's theses articulate a conventional nineteenth-century American Lutheran doctrine of the ministry with certain characteristics reflecting the history of the crisis that had convulsed the Saxon colony. Most important of these was Walther's version of a "transference" theory of the public ministry, which said that the ministerial office, although divinely instituted, was originally committed to the whole congregation and from it transferred or delegated to one of its members.[8] "The ministry of the Word *[Predigtamt]*," Walther wrote, "is conferred by God through the congregation as the possessor of all ecclesiastical power, or the power of the keys, by means of its call, which God himself has prescribed" (Thesis 6, A). In part because Walther linked this view of the ministry to a strongly congregational polity, it has sometimes been suggested that the transference theory results in a public ministry that is purely "functional" in character. This would be an accurate characterization if the term "functional" were taken to connote an instrumental view of the ministry, regarding it as defined by service of the Word of God for which it is designed. It would, however, be inaccurate if this were taken to mean that the ministry is not divinely instituted or that it is merely the creation of the Christian congregation and thus a dispensable element in the life of the church.

Walther, in fact, consistently maintained the divine institution of the ministry. "The ministry of the Word or the pastoral office," he insisted, "is not a human institution but an office that God Himself has established" (Thesis 2). And again, to reinforce the point: "The ministry is not an arbitrary office but one whose establishment has been commanded to the church and to which the church is ordinarily bound until the end of time" (Thesis 3). The conventionally Lutheran character of Walther's theology of the ministry is also apparent in his view of ordination: "The ordination of the called [persons] with the laying on of hands is not a divine institution but merely an ecclesiastical rite *[Ordnung]* established by the apostles; it is no more than a solemn public confirmation of the call" (Thesis 6, B).

Walther's provision for an office of oversight also exemplifies a conventional American Lutheran understanding of *episkopé*. He did not create a separate ministerial office for overseers of the church, but specifically assigned tasks of visitation and oversight to the president of the synod. By means of the provision for this office in the synodical constitution, Walther created for Missouri a powerful instrument for the supervision of both ministers and congregations and, in time, the occupants of this office (and similar positions eventually created for the districts of the church) embodied the spirit of ecclesiastical discipline and ministerial *esprit de corps* that became hallmarks of the Missouri Synod.

Articulating a doctrine of the ministry and an ecclesiastical polity consistent with Lutheran norms and aptly fitted to the American context, Walther helped to create for the Missouri Synod an ethos in which considerable authority and power were vested in the clergy in their role as expositors of the Word of God. While they plainly defined the role of the pastor as preacher and administrator of the sacraments, this theology and polity also placed great responsibility for the leadership of the church in the hands of its people. Aware that this departure from European Lutheran practice might alarm those who wished for more clerical control of the church, Walther took pains to remind his hearers of the primacy accorded to the Word of God by Lutherans. He wrote,

> Don't worry that the adoption of our church polity will lead to an influx of the secular elements of political democracy into the church or that an enslaving rule of the people, a popery of the people, will develop among us. . . . Whenever the pastor preaches, he stands before his congregation with the power of the Word, not as a hired servant but as an ambassador of the most high God. He speaks as Christ's representative.[9]

Missouri's subsequent history would prove the wisdom of Walther's counsel. Certain of the divine institution of their office, its pastors were for generations the authoritative, even occasionally authoritarian, leaders of their flocks. Given its doctrine of the ministry, it is not surprising that the scriptural saying "He that heareth you heareth Me" was often found painted onto the east walls of parish churches of the Missouri Synod during the early years of its history."[10]

CHARLES PORTERFIELD KRAUTH

Like Walther, Charles Porterfield Krauth (1823–83) was compelled to elaborate a doctrine of the ministry in the service of a new church body, the General Council of the Evangelical Lutheran Church in North America. One of a brilliant constellation of leaders who appeared on the American Lutheran scene in the middle of the nineteenth century, Krauth became the theological nestor of this federative body established in 1867 and served as its president from 1870 to 1880.

The General Council owed its origins to conflict in the older General Synod, an alliance of synods established in 1820. Not long after it was created, the General Synod was riven by conflict between advocates of a resurgent conservatism and proponents of a Lutheranism intentionally adapted to the American context. Krauth early emerged as a leader of the rising conservative party which called for a new appropriation of the Lutheran confessions, restorative Lutheran theology, and the liturgical formularies and customs of the sixteenth century. In this Krauth and his collaborators opposed the controversial "American Lutheranism" of Samuel Simon Schmucker (1799–1873) and others who proposed a fundamental revision of the Lutheran tradition in light of the modern, democratic setting in which the church found itself in the United States.

Krauth and his allies, however, were defeated in an effort to gain control of the General Synod and when that body failed to elect Krauth to a theological professorship in its seminary, events were set in motion that would lead to a rupture. Shortly after the General Synod declined to elect Krauth to a faculty post, the Ministerium of Pennsylvania called him to a position at its newly founded seminary in Philadelphia and voted to withdraw from the General Synod. The Pennsylvanians eventually issued a call for the formation of a new general body which resulted in 1867 in the formation of the General Council of the Evangelical Lutheran Church in North America. Krauth played a major role in designing the polity of this new body and in the course of these efforts he addressed himself at length to the doctrines of the ministry.

The need to create a model constitution for the congregations of the General Council was the immediate occasion for a series of articles by Krauth on the ministry in *The Lutheran and Missionary*.[11] In eighteen theses Krauth constructed a theology of ministry with characteristic American Lutheran features, among them, that: the one public ministry is divinely ordained (Thesis 17, 1); the ordained ministry is "rooted" in the priesthood of all believers (Thesis 8); the task of the ministers of the church is to preach the Word of God and administer the sacraments (Thesis 4); the call to the ministry originates in the local congregation (Thesis 16, 7 and 8); the office of oversight is a matter not of divine command but of ecclesiastical convention (Thesis 18). In another series of theses, Krauth discusses ordination in similarly conventional fashion: ordination follows upon and depends on the call; it is solemn and public affirmation of the call; it is necessary but not absolutely so; it is not a sacrament.[12]

Although he advances a view of the ministry much like that of other American Lutheran theologians in this and later periods, Krauth's theology of the ministry is distinct in certain particulars. At least three deserve mention: his discussion of the offices of elder and deacon; his pronounced emphasis on the role of the ministry in the governance of the church; his approach to the question of the historic episcopate.

In rejecting the office of "Lay" or "Ruling Elders," Krauth proposed a departure from an American Lutheran tradition dating from the colonial period. Since the days of Henry Melchior Muhlenberg (1711–87), most Lutheran churches in North America had been governed by church councils composed of elders and deacons in a pattern traceable to the German Lutheran church in London and the Dutch Lutheran congregation in Amsterdam. Considering the scriptural warrant usually cited for this practice (1 Tim. 5:17) insufficient, Krauth proposed that the office of elder be discarded (Thesis 17). Deacons, on the other hand, were to be retained as "executive aids" to the pastor (Thesis 15, 5). The deacons were, however, to be barred from preaching, administration of the sacraments, liturgical service, and the governance of the churches (Thesis 15, 6). These proposals to eliminate lay eldership and refine the definition of the diaconate resulted in a diminished role for lay leaders of the church and drew considerable criticism. One opponent charged, among other things, that the resulting definition of the pastorate was "too autocratic, and the office eminently magnified."[13] The General Council, however, finally approved a model constitution for congregations like that advocated by Krauth.[14]

His opponents in this controversy had, however, identified a characteristic feature of Krauth's theology of the public ministry: its provision for the rule and governance of the church by its ordained ministers. Definite in his opinions on this matter, Krauth refers to the ministers of the church as an official "class" and dwells repeatedly on the "rule" of the church assigned to them (Thesis 17). The same emphasis is also reflected in Krauth's concept of call and ordination. Unlike many other American Lutheran theologians of the nineteenth century, Krauth argues that a valid call to the ministry requires the consent of the standing ministry as well as that of the congregation (Thesis 16, 8). The complementary relation between people and pastor, in Krauth's view, also had a more general but equally definite ecclesiological correlate: "To the NORMAL COMPLETENESS of the local Church, or its full organization, the pastoral relation was essential, and a communion without a pastor was not a congregation organized in the fullest sense, but simply the people of a congregation expectant and with provisional powers only" (Thesis 16, 5).

Turning to the oversight of congregations and pastors, Krauth directs his attention to the question of apostolic succession and episcopacy. "The so-called Apostolical succession or canonical succession," he asserts, "does not exist, would be incapable of demonstration if it did exist, and would be of no essential value even if it could be demonstrated" (Thesis 12). The question of succession aside, Krauth suggests that both the principle of ministerial parity and the history of the church militate against adoption of the historic episcopate. Although polemical in reference to the Episcopal Church, Krauth's discussion of episcopacy is not, however, wholly negative in tone and substance. He proposes that the Lutheran church might adopt a "rightly ordered" episcopal office stripped of historical and theological claims associated with apostolic succession and the historic episcopate (Thesis 18, 44). Given his insistence on ministerial parity and the importance of the presbyter office as the sole ordained ministry of the church, it is probable that Krauth envisioned something like one of the versions of the office of oversight familiar to other American Lutherans in the nineteenth century.[15]

In this as in other fundamental matters, Krauth endorsed the consensus on the doctrine of the ministry which emerged among American Lutherans during the nineteenth century. Distinctive in its emphasis on the status of ordained ministers as an official class charged with the rule of the church and integral to its definition, as well as notable for its circumscription of the role of lay leaders in the life of the church, Krauth's theology of the ministry nevertheless resembles in essential elements that of other mentors of American Lutheranism in the nineteenth century. In working out this theology during a formative moment in the history of the General Council, he helped shape a tradition that would—through the history of the United Lutheran Church in America and that of the LCA—continue to influence the development of American Lutheranism for more than a century.

MATTHIAS LOY

Matthias Loy (1828–1915) served for more than fifty years as a minister of the Joint Synod of Ohio and Other States. In a variety of roles—as parish pastor, editor of the *Lutheran Standard,* writer, hymnist, theological professor, seminary president, university president, and synod president—Loy helped shape a distinct variant of the American Lutheran tradition. In contrast to the Lutheranism originating on the eastern seaboard, on the one hand, and to that of the Missouri Synod and its allies, on the other hand, this strand of Lutheranism in the United States is what might be called the "third tradition." Although diverse in ethnic background, the synods and churches representing this tradition had much in common and eventually coalesced into The American Lutheran Church in 1960–63.

The oldest of the bodies eventually to become part of the ALC, the Evangelical Lutheran Joint Synod of Ohio and Other States, brought a long history to this new church. Organized in 1818, the Ohio Synod owed its origins to emissaries of eastern Lutheran bodies who followed Lutherans into the Midwest during the early national period. These preachers reflected the mild Pietism of the Muhlenberg tradition as it had evolved during the first years of the nineteenth century. By the middle of the century, however, conservative forces were on the rise in the Ohio Synod as they were in the Ministerium of Pennsylvania. This conservative movement occurred just as Ohio closed the pioneering period of its history and entered a stage of rapid growth and expansion. In multiple roles, Loy led the Ohio Synod through both theological and institutional transformations.

Loy was prompted to express himself on the doctrine of the ministry when debate developed in the Ohio Synod over the practice of licensure. Continuing a tradition initiated during the colonial period, the Ohio Synod had followed the practice of licensing candidates to serve as pastors for a stipulated period or periods before finally ordaining them to the ministry. In Ohio as elsewhere, this practice came under sharp criticism as the churches took on stable denominational form, and regular procedures for the preparation of pastors became commonplace. Loy was among the severest critics of this practice, arguing that the system of licensure infringed on the ministerial call by limiting it in time and that it violated ministerial parity by establishing a probationary rank for novice pastors.[16]

Loy, however, had his eye on a wider scene as well. Alert to controversies between the Missouri Synod and its opponents in the Buffalo and Iowa Synods, Loy was also aware of the debate then under way in Europe. Writing expressly for the English-speaking constituency of the Ohio Synod and other American Lutheran bodies, Loy published his own views in a series of articles in the *Evangelical Quarterly Review* which were later gathered into a slender book, *Essay on the Ministerial Office: An Exposition of the Scriptural Doctrine as Taught in the Ev. Lutheran Church.*[17]

For Loy the doctrine of justification is the "sun" of the theological system and all other doctrines are its correlates.[18] This cardinal assumption dictated a doctrine of the ministry emphasizing the instrumental nature of the ministerial office. All Christians, he argued, stand in immediate relation to God and require no mediator of God's grace other than Jesus Christ.[19] All believers, therefore, are priests and possess the powers of the keys of the kingdom. Yet, for the sake of the Christian community, God has ordained a special ministerial calling distinct from the universal priesthood of all believers. The office exists for the sake of order and the proper service of the community: the speaking of the Word of God and the administration of the sacraments. This emphasis on the instrumental character of the ministry was reflected in Loy's explicit repudiation of a hierarchical status for the ministry.[20] Rejecting the notion of the ministry as a separate "class," Loy consistently referred the question of status in the church to the priestly vocation of all believers.

This understanding of the ministry as service pushed Loy toward one startling conclusion. Women as well as men, he argued, possess all the rights of the Christian priesthood and might, indeed, serve in the public ministry of the church in certain emergencies. Loy argued, to be sure, that women were not as well suited as men to the public ministry, but his stress on the universal priesthood nevertheless led him to the conclusion that women might, if no men were available, serve as pastors of the church.[21] Guided by primary postulates of evangelical theology, Loy thus took first, halting steps toward conclusions some American Lutherans would reach a century later when certain of their churches authorized the ordination of women.[22] Essential to Loy's culturally conservative but theologically consistent position were the nuancing of biblical literalism in favor of a more sophisticated hermeneutic, an emphasis on the priesthood of all believers, a repudiation of hierarchical status for the clergy of the church, and the conviction that the office of the ministry is primarily defined by its divinely ordained purpose, the speaking of the Word and the administration of the sacraments.

In extended discussion of the call and ordination, Loy adopts conventional Lutheran positions. He argues that the call to the ministry is both the prerogative of the Christian congregation and the essential factor in the making of a minister. Citing Luther, he argues that the "call and command make a pastor and preacher."[23] Opposed to the notions that ordination imparts a *character indelibilis* and that the rite of induction into the Christian ministry derives its validity from ministerial succession, Loy asserts that ordination is "a solemn confirmation of the call which must precede it, and which is valid without it."[24]

Although Loy does not discuss the office of oversight at length in his essays on the ministry, his role in one episode of Ohio's history is illustrative of his attitude toward the governance of the church. Along with the system of licensure, the Ohio Synod inherited from colonial Lutheranism the practice of convening the ministerium of the church in separate session from the lay members of the synodical convention. Not surprisingly in view of his stress on the priesthood of all believers, his emphasis on the prerogatives of the local congregation, and his insistence that the ministry is defined solely by the tasks of preaching and the administration of the sacraments, Matthias Loy was among the foes of this system of separate meetings. After intense debate in the synod in which Loy took a prominent part, the system of separate meetings was abolished and the principle established of joint governance of the Ohio Synod by both lay and ministerial delegates to its conventions.[25]

Although the practice of convening separate meetings of the ministerium long endured in other precincts, in this instance the Ohio Synod adopted the practice that would eventually come to prevail in most American Lutheran bodies. In a series of theses adopted in 1893, Ohio gave voice to a theology of ministry that would have commanded broad acceptance among other bodies as well. The theses stated that:

> 1. The administration of the means of grace is not the privilege of a special class, but is a right that Christ originally and immediately gave to his whole church, that is, every believing Christian.
> 2. The ministry is an office based upon a special command of the Lord, in force for all times, and by the call transferred to certain persons to administer the means of grace publicly in the name of the congregation.
> 3. The call is a right of that congregation in which the minister is to exercise the functions of office. Ordination is only a solemn and public confirmation of the call and only an apostolico-ecclesiastical order.[26]

In the doctrine of the ministry, as in much else, the Joint Synod of Ohio and Other States stood at the crossroads of American Lutheranism and represented its central traditions.

GEORG SVERDRUP

Georg Sverdrup (1848–1907) brought from Norway to the United States the vision of a church composed of free and living congregations served by educated, consecrated pastors. Scion of a distinguished family of patriots and pastors known for their advocacy of democratic principles and determined opposition to aristocratic privilege, Sverdrup had also been profoundly stirred by the awakening that swept Norway in the middle of the nineteenth century. While distancing himself from the individualism and separatism to which Norwegian Pietism sometimes inclined, he knew and embraced its ardor, its rigor, and its desire to awaken a slumbering church and convert a dying world. The experience of spiritual renewal during the awakening together with family tradition and a considerable theological sophistication combined to produce in this immigrant leader a unique vision of church and ministry.

Central to Sverdrup's conception of church and ministry is the notion of the "free and living congregation."[27] He identified the local congregation, loosely but intimately bound to other congregations, as the fullest realization of the church in history, as the right form of the kingdom of God on earth.[28] Conceiving of these congregations as assemblies for worship and centers for Christian mission, Sverdrup assigned considerable responsibility for the life of the church to both its lay members and its ordained pastors.

An educated ministry was crucial to Sverdrup's vision for the church, and he bent his most creative efforts in the United States to the development of a curriculum for the training of pastors at Augsburg College and Seminary. When a union of three bodies in 1890 appeared to threaten the educational program at Augsburg, Sverdrup assumed the leadership for a movement to protect the school, and within a few years helped organize the so-called Friends of Augsburg into the Lutheran Free Church.

In working out a theology of the ordained ministry in the service of this new body, Sverdrup pondered deeply the import of the new context in which the Lutheran church found itself in the United States. "We are certain," he had said eight days after arriving in America, "that the Norwegian people have here a great and glorious task. It is to declare the truth that freedom is not apart from God but only in God, to bear witness that freedom and Christianity are not two things but one."[29] In this dramatic utterance, he struck a theme as old as the history of the northern European settlement of the continent: that America would be the arena in which God would renew and complete a Reformation aborted in Europe. Confident that American freedom would provide a hospitable environment for the renewal of the Lutheran tradition, Sverdrup suggested that in America evangelical congregations and pastors could seize an opportunity denied them since the close of the apostolic era. He understood, and pressed the realization on his constituency, that this would be to put the church to a test:

> The real struggle about the ministry actually begins within a free church. In the state church the office of the ministry is already distorted, and nobody expects or demands that it be otherwise. In a free church it is essential that the office of the ministry shall have its proper place and function.[30]

The American context, he argued, would constitute a deadly trap for the church if it understood the primary question to be "Is the pastor the servant or the master of the congregation?"[31] If this became the fundamental question, Sverdrup thought, it would inevitably result in the tyranny of either ministry or congregation, in priestcraft or a mob-rule of the church ultimately degenerating into individualism. The proper question to ask, he insisted, has to do with how best to preach the Word of God. "If pastor and congregation are to stand in a right relation to each other, it is essential to maintain the unwavering faithfulness that the ministry of the Word is a service to God and also to the congregation."[32] The dialectic governing the doctrine of the ministry, in other words, is not created by the poles of ministry and church, but by the Word of God and the reality of the congregation created by that Word and ruled by it.

All Christians, Sverdrup insisted, hear and receive the Word of God and all Christians rightfully speak and impart the Word to others. In his providence, God has established the office of the ministry for the sake of the orderly, public proclamation of the Word and the administration of the sacraments in the Christian congregation. When this right has been committed by the call of a congregation to a member of the church, the office may not be usurped by individuals nor may the congregation demand that the occupant of the office do anything other than make the Word of God known in its purity.[33] On the basis of these fundamental considerations, Sverdrup sketched a doctrine of the ministry with features much like those proposed by other nineteenth-century American Lutheran theologians: the church has one, divinely established office of the ministry; the task of the public ministry is to preach the Word of God and administer the sacraments; the call to the public ministry is the prerogative of the local congregation; ordination to the ministry is the ratification of the call and an occasion for prayer on behalf of the ordinand.[34]

While Sverdrup taught a conventional doctrine of the ministry, he proposed a novel departure in the matter of oversight. Arguing that the rule of bishops had made a shambles of the medieval church and that the consignment of the cause of the Reformation to the princes had been a disaster for the development of the Lutheran churches, Sverdrup proposed that Norwegian-American Lutherans abandon the hierarchical structures they had known in their homeland and create a new polity that was both consonant with the witness of Scripture and the theology of the Lutheran tradition as well as appropriate to the American context. As a means to this end, Sverdrup suggested that the congregations of the church unite for mutual support and edification in a voluntary union based on a compact pledging mutual support and subscription to the Lutheran confessions. As a body, this union of congregations would possess no coercive authority over its member congregations or individuals, but would rather relate to them in an advisory capacity.[35] Sverdrup thus proposed that the function of oversight be placed not in the hands of an individual official but that congregations assume the responsibility for the mutual oversight of one another.[36]

In 1897 Sverdrup and a group of colleagues detailed this and other proposals in a brief document, "Fundamental Principles and Rules for Work," which became the charter of the Lutheran Free Church.[37] Guided by these principles throughout its history, the Lutheran Free Church became a part of the ALC in 1963 and through that body conveyed its traditions to the ELCA in 1988. Among the traditions it brought to that new church were a high regard for the office of the ordained ministry and an equal esteem for the life of the congregations and the calling and tasks assigned by God to their lay members.

REFLECTIONS ON A CONSENSUS

Although others might have been chosen, the four teachers of the tradition under consideration here represent both the theological and the institutional mainstream of American Lutheran church life. Each of them served as mentor to a significant church body and each represents the theological tendency of one of the major strands of American Lutheranism. An examination of their views on ministry and oversight indicates that they epitomize the emergence of a considerable consensus on the essentials of a doctrine of the ministry among nearly all American Lutherans in the nineteenth century. Exceptions that might be mentioned—the Laestadian Lutherans or J. A. A. Grabau of the Buffalo Synod, for example—confirm rather than falsify the generalization. The position of neither group ever commanded the support of more than a tiny minority of American Lutherans.

Walther, Krauth, Loy, and Sverdrup, on the other hand, were teachers of commanding influence and in essential elements their views on the doctrine of the ministry are nearly identical. All four of these theologians taught that: (1) the public ministry of the church is of divine institution; (2) there is one such office of the public ministry; (3) the divinely appointed tasks of the public ministers of the church are to speak the Word of God and to administer the sacraments of Baptism and the Lord's Supper; (4) the call to the public ministry normally originates in the local congregation; (5) ordination to the public ministry is the public attestation of the call to the ministry accompanied by the laying on of hands and intercessory prayer on behalf of the ordinand; (6) the office of oversight exists as a practical necessity, but its nature is a matter of ecclesiastical convention rather than of divine institution.

Over and beyond this considerable consensus in essentials, these theologians differed in a variety of matters. They disagreed, for example, about what might be called the etiology of the ministry. With respect to the origin of the ministry, all of them, for example, emphasized the priesthood of all believers, but only Walther thought it necessary to explicate a "transference" theory of the origination of the public ministry.[38] Similarly these theologians disagreed on the place of the ministry in the definition, governance, and ordering of the church. In this matter Krauth's views are obviously at variance from those of his counterparts. Krauth's insistence that the ministry constitutes an official class charged with the rule of the church and integral to its complete definition as well as his determination that the call of a congregation is to be approved by the standing ministry are instances of this marked variance. Finally, while the four theologians in question all agree that there is only one office of ordained ministry commanded to preach and administer the sacraments, they permit varying degrees of latitude with respect to other offices. Krauth, for instance, argues that ordained pastors can divide their labors according to their competence for specialization (Thesis 17, 13) and seems to imply permission for orders of deacons and deaconesses (Thesis 15, 10 and 11). On the other hand, he vigorously denies a place in the church for lay elders of the kind who had figured prominently in American Lutheran congregations since the colonial era. Like Krauth, Walther indicates that other offices might be derived from the one ordained office of ministry (Thesis 8), and more than one hundred years after the publication of *Church and Ministry* and after long debate, the Missouri Synod in 1953 officially designated its parochial school teachers as "ministers of religion" (in part to offer them the same protection from the military draft and the shelter from the provisions of the federal income tax enjoyed by other ordained ministers).[39] Noteworthy here is that neither these significant and real differences nor the pluralism in practice that followed upon them impinge on the essential consensus in the doctrine of the ministry evident in the work of the theologians in question.

These framers of the American Lutheran tradition are also essentially consistent in their views of the question of oversight. All four agree that the office of oversight is without divine mandate but exists as a practical necessity provided for according to a variety of human conventions. Sverdrup is unique among them in proposing that oversight of the church be committed to the congregations on behalf of one another rather than to individual functionaries. Three—Walther, Krauth, and Sverdrup—directly addressed the question of episcopacy. Walther and Sverdrup had personal experience of episcopal governance of the church and rejected it outright. Alert to the rise of the high-church movement among Anglicans, Krauth is a caustic critic of arguments for the historic episcopate (Thesis 18), but envisions the possibility of such an institution for American Lutheranism if it could be parted from a historical and theological rationale he thought improper to it. In theological reflection on the office of oversight, in fact, all four of these theologians endorsed a considerable and real consensus in essentials which was ultimately reflected in practice as well. The Lutheran Free Church, for example, differed considerably in polity from the Missouri Synod, the General Council, and Joint Synod of Ohio, but like its counterparts the Free church nevertheless practiced presbyteral ordination (in the setting, it should be noted, of its regular conventions) and informally vested considerable authority in its president and other officers.

Here it might be appropriate to pause and ask why American Lutherans moved with relative ease toward a consensus on the doctrine of ministry. Why did American Lutherans reject both the sacramental clericalism and the juridical functionalism which dominated the European debate? Why does the European typology fail to explain the unity and diversity of American Lutheran thinking on the ministry? Georg Sverdrup's analysis of the development of the Lutheran tradition in the United States may at least point the way toward answers to these questions. The American context, he argued, provided the opportunity for Lutherans to free themselves from the political determinants that had complicated the European debates. With establishment and all that it entailed behind them, Sverdrup proposed, American Lutherans were free as Christians had not been since the opening of the Constantinian era to think and experiment their way toward fully evangelical views of church and ministry. In particular, Sverdrup maintained, the American context made it possible for the Christian congregation and the pastoral office to find their true forms as never before. In this, the American regime made possible a realization of the goals of the Lutheran Reformation—an upheaval occasioned by tracts with programmatic titles like the one Luther wrote for the Christians of Leisnig in 1523, *That a Christian Assembly or Congregation Has the Right and Power to Judge All Teaching, and to Call, Appoint, and Dismiss Teachers, Established and Proven by Scripture*—still denied to many European Lutherans and for which some of them made a heroic stand against apostate bishops and civil authorities during the German *Kirchenkampf* of the twentieth century.[40]

Whether or not Sverdrup's analysis is entirely apposite or accurate, it is in any event true that a consensus on ministry and oversight made possible by the conjunction of the American context and a renewed appropriation of the theology of the Lutheran Reformation served to undergird church life among American Lutherans through the middle of the twentieth century. While on occasion synodical bodies addressed questions concerning the ministry, these deliberations did not stir the sort of controversy that accompanied discussion of other topics including pulpit and altar fellowship, predestination, Scripture, and unionism. It is not, then, surprising that Conrad Bergendoff of the Augustana Lutheran Church could suggest in 1956 (in an official publication of the United Lutheran Church in America) that all American Lutherans could agree to a simple definition of the ministry which he had discovered in the pages of Walther's *Church and Ministry*. Quoting from Luther's explanation of Psalm 110 in 1539, Bergendoff proposed this statement from the Reformer as the basis for a modern American Lutheran consensus on the ministry:

> Whoever exercises such a ministry is not a priest on account of his ministry, but a servant of all the others who are all priests. When he no longer can or desires to preach and serve, he becomes again one of the congregation, gives the ministry to another, and is no more than any other ordinary Christian. In this way one must distinguish the office of ministry or of service from the universal priesthood of all baptized Christians. For such a ministry is nothing else than a public service entrusted to a single person by the whole congregation wherein each one is a priest.[41]

Among theologians, a general agreement on the nature of the ordained ministry sketched in terms like this appears to have endured, with isolated exceptions, until about the time of the opening of the Second Vatican Council of the Roman Catholic church. Responding to discussion with Roman Catholics during and after Vatican II (1962–65), some Protestant thinkers sponsored a major revision of traditional theologies of ministry and oversight. American Lutheran theologians played a leading role in this effort, and as early as 1969 one of them was prepared to say that, "While the structure of the Lutheran understanding of the ministry is very different from the traditional Roman Catholic one, there are few, perhaps no, points of irreducible conflict."[42] While largely novel in form for American Lutherans, this understanding of the ministry was not entirely without precedent. It drew on selected strands of earlier American Lutheran thinking as well as on the longer history of Lutheran confessional theology and was also influenced by the Protestant theological renaissance that had occurred earlier in the twentieth century in Europe.

In the train of these developments on the theological scene, proponents of an understanding of the ministry that was, however, novel to most American Lutherans appeared in various churches during the next two decades. They characteristically argued that: the ministry as a distinct order within the economy of the church is of divine institution; the ministry is an essential, independent factor in the constitution of the church; the unrepeatable and necessary rite of ordination in which charismata are conveyed is sacramental in character if not actually a sacrament; ministerial succession is essential to ordination; ministers are called to the service of the church at large as well as to particular offices in congregations and elsewhere; the office of bishop is essential to the full being of the church and emblematic of its visible unity.[43] Many proponents of this position have argued that American Lutherans ought to adopt one or another version (though which one has been a matter of debate) of the historic episcopate and some argue that Lutherans ought to recognize the primacy of a reformed papacy.[44] Occasionally more extended theological claims have been advanced on the basis of this view of ministry, including the argument that the church and its ministry are aspects of a second incarnation.[45] While not all who claim the name (borrowed from predecessor movements in Europe) agree on all particulars and not all who hold this view of ministry claim the name, it has generally become a fundamental tenet of the contemporary "evangelical catholic" movement among American Lutherans.[46]

These views have not gone unchallenged, and from the late 1960s to the present there has been steadily escalating tension among American Lutherans over the doctrine of the ministry. As it has taken shape, the debate over ministry has often engendered a polemical spirit and the argument has from time to time descended from its original sophistication to caricature and canard. There have been, for example, renewed attempts to impose the terms of the European debate of the nineteenth century onto contemporary American Lutheran theologies of the ministry, and advocates of a sacramental conception of the ministry have often taxed proponents of the conventional American Lutheran position with holding "functional" views of the office.[47] The atmosphere was made yet more volatile by the emergence in the 1980s of strident, open debate over whether Lutherans ought to make relations with Roman Catholics, Anglicans, and the Orthodox their first priority in ecumenism or whether they ought not pursue and enter closer ecumenical relations on all fronts as and when possible. In spite of this increasing division, however, it was possible as late as 1974 for theologians representing the ALC, the LCA, and the Lutheran Church–Missouri Synod, working under the auspices of the LCUSA, to issue a statement reflecting general agreement on the doctrine of the ministry in terms that their nineteenth-century predecessors would have easily recognized.[48]

In the meantime, however, two new factors had entered into American Lutheran debates about the ministry. First, by the end of the 1970s most informed observers of the American Lutheran scene took it for granted that the ALC, the LCA, and the newly formed Association of Evangelical Lutheran Churches were on the way toward a merger. Second, in 1982 the World Council of Churches issued its Faith and Order Paper No. 111, *Baptism, Eucharist, and Ministry (BEM)*, which among other things called upon the churches not embracing the threefold ministerial order of bishops, priests, and deacons to consider accepting this scheme. The publication of *BEM* and other ecumenical statements during deliberations that would eventually result in the formation of the ELCA in 1988 proved to be of momentous significance for the constituting of the new church.

As negotiations toward merger proceeded in the 1980s, proposals on the ministry before the Commission for a New Lutheran Church reflected variations of the conventional American Lutheran position first articulated in the nineteenth century and expanded in the twentieth century to accommodate and recognize various other professional servants of the church. Although there appeared to be a majority in support of a settlement based on the inherited consensus, a determined minority entrenched itself in defense of the 1953 decision of the LC-MS to designate schoolteachers "ministers of religion." This standoff resulted in a compromise referring discussion of the doctrine of the ministry and the status of unordained professionals to the new church. To this compromise there was appended a provision that the ELCA undertake study of the ministry, specifically including examination of "the possibility of articulating a Lutheran understanding and adaptation of the threefold ministerial office of bishop, pastor, and deacon and its ecumenical implication."[49] This provision, of course, indicated the significance of *BEM* and the ecumenical movement as a whole for the formation of the new church and the development of its official position on the ministry of the church.[50]

Before the ELCA assumed its place on the American scene in 1988, it had thus been committed to debate and decide momentous questions of ministry and polity—contemporary events once again repeating the American Lutheran pattern of debate over ministry and polity in the context of the creation of new denominational structures. It may also happen that the period of 1960 to the close of the century will prove to be a moment of transition from one phase of American Lutheran history to another, a revolutionary interlude in which the meaning of being Lutheran in the United States will dramatically change. This will depend in part on whether the people of the ELCA and of the LC-MS decide to abandon or endorse the consensus on the doctrine of ministry they have inherited from their forebears.

A variety of considerations will be at play as American Lutherans make this decision: matters of order and rank within the churches, opportunities and challenges presented by the ecumenical movement, and the call to express the visible unity of the church. Their tradition, however, argues that for American Lutherans all of these considerations will be subordinate to another more important one. The question of whether American Lutherans will, as Matthias Loy put it, make the doctrine of justification the "sun" of their theological system is, their history insists, the most pointed question before them. In other things they have thought of themselves as blessed by a freedom created by the gospel of Jesus Christ and, in the providence of God, recognized by the political regime under which they live. If the need to articulate a doctrine of the ministry consistent with the doctrine of justification and conformable to the confessions of the Lutheran church constitutes the chief theological task presently before the American Lutheran churches, the corresponding practical task, their heritage would have it, is to structure a ministry whose chief end will be the proclamation of the gospel. The theological tradition developed by American Lutherans over the course of three centuries insists that it is for this end and this alone that the public ministry of the church exists and for which God has given it a definite mandate. For the rest, American Lutherans have consistently understood both church and ministry to be committed to freedom for the sake of their proper service to the world.

NOTES

1. Perhaps best known of these episodes have been the controversies of the Missouri Synod with the Buffalo and Iowa Synods.

2. Examples might include disputes about lay participation in the proceedings of the Ministerium of Pennsylvania, debates in various bodies about the system of licensure, the Augustana Synod's repeated rejection of the historic episcopate, and conflict among Norwegian-American Lutherans over the proper place of lay preaching in the church.

3. On the European debate, see Holsten Fagerberg, *Bekenntnis Kirche und Amt in der deutschen konfessionellen Theologie des 19. Jahrhunderts* (Uppsala: Almquist & Wiksells Boktryckeri AB, 1952).

4. Commenting on an earlier version of this essay presented to the Task Force for the Study of Ministry of the Evangelical Lutheran Church, John H. P. Reumann argued that the inclusion of Wilhelm Löhe among the mentors of American Lutheranism in the matter of the ministry would require qualification of the conclusion that from the middle of the nineteenth century to the middle of the twentieth American Lutherans enjoyed a considerable consensus in the doctrine of the ordained minstry. For Reumann's remarks see "Synopsis III, Evangelical Lutheran Church in America, Task Force on the Study of Ministry, June 8-10, 1989, The Lutheran Center, Chicago, Ill.," p. 3.

Löhe's importance in American Lutheran history is difficult to overestimate. His name graces the chapel of a prominent Lutheran seminary in the United States and his works have stirred the imaginations of American Lutheran theologians for generations. Furthermore, Löhe's views on the ministry were, to be sure, different in important particulars from those of the mentors of the American Lutheran tradition mentioned here, not the least of which differences is reflected in Löhe's favorable attitude toward patriarchy and ecclesiastical hierarchy. In many respects, nevertheless, he shared common presuppositions and conclusions with his American counterparts. He was, for example, an adamant foe of the historic episcopate in its Anglican, Roman Catholic, and Orthodox forms. On this matter, see *Three Books About the Church*, trans. and ed. James L. Schaaf, Seminar Editions, ed. Theodore G. Tappert (Philadelphia: Fortress Press, 1969), 131-40.

Ultimately, however, Löhe cannot be identified as a mentor of the official American Lutheran tradition in the matter of the doctrine of the ministry. Among other things, he never visited the United States, he opposed (unlike those who came after him in the missionary institute he founded) a transition to the English language, and he regarded the developing polities of American Lutheranism as an exercise in "mob rule."

More importantly, however, when the Iowa Synod, the American group most intimately linked to Löhe, assumed its final form, its official posture on the ministry resembled not that of Löhe, but rather that of other American Lutheran bodies. As one of its principal theological mentors said of Iowa's developed position on the ministry, it represented an American Lutheran "consensus which is also the consensus of the Lutheran Church in the doctrine of the ministry" [*diesen Konsensus, der auch der Konsensus der lutherischen Kirche in der Amtslehre ist*]." See Sigmund Fritschel, "Die Thesen von Michigan City noch einmal," *Kirchliche Zeitschrift* 20 (1896), 30. It is not surprising, for example, to find Charles Porterfield Krauth's "Thetical Statement of the Doctrine Concerning the Ministry of the Gospel" (see n. 10), reprinted in a journal widely read by Iowa's pastors. See "Thesen über das Predigtamt," *Theologische Monatshefte* 2 (June 1869): 161-70. The work of J. M. Reu, Iowa's chief dogmatician for decades, represents the position characteristic of that body in its mature form. To measure the distance between Löhe's views and those of the Iowa Synod, compare the synopsis of Löhe's developing views presented in Siegfried Hebart, *Wilhelm Löhes Lehre von der Kirche, ihrem Amt und Regiment; Ein Beitrag zur Geschichte der Theologie im 19. Jahrhundert* (Neuendettelsau: Friemund-Verlag, 1939), 39–392 with J. M. Reu, *Lutheran Dogmatics*, rev. ed. (Dubuque, Iowa: Wartburg Theological Seminary, 1951), 432–38, and "Die Aufrichtung des evangelischen Predigtamtes zu Luthers Zeit," *Kirchliche Zeitschrift* 61 (1937): 193–218. This article replicated a lecture delivered in Rock Island, Illinois, on February 10, 1937. A slightly abbreviated English version appeared in the official theological journal of the Augustana Synod. See J. M. Reu, "The Office of the Ministry," *The Augustana Quarterly* 16 (1937): 195–214. Reu's discussion of the history of early Lutheranism in ibid. is notable for its emphasis on the early Lutheran reluctance to introduce the practice of ordination into its emerging church order. The Iowa Synod experienced no difficulties over the ministry with the Ohio and Buffalo Synods when it merged with those bodies in 1930, nor did the matter arouse controversy during the merger that produced the ALC in 1960–63 when these German bodies united with three Scandinavian-American bodies, including the Lutheran Free Church to which Georg Sverdrup was mentor. For an extended discussion, see Todd Nichol, "Wilhelm Löhe and the Iowa Synod on Ordained Ministry," *Lutheran Quarterly* 4 (Spring 1990): 11–29.

In short, the figures selected for examination here do represent a considerable consensus on ministry and oversight in the American Lutheran tradition. It would be difficult to name another figure whose addition or absence would qualify a historical argument for the emergence of denominational American Lutheranism in the nineteenth century and its maturation early in the twentieth century. Were Henry Melchior Muhlenberg taken into consideration, the argument would be extended and reinforced to include the eighteenth century. For a brief introduction to Muhlenberg on the ministry and the evolution of early American Lutheran views of ministry and oversight, see Theodore G. Tappert, "The Church's Infancy, 1650–1790," in E. Clifford Nelson, ed., *The Lutherans in North America*, rev. ed. (Philadelphia: Fortress Press, 1980), 39–57.

5. Carl S. Mundinger, *Government in the Missouri Synod: The Genesis of Decentralized Government in the Missouri Synod* (St. Louis: Concordia Publishing House, 1947), 63.

6. The English title of a recently published translation is *Church and Ministry (Kirche und Amt): Witnesses of the Evangelical Lutheran Church on the Question of the Church and Ministry*, trans. J. T. Mueller (St. Louis: Concordia Publishing House, 1987).

7. Walther's theses on the ministry are in ibid., 21–23.

8. Edmund Schlink attributes the invention of the transference theory to Justus Henning Boehmer. See *The Theology of the Lutheran Confessions*, trans. Paul F. Koehneke and Herbert J. A. Bouman (Philadelphia: Fortress Press, 1961), 244 n. 13.

9. Quoted in Mundinger, *Government in the Missouri Synod*, 202.

10. See ibid., 197.

11. See "Thetical Statement of the Doctrine Concerning the Ministry of the Gospel," *The Lutheran and Missionary*, 31 December 1874; 7 January 1875; 21 January 1875; 18 February 1875. Titles vary. The articles are unsigned, but on their authorship see Adolph Spaeth, *Charles Porterfield Krauth* (Philadelphia: General Council Publication House, 1909), 2:194.

12. A synopsis of theses on ordination by Krauth appears in Revere Franklin Weidner, *The Doctrine of the Ministry: Outline Notes Based on Luthardt and Krauth* (Chicago: Fleming H. Revell Company, 1907), 107–10.

13. B. M. Schmucker, quoted in Spaeth, *Krauth* 2:193.

14. For the history of these debates and the text of the model constitution for congregations, see S. E. Ochsenford, *Documentary History of the General Council of the Evangelical Lutheran Church in North America* (Philadelphia: General Council Publication House, 1912), 190–203.

15. For a brief survey, see Theodore G. Tappert, "Lutheran Ecclesiastical Government in the United States of America," in *Episcopacy in the Lutheran Church? Studies in the Development and Definition of the Office of Church Leadership*, ed. Ivar Asheim and Victor R. Gold (Philadelphia: Fortress Press, 1970), 155–74.

16. For a brief summary of his views on licensure, see Matthias Loy, *Story of My Life* (Columbus, Ohio: Lutheran Book Concern, 1905), 199–202.

17. Columbus, Ohio: Schulze and Gassmann, 1870.

18. Ibid., 72.

19. Ibid., 70–74.

20. Ibid., 23.

21. Ibid., 40–41.

22. For an extended discussion of Loy's very conservative position on the matter of women in the public life of the church and the exception he was prepared to condone, see *The Rights of Women in the Church: An Essay Prepared for Discussion at the Meeting of the English District of the Evangelical Lutheran Joint Synod of Ohio, held at West Alexandria, Ohio* (Columbus, Ohio: Lutheran Book Concern, 1896), especially 28–29. I am indebted to Professor L. DeAne Lagerquist for bringing this essay to my attention.

23. Ibid., 77.

24. Ibid., 197.

25. For commentary by Loy on this matter, see *Story of My Life*, 202–8.

26. These theses are conveniently reprinted in "Current Religious and Theological Thought," *Columbus Theological Magazine* 13 (1893): 306.

27. For an accessible sample of Sverdrup's thinking on this topic, see *The Heritage of Faith: Selections from the Writings of Georg Sverdrup*, trans. Melvin A. Helland (Minneapolis: Augsburg Publishing House, 1969), 37–63. A more extensive selection is in

Sverdrup's *Samlede Skrifter i Udvalg*, vol. 2, ed. Andreas Helland (Minneapolis: Frikirkens Boghandels Forlag, 1910).

28. Sverdrup did not, however, restrict the signs or the work of the kingdom of God to the local congregation. On this, see James S. Hamre, *Georg Sverdrup: Educator, Theologian, Churchman* (Northfield, Minnesota: The Norwegian-American Historical Association, 1986), 137–38.

29. Quoted in Hamre, *Georg Sverdrup*, 3.

30. Georg Sverdrup, *The Heritage of Faith*, 43.

31. Ibid., 44.

32. Ibid., 48.

33. Ibid., 43–53. In addition to the one office of ordained ministry, Sverdrup also proposed the creation of the office of deacon for the prosecution of the work of the congregation and the assistance of the pastor. See *Samlede Skrifter* 2:79–84.

34. Sverdrup does not dwell at length on ordination, but the care expended on the question of ordination throughout the history of the Lutheran Free Church, its continuation of the office of ordinator it had inherited from a predecessor body, and the practice in the Free church of holding services of ordination during its regular conventions indicate the importance assigned to ordination in this tradition. See Eugene L. Fevold, *The Lutheran Free Church: A Fellowship of American Lutheran Congregations, 1897–1963* (Minneapolis: Augsburg Publishing House, 1969), 85–86, 108–9.

35. *The Heritage of Faith*, 53–63.

36. Ibid.

37. The first and final versions of this document approved by the Lutheran Free Church are conveniently reprinted in Fevold, *The Lutheran Free Church*, 303–12.

38. Here it might be observed, however, that in practice the LC-MS and nearly all other Lutheran bodies in the United States actually endorse presbyteral succession in practice if not in official doctrinal statements.

39. *Proceedings . . . Lutheran Church-Missouri Synod . . . 1953*, 323–24.

40. For the dramatic history of one German congregation tried in the fire of the *Kirchenkampf*, see Gert Haendler, *Luther on Ministerial Office and Congregational Function*, trans. Ruth C. Gritsch, ed. Eric W. Gritsch (Philadelphia: Fortress Press, 1981), 91–102.

41. Quoted in Conrad Bergendoff, *The Doctrine of the Church in American Lutheranism* (Philadelphia: The Board of Publication of the United Lutheran Church in America, 1956), 36. Unless development of a consensus is assumed, it is difficult to reconcile this assertion with Bergendoff's earlier comment about American Lutheran difficulties with the understanding of the minsitry. See ibid., 19.

42. George Lindbeck, "The Lutheran Doctrine of the Ministry: Catholic and Reformed," *Theological Studies* 30 (December 1969): 588.

43. A characteristic statement of this position including most of the elements mentioned is Carl Braaten, *The Apostolic Imperative: Nature and Aims of the Church's Mission and Ministry* (Minneapolis: Augsburg Publishing House, 1985), 138–63.

44. See, for example, William H. Lazareth, "Evangelical Episcopate: An Argument from the Lutheran Confessions," *Lutheran Forum* (Advent 1988), 13–17 and Richard John Neuhaus, "Healing the Breach of the Sixteenth Century: An Imperative Possibility," *Dialog* 25 (1986): 39–43. A characteristic discussion of both episcopacy and papacy appears in Richard John Neuhaus, *The Catholic Moment: The Paradox of the Church in the Postmodern World* (San Francisco: Harper & Row, 1987).

45. So, for example, Carl Braaten: "It is always the gnostic-docetic heresy that separates what God has joined together in the foundational events of two incarnations—first, the Word made flesh in Jesus and second, his gospel becoming history through the once-for-all apostolic witness and its continuing succession through the church as a whole and through an evolving plurality of ministries of service." *The Apostolic Imperative*, 123.

46. On the history of the concept of evangelical catholicity, see Sven-Erik Brodd, *Evangelisk Katolicitet: Ett studium av innehåll och funktion under 1800– och 1900–talen* (Lund: C. W. K. Gleerup, 1982). On the broader topic of the ancestry of this American Lutheran movement, see N. P. Williams and Charles Harris, eds., *Northern Catholicism: Centenary Studies in the Oxford and Parallel Movements* (London: Society for Promoting Christian Knowledge, 1933); and David L. Scheidt, "The 'High Church Movement' in American Lutheranism," *The Lutheran Quarterly* 9 (November 1957): 343–49.

47. See Braaten, *The Apostolic Imperative*, 138–63. Braaten, for example, describes what he calls the "functionalist" approach to ordination this way: "As ordination is taking place, they mutter to themselves, 'It is not a sacrament; it bestows no *character indelebilis;* this is not a *sign* of succession leading back to the apostles.' It is just a ceremony, but they do not know what they are doing, or what for" (ibid., 141).

An attempt to destroy the intellectual hegemony of the European typology is Roy A. Harrisville, *Ministry in Crisis: Changing Perspectives on Ordination and the Priesthood of All Believers* (Minneapolis: Augsburg Publishing House, 1987).

48. See "The Ministry of the Church; A Lutheran Understanding," a study document adopted by the standing committee of the DTS of the LCUSA in March 1974.

49. *Constitutions, Bylaws, and Continuing Resolutions: Evangelical Lutheran Church in America . . . 1987*, 48.

50. For a complete account of the history leading to this compromise, see John H. P. Reumann, "Toward the Evangelical Lutheran Church in America (1988)," in *Ministries Examined: Laity, Clergy, Women, and Bishops in a Time of Change* (Minneapolis: Augsburg Publishing House, 1987), 199–223.

THEMATIC PERSPECTIVES

Part

2

8

GERHARD O. FORDE

> Of this gospel I was made a minister according to the gift of God's grace which
> was given to me by the working of his power. To me, though I am the very least
> of all the saints, this grace was given, to preach to the Gentiles the unsearchable
> riches of Christ, and to make all people see what is the plan of the mystery hidden
> for ages in God who created all things; that through the church the manifold
> wisdom of God might now be made known to the principalities and powers in the
> heavenly places. This was according to the eternal purpose which he has realized
> in Christ Jesus our Lord, in whom we have boldness and confidence of access
> through our faith in him. So I ask you not to lose heart over what I am suffering
> for you, which is your glory. (Eph. 3:7-12)

Lutheran difficulties with the doctrine of ordained ministry have been persistent and notorious. Lutheran thinking, writing, and practice has halted between understandings inherited from its Roman Catholic past on the one hand
and those propounded by reformers of a more pronounced Protestant stamp on
the other. Are the Lutheran views of the ordained ministry Catholic or Protestant? A confident answer does not appear forthcoming even though Lutherans
are constantly redoing and studying the ministry. In spite of the volumes dedicated to the subject, it is still necessary to have another go at it.

What is the problem? The premise from which this essay works is that the
Lutheran doctrine of ministry has been batted from pillar to post and back again
because it has not been worked out consistently and consequently in terms of
its own fundamental theological and hermeneutical principles. So it has wavered
back and forth, sounding now more Catholic and now more Protestant notes,
depending on winds of fancy or the spirit of the times. The ambiguity and
uncertainty in the Lutheran doctrine of the ministry are rooted in the very same
ambiguity evident within Lutheranism itself over what the speaking of the gospel
and the administration of the sacraments mean. That is, the ambiguity and
uncertainty in the office of saying the gospel are rooted in the ambiguity and
uncertainty about what in fact is to be said and what such saying involves and

is to accomplish. What is needed is to work out a view of ministry consequent to and consistent with the fundamental theological doctrines that gave birth to the Lutheran movement in the first place.

ROOTS

The roots of the doctrine of ministry in Lutheranism lie in the doctrine of divine election. That, however, is to state the matter theologically, that is, with reference to God. Anthropologically stated, that is, with reference to the human predicament, the roots lie in the doctrine of the bondage of the will. Christologically stated, they lie in the theology of the cross. To say that about roots is, of course, to suggest at once the reason for ambiguity in Lutheran views about ministry. Lutherans, like other Christians, never are so nervous and divided as when it comes to these doctrines and their consequences. Such nervousness and division, however, are bound to surface in the understanding of ministry. When one views Lutheran history it is perhaps not strange that a view of ministry has never been worked out consistently from these roots. This is what now needs to be attempted.

Why is the ministry of Word and sacrament necessary? Why is it necessary to have a preacher who is to say something from God to us? Most other religions do not do that. To be sure, they have teachers. But for the most part they seem to be gurus of some sort who instruct in how to conduct oneself appropriately or perhaps in how to approach or become one with the desired religious goal or god. They are not what Christians call ministers or pastors. Why do we have such? The answer and also the problem are rooted in the fact that God is a God of election, a living God who chooses and who thus speaks. Since God is an electing God, it is necessary that someone come to speak to us who can actually do the electing in the name of God. It is necessary that there be a minister, a speaker of the Word of God. If there is no actual speaker, election becomes an abstract idea that only threatens and destroys us. The only solution to that threat and that destruction is for someone to come to us and actually do the electing. That is the theological root of the doctrine of ministry.

Usually, however, the doctrine is not so rooted. And that is the reason for much of the trouble. The problem surfaces because we do not get on well with the idea of an electing God. In attempting to think and speak about God we run into that collection of magnificent abstractions which threatens to undo us. God is timeless, almighty, unchanging, infinite, unsuffering, omnipresent, omniscient. The idea that such a God elects becomes just the last straw. As an idea it is simply taken to mean that God has decided things once and for all from timeless eternity. And so it is usually thought that an electing God leaves no room for ministry or preaching or sacrament. Why preach if all has been decided from eternity? Rather than the foundation of the doctrine of ministry, election becomes the rock on which it is shipwrecked.

Precisely here the doctrine of ministry stands at the crossroads. If one is true to the Lutheran understanding of the matter, the ministry of speaking the Word and administering the sacraments is the carrying out of the divine election and thus the concrete solution to the problem posed by the electing God. Ministry so understood does not have to do with constructing and conveying better or more accommodating ideas about God, but speaking precisely the living Word of God. God does not call off the election but simply goes ahead and does it concretely in and through the ministry of the church. "The plan of the mystery hidden for ages in God who created all things" is now made known to all, even principalities and powers in heavenly places, through the church of Christ and its ministry. Election is the *fons et radix* of ministry.

Where this is not understood or accepted, however, ministry will take a quite different shape. Being scandalized by the idea of God and especially election, and having no apparent solution for the threat of it all, the "minister" can "serve" only by attempting to undo it. There is a marvelous irony here: the minister enters into competition with the God who is to be served. To establish the significance of such ministry the minister can only seek to make the claim stick that God does not in fact elect and that our only real hope lies in the possibility of altering (and thus unmasking or rationalizing) "the mystery hidden for ages." Ministry tends to become the business of doing that or explaining how to do it. To carry this off the minister appeals to whatever degree of "free will" is deemed to have survived in the hearers. If God does not elect we must do so for ourselves. Ministry becomes appeasing or explaining rather than proclaiming.

Here lies the reason for the ambiguity in Lutheran views on the ministry. From the beginning Lutherans have been nervous about the doctrines of election, the bondage of the will and the theology of the cross that fired Luther's Reformation. When ministry is not the concrete carrying out of divine election it becomes a matter of appealing to human wills. Two possibilities tend to emerge. We may roughly call them the Catholic and the Protestant tendencies. The Catholic tendency is to understand the ministerial office as the divinely ordained means for continuing the work of reconciliation between humans and God. This means that the minister is primarily a priest involved in the ritual of sacrifice, either repeating or re-presenting the atoning deed. Grace is proffered to move the at least partially free will.

The Protestant move generally has been to object to the presumption of such claims on the grounds that mediation has been accomplished by Christ "once and for all." While legitimate as criticism of clerical presumption, the objection all too often threatens to undermine the very possibility of ministry itself. Where, for instance, one holds doggedly to supralapsarian divine election as an idea, ministry gets reduced to the more cognitive task of informing the elect about such matters and the consequences thereof. The mystery remains essentially hidden and waits on the secret and internal witness of the Spirit for disclosure. Most of Protestantism, however, has found such theology unbearable, and so has tended to render the idea of election inoperative either practically or theoretically, insisting on some degree of human ability to choose or contribute to salvation. The Protestant minister then becomes either the persuader appealing to the will for its decision or the homiletical apologete for faith, morals, and the "Christian view of life." Many of the useful and meaningful tasks of caring for one another may thereby be encompassed, but the essential purpose of ministry gets obscured and/or forgotten.

Having largely lost its rootage in the doctrines that gave it birth, the Lutheran understanding of ministry has been batted back and forth between Catholic and Protestant tendencies. Sensing instinctively that ministry involves something more than just the function of persuading or teaching, Lutherans are often pulled in the direction of more Roman Catholic tendencies, attempting to shore up the office with more weighty ecclesiastical distinction. Ecumenical pressures from the Catholic side also tend to reinforce such moves. Traditional Reformation critique, however, makes it difficult for Lutherans to embrace these tendencies without reluctance or suspicion. So there is always reaction that moves in a more Protestant direction. Lacking a clear understanding of the purpose of ministry, there is constant argument over whether the office of ministry should be understood in an "ontological" or in a merely "functional" sense, whether the minister is granted the ontological qualification to assist in effecting or representing divine-human reconciliation or merely delegated the function of making the fact of its accomplishment known.

If Lutheranism is finally to escape this vacillation between Roman and Protestant tendencies it will have to reconstruct a view of ministry on the foundations laid by the Reformation that gave it birth. That is, it will have to work clearly and consistently from the realization that the reality quotient of ministry, if we may so call it, is that ministry is the concrete carrying out of the divine election now authorized and commissioned by the crucified and risen Lord Jesus. "All authority has been given unto me in heaven and on earth . . . ," Jesus said, and that is quite a lot. Ministry is neither the completion of an insufficient reconciliation or representation of an absent reconciler, nor is it merely explanation of an ancient fact. It is neither "ontological" nor merely "functional" in an educational sense. It is the actual doing of the deed authorized and commanded by Jesus. It is the service rendered by the church to what God has done to accomplish the election and precisely thus the salvation of humankind in Jesus. The sacrifice does not need to be repeated nor the reconciler made present again by those ontologically endowed. Everything has been accomplished. It is out in the open. The mystery hidden for ages is now revealed, not smuggled away again, in the church. It is to be made public. Surely Protestantism is right about that. But ministry is not merely the business of explaining that idea to the supposedly free, or of the informing of the elect about what took place in eternity. It is rather the actual doing of the electing deed to bound and unbelieving sinners here and now. Surely the entire heritage of Lutheranism, its insistence on the living Word of preaching as the Word of God here and now, absolution "for you," and its view of sacraments as imparting the reality of what they promise, all point unmistakably in this direction. Ministry is obedient service to the revealing of the mystery of God's election through Jesus Christ in a fallen world.

MAKING THE MYSTERY PUBLIC

The commission that impels ministry in this fallen world is to do the electing authorized by the death and resurrection of Jesus Christ. He to whom all authority in heaven and on earth is given says, "Go, baptize, preach, teach, absolve!" "As the Father sent me, so I send you." The entire drive behind ministry is toward making public, bearing witness to, the mystery hidden for ages but now revealed in the church. It is important to stress this for at least two reasons. First, because it means that ministry as service to the revealing deed in Jesus cannot mean some kind of cultic or ecclesiastico-political re-mystification. It cannot mean, for example, that ministers are gurus or specially endowed cultic custodians of private mysteries available only to initiates. Ordination to ministry in the church of Jesus Christ cannot mean induction into a secret society bent on keeping its mysteries hidden.

Second, it is important to stress the fact that ministry as service to the electing deed of God in Christ means the constant drive toward publicizing the mystery because such publication is by no means a simple matter. For our world lives in mortal fear of the mystery. Perhaps another way of putting it is that we live in a world that simply cannot believe its good fortune. So the world prefers to keep the mystery hidden, to deny it, or to rationalize it. To repeat what was asserted earlier, the idea of an electing God is a terror because the only God the world knows is hidden behind the mask of all those magnificent abstractions. So the truth is that the world is alienated from God and will not, cannot, believe. Consequently it is no simple matter to make the mystery public, to bring it out into the open. There is a kind of conspiracy, sometimes unwitting and unconscious but sometimes quite conscious, to keep the mystery hidden away. It is not merely accidental that the passage from Ephesians herein taken as a leitmotif ends with some words about suffering. Service to the divine deed involves suffering. That is the nature of this age.

Historic Lutheranism has always recognized the world's recalcitrance in its teaching about the bondage of the will, the theology of the cross, and the preaching of law and gospel. This is not the place to attempt a treatment of those teachings, but it is necessary to point out their bearing on the understanding of ministry. To say that the world will not hear of an electing God, that it will not and cannot of "its own reason or strength believe," is to say that it is afflicted with the bondage of the will. It is not possible therefore in publicizing the mystery just to content oneself with "explaining" things or unloading supposedly authoritative direct and dogmatic statements, however astute or even biblical, about God upon which hearers are to exercise their wills. Since we are not reconciled to God by our own machinations or explanations all reconciliation can proceed only through the crucified and risen Christ. Only Christ, the one to whom all authority has been given, is God for us. We cannot be reconciled to God by our theological or philosophical explanations or our religious deeds. A ministry is necessary; there must be someone who actually does the deed to us. God was *in Christ* reconciling the world unto himself. The deed has been done.

Ministry, therefore, can only be the service of this deed and thus must be shaped by the theology of the cross. Old beings, trapped by the bondage of the will, can only be put to death in order to be raised to the newness of life. The concrete doing of the electing deed in the living present means, therefore, the proclamation in Word and sacrament of the crucified and risen Christ who is the end of the old and the beginning of the new to faith. It is the coming of the kingdom of God among us. Ministry is the work of making this public in a world that prefers that it be forgotten or kept hidden or at the most tolerated as a private opinion.

Ministry as obedient service to the divine electing and reconciling deed in Jesus means therefore the announcement of the end of the old and the beginning of the new. Its proclamation, shaped by the theology of the cross, is governed by the distinction between law and gospel. This distinction comprehends the fact that publication of the electing deed cannot proceed directly to a world that crucified Jesus, but must first bring it to an end. Ministry as service to the divine deed has no interest in prolonging the world's religious agony or hiding the mystery under cultic mystification. Preaching of the law is the end of all that, it brings old beings to an end that they might hear the gospel of the new life in the resurrected Jesus. The point of the distinction is once again the making public of the divine deed, making it hearable in a world that will not hear it. The distinction is made so that a new kind of speaking might be heard in this world: gospel speaking. The drive behind ministry is to say it, to have the courage to do the electing deed, to bear witness to it, to make it public, "to make all people see."

THE PUBLIC OFFICE

Now that we have said something about the foundations of the doctrine of ministry we are finally in a position to talk about ordained ministry, the main topic of this essay. Up to now we have not been talking specifically about ordained ministry, but rather about the ministry of the church and therefore of all the elect in Jesus Christ. All are called by virtue of baptism to the ministry of publicizing the mystery hidden from the ages but now revealed in Jesus Christ. All are authorized and obligated to do it. This is entailed in the teaching of the priesthood of all believers.

But we should be careful here. The fact that all are called to this ministry does not mean that everything the baptized do is to be called ministry. If ministry as we have defined it is indeed service to the electing deed of God in Christ, it is best to avoid the current inflation in terminology which defines anything and everything Christians do as ministry. Where everything is ministry, the quite specific and concrete service to the deed of God in Christ can easily be lost once again, on the one hand, and the quite worldly nature of the God-given tasks of daily life obscured, on the other. The doctrine of ministry has to be augmented by the doctrine of vocation. The elect are called to serve God in the world for the time being. Their election in Christ will be reflected in their worldly tasks but not confused with them. Every Christian is to do ministry, but not everything Christians do should be called ministry.

Ordained ministry takes the cause of publicizing the mystery one step further. Here the drive to publicize the mystery culminates in a public office. It is the point at which, we might say, the Christian vocation to ministry "crosses the line," converges upon, or coins itself in a this-worldly calling and all that is involved in that. In the public office the age to come, the kingdom of God, makes its claim known in this age, to the powers that be. Ordination to the public office is thus an extremely precarious and at the same time audacious move. Precarious because the possibilities are legion for abuse, pretense, perversion, and all species of clericalism, on the one hand, but also slighting, demeaning, disdaining, or just plain neglect of office, on the other. The temptation to politicize the office, to lend it too much of this world's power, always lies near at hand. Formerly that was done by making it virtually a state office. More recently, it seems, the temptation is to make the office one whose main public function is political advocacy. On the other hand is the temptation to mystify it, to claim too much for it by ecclesiastical power plays. The move is audacious because a claim is made, an authority asserted in the trappings of this age, so to speak, which is not of this age. The public office announces the end, the limit, the goal, the telos, of all offices. This precariousness and audacity means that the church must take the utmost care in how it orders the public office. This brings us to the place of ordained ministry per se.

Ordained ministry is ordered ministry, and that in a double sense. It is a ministry that one is ordered, that is, called, to do, and it is to be done in ordered fashion. Ordained ministry is ministry incarnated, so to speak, in the order of this world, this *publicum*. It is better, in this light, to look upon ordained ministry not as one somehow elevated above this world as is our ecclesiastical wont, but rather as the instance in which one is called to penetrate the order of this world. Articles 5 and 14 of the CA (*BC* 31, 56–61) tersely set forth the contours of the

Lutheran doctrine of ministry. Article 5 says that in order for justifying faith to be obtained, "God instituted the office of ministry, that is, provided the Gospel and the sacraments. Through these, as through means, he gives the Holy Spirit, who works faith, when and where he pleases, in those who hear the Gospel." But Art. 5 does not yet speak explicitly about the ordained ministry, even though it seems strongly to imply it. Article 14 provides the conclusive note on ordering the public office: "Nobody should publicly teach or preach or administer the sacraments in the church without a regular call."

Now we must dwell a bit on what is said in these articles and the relationship between them to fix the contours of the doctrine as clearly as possible. To begin with it is clear for the confession that the office of ministry is a divine institution, not a human invention nor an option that churches or congregations may or may not exercise. The office of ministry is God's idea, not ours. But how or when was the office instituted? It is always a temptation here to look for some particular instance in "holy history" or perhaps for a crucial moment in the life of Jesus when something like an act of institution is supposed to have taken place. So many, particularly Roman Catholics, have looked to Matt. 16:18: "You are Peter, and on this rock I will build my church." Others may seek different instances for an "institution," or at least an indication that Jesus must have had church and ministry in mind. But if, subsequently, historical investigation calls talk of the church and ministry by Jesus himself into question, we appear to be on shaky ground.

The confession, however, avoids this impasse. Divine institution is not identified with an isolated moment or act, even of Jesus, but rather with the giving of the gospel and the sacraments. The gospel and the sacraments were given when God went public in Jesus. God thereby instituted the office. As we maintained above, the gospel and the sacraments drive to the publication of the mystery. They are the concrete means through which the divine electing deed is done. "Through them, as through means, [God] gives the Holy Spirit, who works faith, when and where he pleases." The gospel and the sacraments demand the office. Somebody has to say it, do it. The drive toward publication is perhaps even more explicit in the original of the German version of the confession which says that God has instituted the office of *preaching* (*Gott hat das Predigtamt eingesetzt*). The anathemas attached to Art. 5 are directed against all attempts to obscure or subvert the drive toward publication by internalizing it once again or reducing it to some secret agenda of the Spirit. All teaching "that the Holy Spirit comes to us through our own preparations, thoughts and works without the external word of the Gospel" is rejected. In making gospel speaking possible and indeed necessary, God instituted the office. The gospel comes to us from without through the external word and must be made public.

Ordained ministry is the culmination of the drive to make the gospel public. Ordained ministry is one properly "ordered" to exercise the office publicly. The move from Art. 5 to Art. 14 is quite consequent and natural. God has instituted the office by making the gospel public, says Art. 5, but no one, says Art. 14, should teach or preach or administer the sacraments publicly without a regular call. The confessors see no inconsistency at all between divine institution and churchly ordering of the public office. For them all public offices are divinely instituted even while the particular ordering of these offices was left for determination according to the needs of times and places. On this score, the public office of ministry is no different from other public offices. God institutes; the church orders, just as in the state God institutes the political office, which is ordered by the circumstances of time and place. Nor can there be any cause for competition between lay and clerical exercises of the office. All the members of the church are to be involved and dedicated to the drive to publicize the gospel and so are to be concerned about the public exercise of the office. Therefore the church through its ordering calls those appropriately qualified to exercise the office publicly. It is not possible to arrogate to oneself such a public exercise. Ordained ministry is not a private matter. The church through its quite public structures calls to the office.

At the same time, the congregations of the church do not own the office nor do they "transfer their authority" to it. The gift of the office has been given by divine institution to the church and demands filling. The church through its organized and public structures is to do this, and in that sense has the "authority" to do it. But it does not give the office its authority.

It may be helpful to make a distinction here between two kinds of authority: the authority to fill and regulate the public office, and the authority of the office itself. The organizations of the church have the authority to fill and regulate the office and the responsibility to support it. The authority of the office itself is rooted in the Word its holders are called to proclaim. The organizations of the church are not to usurp or privatize or smuggle away this authority. They are to see to it that the Word may have free and public course to establish its own authority.

Now we must say something about what is meant by the public exercise of the office. This does not mean merely that the ministry in question is done "in public," out in the open, standing on a soap box, for example. It means rather that for the confessors Christianity was a *cultus publicus,* a public cult. It belonged to the *res publica.* The ordained minister was in that sense something akin to a public official who was thus authorized to perform the public acts of the cult and for the benefit of the public. The ordained minister was to make public proclamation of and public argument for the Word of God, to administer the sacraments as public acts, and to call the public and its magistrates to judgment before divine law.

Such public exercise of the office was set in sharp contrast to a more private exercise in which one speaks as an individual to others, as a parent to a child, perhaps absolves another and so on, what Luther in his catechism called mutual consolation among Christians. In such instances one has to do with Christianity as a *cultus privatus*. Since we have put so much emphasis in this essay on the publicizing of the mystery there is potential for confusion here. Everyone is called upon to do what we have called publicizing the mystery, speaking the Word of God to another, making the message hearable for as many as possible in as many appropriate ways as possible, but apart from the ordained public office that occurs as a *cultus privatus*, a private exercise. Only one who is regularly called and ordered by the community can exercise the office publicly, speaking to and for the community. In the Lutheran view, this distinction between private and public exercise of the office marks the primary difference between lay and clergy.

The difficulty we encounter in the modern world, however, is that Christianity (or any religion for that matter) is no longer accorded status as a *cultus publicus*. The modern state, at least in the West, is more or less concerned only with providing for the physical well-being of its citizens. It is concerned with the economy, defense of the realm, just distribution of goods and services, and so forth. Only such matters are considered "public affairs." The modern state cares little about religion as long as it does not interfere with justice or public business. No doubt this is also a major reason why so much difficulty is encountered in sorting out the relationship between "religion and politics," church and state. Since the meaning of the public office is lost, ministry is limited to the private sphere. Willy-nilly Christianity becomes simply a private cult and the rationale for ordained ministry in Lutheranism threatens to disappear altogether.

Here I expect is a major reason for the erosion of the understanding of ordained ministry among us. When the church becomes merely a private cult it is difficult to say why just any Christian cannot perform most if not all the functions ordinarily assigned to the ordained. It appears presumptuous in a democratic society to suppose that some are raised to a different level by ecclesiastical monkey business. And since it is, after all, only a "private" matter, what difference does ordination make? Furthermore when members of the clergy themselves capitulate and no longer do what can be called public preaching, teaching, or absolving but rather just make public display of private emotions and experiences or invest most of their effort in private counseling, what does one need ordained clergy for? What matters is not the public exercise of the office but what "personal skills" or what kind of a (private) person the leader is. There is no way that ordination automatically imparts any skills or makes a person nice. So what is it for? Cannot properly sensitized or trained lay persons do just as well, or better? It is ironic that the state turns out to be one of the last holdouts here. The state, clinging to the vestigial remains of the public office, will not allow just any lay person to marry or get tax exemptions or serve as chaplain or do visitation in institutions and so on. For more "public" functions the state wants the assurance of ordination. The state, at least, recognizes a public office when it sees one.

Since the idea of a public exercise of the office has virtually disappeared from the church the ordained office tends to go begging for a rationale. Quite naturally, perhaps, it takes refuge in the one manifestly public act left, the Sacrament of Holy Communion. The church has always held that baptism may in emergency be done by any Christian and, since it is done to an individual, may be more or less private. Holy Communion, however, is public at least in the sense that it involves the community and thus some sort of public office. Of course even here there are determined efforts of late to privatize, to "do the Eucharist" preciously in small and cozy like-minded groups. The church becomes a private "support group." So the question inevitably arises once again whether the ordained are really needed for such private "sharing." The church still tends to resist such privatizing, or at least it ought to where it does not. But even in public celebrations of Holy Communion the ordained pastor is increasingly put on the periphery. Since it is apparently no longer an eminently public instance of doing the electing deed, a Holy Communion in the body and blood of Christ given and shed for us, but rather something more like our private "sharing" with one another, it is of course more meaningful to have it distributed by such persons as like-minded friends or the newly confirmed or one who has suffered through a divorce and needs to be reaffirmed or a five-year-old. It is supposed to mark a great advance in lay participation in ministry to have the unordained do virtually everything but "preside." Why the laity cannot preside remains, of course, something of a mystery. Isn't it just a matter of saying the proper words? Since the words are in the book, should that not be much easier to do without mistake or heresy than praying or imitating a sermon!

The general result of all this sentimental privatizing is that the sole remaining mark that distinguishes ordained ministry is that the ordained for some unknown or forgotten reason get to preside at the Holy Communion. Even the eminently pastoral act of the concrete giving of the body and blood has been largely preempted. It is not entirely strange therefore that in order to preserve some sort of justification for an ordained clergy and bolster its sagging morale there is a strong tendency to resort to a more Roman Catholic understanding of the significance of ordination. If the ordained pastor is the one whose sole distinguishing privilege is to preside at "the Eucharist," then ordination must evidently mean the conveying of some secret power by the church to do this. So the office gets re-mystified, so to speak, and in spite of the intention to hang onto the one public act left, disappears behind a cloud of sacred smoke. Ordination here does not mean being called to and ordered in the public office of revealing the mystery, declaring the gospel, but rather the mysterious bestowal of secret power. One may rescue some prestige for the office by such a move but its essence is only frittered away.

There is widespread concern today over the general loss of self-confidence and sense of importance or purpose among ordained clergy. They begin to feel that they are only the hired hands of congregations on the one hand or the end of the line in the ecclesiastico-bureaucratic pecking order on the other. Some seem to think this can be remedied by reverting to a more Roman and episcopal understanding of the ordination. But that is simply to return to the view of ordained ministry which caused the trouble in the first place.

If this essay is at all on target, the way forward would be to work out more consistently a view of ordained ministry as a public office, the culmination of the commission given the church to publicize the mystery of divine election in Jesus Christ. Ordained ministry will regain its reason for being and the ordained a sense of direction and purpose only if the vocation to public office is reclaimed. True, the idea of a public office is quite contrary to the modern Western attempt to relegate religion to the private sphere. But Christians must not capitulate to this privatizing. It is indeed an audacious thing to ordain people to a public office. But by so doing we are staking out the claim made on this world in Jesus, we serve notice in this age that the new age, the kingdom of God, is the end, the goal, the telos, of the created order.

ORDINATION

Ordination is the act by which one is placed in the public office of ministry. Here ministry as service to the electing deed of God in Christ impinges upon, invades, the order of this age. When ordination is understood in this manner perhaps some of the persistent arguments surrounding it can be shown to be needless. Usually, perhaps misled by the Latin concept of *ordo*, we assume ordination means elevation to a higher order, a higher class. In the church, therefore, ordination is taken to mean elevation to a higher spiritual order. When understood as a sacrament it even takes on salvific power. The ordained are somehow closer to God or have more "grace," and can perhaps be more certain of salvation.

So the trouble starts. Not only does this provoke resentment and anticlericalism among the unordained, it also opens a Pandora's box of nagging questions. Who possesses the authority or power to distribute such extraordinary favors? How was it obtained? How is it passed on? Where does the right and the power to ordain in such fashion reside? Who has the sacred "mana"? The hierarchy? The bishop? The congregations? How shall such matters be decided? On the basis of Scripture, tradition, practicality? Those who rightly enough desire to support a high doctrine of ordained ministry often buy in on sacramental or hierarchical high jinks which ultimately provoke anticlericalism. On the other hand, those who again rightly enough resist ecclesiastical mystifying end up saying things that in fact only demean or undercut the purpose of the public office.

Where it is understood that ordination to the public office does not mean the bestowal of special or mysterious sacramental favors, an elevation to a higher spiritual order or some such, but rather an entry into the order of this world with the Word of the gospel it would seem that most of these arguments are needless. We must indeed be very careful in what we say about this office today. What is needed is a high doctrine of ordained ministry which comprehends its crucial importance at the same time as it removes the ecclesiastical mythology that only provokes disdain and anticlericalism. If it is clearly perceived that ordination does not mean extraordinary elevation but rather being called and prayed over to enter into this precarious and audacious public office, thus to enter into the order of this world, as "sheep among wolves," we can arrive at a high doctrine of ordained ministry shorn of the mythology that obfuscates and discredits.

Ordination means that the church through its ordered structures calls and orders qualified members into the public office. What are these ordered structures? Lutheranism has never been dogmatic about this, and should not be. The structures will no doubt vary with time and place. However, the calling to and ordering in the public office should be done in such a way as to enhance rather than undercut the public purpose and posture of the office. Starting from the basic tenet of the priesthood of all believers, Lutheranism has always insisted on the place and importance of the people of the church and thus the rights of the congregations for the structuring of the church. However, with the consent of the people (sometimes more, sometimes less, perhaps) the church can be structured in various ways. Sometimes it has been more episcopal, sometimes more of a state church or folk church, sometimes more congregational, and so on. The exact determination of the structure is not crucial so long as the public nature of the office is upheld and enhanced.

The problem has always been how to prevent lapsing into mere congregational functionalism where the pastor can easily become just the hired hand of the congregation, the pawn of collective private opinion on the one hand, or attempting to escape that by reverting to a Roman sacramental hierarchicalism on the other. Perhaps the question can be put like this: In what way does the ordination, though done through the congregations and given structures of the church, admit to an office that somehow transcends, and if need be, stands over against those congregations and structures?

The whole direction of this essay indicates where the answer has to be. It is in the very point and "logic" of the public office itself. What needs to be recaptured, understood, and worked out in the church is that the office instituted by the giving of the gospel now lent public voice is that which transcends and stands over against the congregations and structures. That is, by calling and ordaining to this office, the congregations and structures place themselves under the hearing of the Word, the proper public exercise of this office, under the proclamation in Word and sacrament of the law and the gospel. They recognize that what transcends them is the divine Word publicly proclaimed. In explicit terms, neither the authority of alleged autonomous congregations whether delegated or transferred, nor episcopal succession or alleged bestowal of ontological sacramental favors are a guarantee of anything conclusive in this regard. The public office and the proper ordering of that office, demanding as that ordering may be, comprise the instance through which final authority is exercised in the church. The authority establishes itself through the Word preached and heard, the sacraments given and received. The point of the office is to see to it that what is preached in the church is the gospel of Jesus Christ. This is the final exercise of "authority." The only defense against anticlericalism is not to demean or belittle the office but rather to have a clergy that distinguishes properly between law and gospel and so preaches the gospel as God's final Word to us.

The proper ordering of the public office is therefore an exceedingly important and at the same time hazardous task. But ordination is itself the means through which the church and its congregations actually do this ordering. It is not just the instance in which some mysterious gift is supposedly bestowed upon the ordinand. As stated at the outset, ordination means both ordering in the sense of calling, and ordering in the sense of regulating or establishing order. In confessional Lutheranism this is reflected in the fact that ordination involves not just one but at least four operations: the call; the examination; the laying on of hands; and prayer. All of these belong to the "regular call," the *rite vocatus* of the CA's Art. 14, and are a part of ordination and thus necessary for the proper ordering of the public office. One could also add to this list the public questions put to and the response requested from the ordinand, the promise faithfully to fulfill the conditions of the office.

The church orders its public office by calling properly qualified persons to that office. This call comes "from without," through the congregations and structures to be served. It is in this sense a public matter. The "private" or "inner" sense of calling of the individual is of course of prime importance both for the church in that it desires committed candidates and for the individual in contemplating candidacy for the public call, but all that is presupposition. It belongs to the question of qualifications. The call is to serve in the public office. Thus the examination by those who have been entrusted with the care and furtherance of the office follows. The candidate is to serve, proclaim, care, and make argument for the public message and theology of the church. This cannot be stressed enough. One is not called to this office to peddle private opinions. So the examination is to determine the personal, intellectual, and spiritual fitness of the candidate for the public office and the ordination ceremony requires the promise to preach, teach, and exercise the office in accord with the church's public theology, the Holy Scriptures, the creeds, and the Lutheran confessional writings. The ordained are to care and seek to gain hearing for the public theology of the church in a particular time and place.

In the laying on of hands those to whom this public office has been entrusted by the church invoke the Holy Spirit to attend, empower, and enliven the new ordinand's exercise of the office. The occasional modern practice of having unordained persons involved in the laying on of hands is a sentimentalized misapprehension of what ordination means. In perhaps justified zeal to counteract the idea that only the ordained have the power to bestow charisms, the practice undercuts the institution of the public office altogether. It is consonant with the public nature of the office that those who are entrusted with its care in the church are also the ones who ordain. Whatever meaning there is in the idea of succession is involved here. It is not that there is some sort of unbroken succession of bishops, perhaps, or sacramentally charged persons as such who possess the "mana" of the office and alone have the power to pass it on. But there are indeed persons and the office is handed on by persons. The point is simply that those who have been entrusted with the exercise of the office in the present also care for its future and see to its perpetuation.

But what, in the end, does ordination grant? Does it infuse a special sacramental grace or grant a perhaps indelible ontological status or bestow a particular "charism" of some sort not available to others? Here we must be careful how we speak lest we overshoot the mark on the one hand or demean the office on the other. There is need for some demythologizing of ordination at the same time as there is need for establishing its true significance and restoring proper regard for the office. We can accomplish that if we can establish the meaning and importance of being entrusted with, gifted with, the public office. The office itself is the gift of the Spirit to the church, the calling, the empowering to speak, teach, administer the sacraments publicly. In that sense, it is no doubt appropriate to speak of it as a charism if one so desires. But it is the charism of the public office, the calling and the gift to which one is ordained. One so called is emboldened to speak in the Spirit to the public. It is not that the individual is given some special infusion of grace or spirit as such or granted indelible ontological character, but rather entrusted with the gift of the office. The office, so to speak, makes and shapes the person, not vice versa. Through the office one is called publicly to say and do the audacious words and deeds authorized by the divine election through the crucified and risen Jesus. The office is itself the charism, the gift of the Spirit to the church and thus to the ordinand.

To whom may this office be given through ordination? Basically it may be entrusted to anyone who is called, properly prepared to meet the demands of the examination, and ready to make the promises to preach and teach according to the public and confessional theology of the church. Since the office is rooted in the divine election manifest in the crucified and risen Christ and therefore bears witness to the eschatological age—where there is no longer Jew nor Greek, bond nor free, male nor female, but all are one in Christ—candidacy for ordination cannot be dependent on distinctions rooted in the old age, such as gender, class, race, or even supposed religious superiority, that is, fitness for a sacrificial priesthood. Men and women are equally open to the call of the church if the demands of the office are met. By the same token, since one cannot claim the office for oneself, no one possesses any automatic rights to the office which are rooted in the natural or religious claims of this age. Ordination is to the public office that announces the coming of the new age, not the prolongation of the claims and distinctions of the old.

Is such ordination for life? Perhaps if we look more closely at what actually takes place in the ordination to the public office we can handle this tricky question in a more useful manner. It is not for life in the sense that it supposedly imparts an "indelible character" that inheres in the ordinand come what may. Nevertheless, we must again be careful that we do not disdain or destroy the integrity of what actually occurs in ordination by overreacting. In ordination the church asks for and receives a promise from the ordinand faithfully to carry out the office. Such promises certainly should not be regarded as temporary either by the ordinand or the church. Neither the promise nor the entrusting with the office should in that sense be treated as transitory or subject to congregational or bureaucratic whim and fancy. At the same time, however, the promise can be broken or revoked. Persons can be denied or removed from the office for failing to exercise the office properly. Ordination, we might say, is "for life," in the sense that the relationship established promises and is intended to be permanent, but in this age cannot yet be removed from the ravages of sin and time by some sort of automatic ontological guarantee.

What sort of guarantee of the proper exercise of the office then does ordination establish? The efficacy of the office depends, of course, on the promises of God in Christ and not on the sincerity, skill, dedication, or faith of the one ordained. That is never at issue when the question of guarantee is raised. Nor, to reiterate, does ordination confer ontological gifts that qualify one automatically to do or represent "the sacrifice" or some such. Here we can only look once again to the particular kind of ordering involved and to what actually occurs in the ceremony. There is the call, the examination, the laying on of hands, the prayer, and the promise. The church as hearer and receiver of the Word and sacrament is called to constant concern and prayer for those in the office, and through its appropriate structures to watch over its proper exercise. Those ordained must live under the promises made, and thus must care for the gospel and for one another in this regard. For the time being there can be no automatic guarantees. There can only be constant care, vigilance, prayer.

Before we leave the subject of the ordained public office we must enter something of a caveat. Increasingly one hears the claim advanced by those involved in ecumenical dialogues that the ordained public office is "constitutive" of the church. To be faithful to the confessional view one must be quite clear that the office constitutes nothing. Christ is the head of the church and as the sheer giver of all good constitutes the church. The office is constituted by this sheer act of divine giving, not vice versa. The office is simply *ministry:* service inspired by the divine deed. To say more than that is to confuse the giving and the gift. The delivery of the gift, and, indeed, even a "delivery boy" is quite necessary, but it does not *constitute* anything.

The claim that the ordained office is constitutive of the church that seems to be gaining currency for the sake of ecumenical rapprochement results only in a messy confusion of this age with the next. The office and its holders take on a status that suggests a transcendence of the eschatological limit. A "hierarchy" emerges which reaches above or beyond this age and/or mirrors that of "heaven," and so threatens the eschatological promise of the gospel itself. Soon one begins to invest theological capital in the status and authority of the delivery boy rather than in the gift. One spins theories and argues about delivery systems. The "office of delivery boy" intrudes itself as a more or less independent reality between the giver of the gift and the receiver. Soon the delivery boys begin determining the nature of the gift and the conditions under which it can be given. The church becomes dominated by and defined as a delivery system ruled by the delivery boys, not the assembly constituted by the actual giving of the gift. The postal service does not constitute the correspondence between lovers. It exercises its office when it simply delivers. In spite of the necessity of the office it is quite mistaken to hold that the office constitutes anything. It is the need and desire of the lovers to correspond which calls the office into being, not the office that somehow constitutes the correspondence or the relationship. We would do well to remember some words from Luther's Advent Sermon in the Church Postil:

> That the gospel is preached and your King comes is not due to your power or merit, God must send it out of sheer grace. Thus there is no greater wrath of God than where He withholds the gospel and nothing but sin, error and darkness remain. . . . "Behold," that is: "Your King comes"; you do not seek him, he seeks you. You do not find him, he finds you. For the preachers come from him, not from you. Their sermon comes from him, not from you. Faith comes from him, not from you. And everything that faith works in you comes from him, not from you, so that you see clearly that where he does not come, there you remain on the outside, and that where the gospel is absent, there is no God, but only sin and corruption, even though free will does, suffers, works, lives, as it pleases and wants. (*WA* 10 I/2, 30, 13-28)

Perhaps the question of whether the office constitutes the church leads naturally into questions about higher and lower offices. Does the problem of guarantees, the task of watching over the public office, require perhaps a higher instance of the office, an overseer, or as developed in the church, the office of the bishop, the so-called historic episcopate? Or, to get the whole question before us, should there be three ranks of ordained clergy to carry out the tasks of the public office: deacons, presbyters, and bishops? In good Lutheran fashion the question might simply be disposed of pragmatically: if it is useful at a given time and place so to distribute the dimensions of the public office, it could possibly and quite innocently be done. Historical precedent and ecumenical posturing, however, no longer allow such pragmatic innocence. Where it is insisted that the threefold office is necessary in order to have a valid ordained ministry according either to the New Testament or the historic tradition, we must press further questions. The office begins to intrude itself between the giver of the gift and the receiver.

It is not the assignment of this essay to deal extensively with questions about deacons and bishops, but it may at least be to the point to ask what insistence on a threefold order does to the understanding and place of the public office as herein developed. It is certainly contrary to the Lutheran hermeneutic of both the New Testament and church history that the church must have a threefold office. It is dangerous to argue that it could be introduced as an ecumenical concession when one may thereby be acceding to quite different presuppositions about Scripture, tradition, church, and order. It is vital for the mission of the church to keep the understanding of ordination to the public ministry of Word and sacrament clearly in view as the culmination of the command to publicize the mystery, to get the gospel heard. This ministry is the apex, the "highest" exercise of the church's office and must not in any way be undercut, carved up, or watered down by mixing it with or subordinating it to other orders. The office of ordained pastor should not be further eroded or marginalized as current practice threatens to do, by privatizing and laicizing from within and by bishops from above and deacons below. Other offices or orders can be considered legitimate only as they enhance and support this office.

The office of bishop is not a higher office than that of the parish pastor which then supposedly requires a new ordination or laying on of hands. Ordination is to the public ministry, nothing else. Indeed, the parish pastor is really the local bishop. Those who have come to be called bishops over synods, for example, are really supposed to be nothing other than pastors whose jurisdiction has come to be extended over a wider area. There is some question whether a bishop who is not actually a parish pastor involved in the public ministry of Word and sacrament should be called a bishop at all. But it is perhaps too late or fruitless to argue about that. The functions such "bishops" perform are rather more like those of an archdeacon, an administrator of diocesan affairs. No doubt that is why early Lutherans almost unanimously chose to call such functionaries superintendents and presidents rather than bishops. In any case care must be taken not to allow the supposedly weighty and impressive business of the bishop to appear as the "real" public business of the church while the public office of Word and sacrament goes begging. Most of what the bishop does belongs to the more or less private business of internal administration rather than to public ministry.

When the bishop's office is overwhelmed by bureaucratic affairs it may not be entirely beside the point to ask once again the question about the bishop and the gospel. If bishops are to oversee anything at all they should be there to see to it that the gospel is given public voice in their jurisdiction. But bishops hardly busy themselves with that. Recall that the sixteenth-century Reformers expressed willingness to go along with the bishops if they would allow the preaching of the gospel. But not one of them did. Was that only accidental? When a bishop becomes something "more" than a pastor has the gospel simply been eclipsed? Is that why the pastor becomes hostage to directives, programs, plans, and schedules from above?

The question of the teaching office in the church today ought to be reexamined in the light of the experience of history. It is clear that there is a crying and desperate need for vital and confessional teaching in the church. It is not clear, however, that the contemporary bishop is the one to do it. We ought to beware the assumption that proper exercise and oversight of the teaching office is somehow automatically bestowed by installation into the office of bishop. More attention needs also to be given to the place and ordering of those who actually do the teaching in the institutions and seminaries of the church. No doubt this should be done in conjunction with bishops, but not necessarily under their sole jurisdiction.

If ordination means being ordered in the public office of Word and sacrament as herein developed it would also seem that deacons would hardly qualify for such ordination. This is in no way to question the utility of a diaconate as such, but only its placement somewhere within the ordained ministry. Not only are deacons restrained traditionally from performing the public acts for which one would be ordained, such as public absolution and sacraments, but also for the most part the acts they are to perform would, at least in the classical sense, be deemed more "private," "in-house," and domestic than public. Where they do have public significance or import would more likely be in some profession for public benefit—perhaps in medicine or education or social service—and would call for appropriate professional certification, not ordination.

The ordained diaconate has, in the history of the church, been a very unstable order. That is no doubt because there has been a contradiction within the very idea. Deacons are ordained supposedly to the public ministry of the church, and yet subsequently severely restricted in doing the public aspects of that ministry. It becomes an order defined primarily in terms of what it cannot do. That is not an attractive situation. So it has tended to become just a steppingstone to the "full" ordained ministry. Where it has been something more than that, it has often been suspected by the ordained as a competitor. Rarely has it found stability as an order. Arguments for a diaconate as a part of the ordained ministry would, at the very least, have to be much more carefully made than heretofore. Past history does not indicate it greatly to have enhanced the public ministry of the church.

CONCLUDING WORD

The aim of this essay has been to attempt a reconstruction in the understanding and purpose of ordained ministry on more strictly Lutheran and confessional principles. I hope that it represents at least a beginning along those lines. I have sought to avoid, as much as possible, many of the traditional alternatives and standoffs in argument because much of the time they seem to me to be misplaced, if not sterile. So I have also avoided footnotes and citation of other authors even though indebtedness will no doubt be detected here and there. The territory is so pockmarked with craters from previous battles that one is likely to be prematurely labelled and unfairly dismissed by quoting this or that authority. I have chosen rather to attempt thinking through the problems with as little distraction as possible. It would be vain, no doubt, to pretend I have succeeded entirely in my aim. I hope, however, that it is a beginning.

My intention has been to support, enhance, and encourage the ordained ministry of Word and sacrament in the church, to restore to it some sense of purpose, self-understanding, and direction in a time when it is beset from within and without by self-serving detractors and ecclesiastical con artists. Ordained ministry is the culmination of the church's commission to get the gospel heard properly and well. The ordained pastor is essentially a public absolver, doer of the electing deed, preacher, and giver of the sacramental Word. This is the office to which the church calls and about which it must be concerned. It may be well to pursue this fact with some singlemindedness once again in an age that seems bent on reducing the office to that of social worker, enabler, presider at "the eucharistic sacrifice," or some such. Could it be such reductionism is at least partly responsible for the church having to go so far as to launch special campaigns to promote speaking the gospel, and then fall into the perilous business of turning the evangel into an "ism"? It is quite possible that renewed understanding of what the office of ministry is about could contribute to renewed understanding of what the church and its mission is about. At least one hopes so.

9

Is "evangelical episcopate" an oxymoron, a contradiction in terms? That depends on what the term includes. Apparently the term includes, according to its advocates, ways of adopting the historic episcopate without running into the problems Lutherans usually have with it. What is the historic episcopate? Generally speaking, only those bishops who have been ordained through the laying on of hands and the invocation of the Holy Spirit by bishops in historic continuity with the bishops ordained this way down through the ages can be said to belong to the historic episcopate.[1] The historic episcopate is to be distinguished from apostolic succession, which refers to general continuity with the apostles, either with their teaching or with structures in the church that one traces back to the apostles.

WHAT IS REALLY AT STAKE? THE FREEDOM OF THE GOSPEL

Lutherans can of course adopt any form of church structure, up to and including the papacy, as long as the primacy of the gospel and Christian freedom are allowed. Salvation is the only non-negotiable. What is salvation? Justification by grace alone through faith alone in Christ alone. All else, such as forms of worship and structures of the church, although important and varying in appropriateness, remains within the arena of Christian freedom unless someone makes it a requirement for salvation; then it has become a new law and is to be rejected.

This is called the *adiaphoristic* principle. That there will be worship and forms of worship is essential. The actual forms may vary, and no particular form may be required for salvation. It remains within the arena of Christian freedom to dispute which forms are more appropriate. The same is true for church structures. The gospel must be proclaimed, and for this structures are essential, including oversight *(episcopé)*. Again, the actual structures may vary, and no particular structure may be required for salvation. It remains within the arena of Christian freedom to dispute which structures are more appropriate. If anyone claims that a particular form or structure is required for salvation (the gospel), this is a new law and is to be rejected.

In other words, no particular form or structure is part of revelation and thus exists by divine law (*iure divino*). Certain developments within church history, to be sure, are ancient and venerable, but are not for that reason mandated by divine law unless the notion of divine law is expanded to include a great many things, such as the papacy. And when the meaning of divine law is expanded, the problem is deciding what principle is to be used to sort out the various developments. Lutherans clearly do not allow either antiquity or the majority to be decisive, for neither the length nor the breadth of the tradition, for example, supports the ordination of women. Only the gospel is decisive; all the rest is a matter of Christian freedom, allowing for disagreement among those of good will. *Baptism, Eucharist and Ministry*, produced by the Faith and Order Commission of the World Council of Churches, summarizes a kind of ecumenical consensus in stating:

> The New Testament does not describe a single pattern of ministry which might serve as a blueprint or continuing norm for all future ministry in the Church. In the New Testament there appears rather a variety of forms which existed at different places and times. As the Holy Spirit continued to lead the Church in life, worship, and mission, certain elements from this early variety were further developed and became settled into a more universal pattern of ministry. (M 19)

How to discern which elements after the New Testament were from the Holy Spirit is the problem, because what is "more universal" runs into the difficulty of the papacy, which is in fact a more universal development, on the one hand, and the ordination of women, which is a less universal development, on the other.

WHAT DO LUTHERANS SAY?

Martin Luther favored congregational structures, yet he was willing to accept either presbyteral or episcopal structures.[2] One might respond: We do not follow Luther, but the *Book of Concord*, especially the Augsburg Confession. Of course this is true, although we must remember that Luther wrote key parts of the *Book of Concord* and the Formula of Concord uses Luther as a major authority, as its index shows. But what of the Augsburg Confession, authored by Philip Melanchthon? Does "bishops or pastors" (CA 28.30, *BC* 85; CA 28.53, *BC* 90; also 28.55, *BC* 90 in the German text) mean that—reading "pastor" as shepherd, an episcopal function, and not as a technical term for the local minister—bishops and pastors are equated? Did the Augsburg Confession not simply assume that a reunited church would continue to have bishops?

The Reformers had no objection to oversight *(episcopé)*, but they did object to the way in which episcopacy was conceived and filled at that time. When one looks back at the Torgau Articles (from early in 1530) and then forward to later statements, such as the Smalcald Articles (SA 10.1–3, *BC* 314) and the Treatise on the Power and Primacy of the Pope (Tr 60–62, *BC* 330-34; the Treatise was officially adopted as a Confession and was intended to be a supplement to the CA), there is no question that in these documents bishop, pastor, and presbyter were equated (Tr 63–65, *BC* 131).

Article 28 of the Augsburg Confession on bishops was one half of a compromise proposal, which ran: If you give us Articles 22–24 (on both elements in the Mass, married clergy, and the Lutheran form of the mass), we will agree to the kind of bishops described in Article 28: bishops who do what they do "simply by the Word" (CA 28.22, *BC* 84), that is, who do what every pastor or presbyter does. This was not to be simply an episcopate in the old style, but an actually reformed office of oversight. What was this "episcopate"? Lindbeck, in the Lutheran responses to Catholic questions during the fourth round of dialogue in the United States, spells out the Lutheran stance:

> Episcopacy is therefore the normal polity of the church. Yet it is a subordinate, instrumental, and fallible sign of apostolicity which may be misused by being made superordinate and constitutive. A part of the church which through unfavorable historical circumstances loses the episcopate does not necessarily for that reason lose apostolicity. (This may differ from the Roman Catholic position as presented in [George] Tavard's memorandum, which denies that "the *res* of apostolicity may be absent even when the *signum* of episcopal succession is present.") Lutherans, of course, believe that this happened in the sixteenth century. And many of them, like Joest, think that this exceptional situation is not yet ended. . . . In short, these Lutherans regard the historic episcopacy as still so widely "absolutized" that it remains unacceptable even though it is in itself normal and desirable.
>
> This objection would be largely removed by Roman Catholic admission of the possibility of full recognition of presbyterial orders. It would not, to be sure, be entirely removed. Lutherans would still insist that the *signum* of succession can exist where the *res* of apostolicity is absent (or, at any rate, so seriously distorted and obscured that the presence of the *signum* is misleading rather than helpful).[3]

"[A] subordinate, instrumental, and fallible sign of apostolicity . . . the *signum* of succession can exist where the *res* of apostolicity is absent"—these words from Lindbeck hardly describe a sacramental view either of the episcopate or, for that matter, of the presbyterate. Further, the historic episcopate has normally been "misused by being made superordinate and constitutive" instead of "a subordinate, instrumental, and fallible sign of apostolicity." The historical norm has been to make the historic episcopate "superordinate and constitutive," and the occasional exceptions prove the rule.

The Lutheran compromise was largely rejected and, as a consequence, the Lutherans were not, strictly speaking, bound to what had been proposed in

Article 28. Yet Lutherans have made the Augsburg Confession their main statement of faith, including Article 28 and its radical reshaping of episcopacy, with no sense that the church lacked anything essential without the historic episcopate.[4]

Lutheran practice in the first and second generations of the Reformation confirmed this theological standpoint. There was no sense of having an "emergency situation," of trying to patch something together until they could have "real bishops" once again. The "emergency situation" existed for that part of the church where through most of church history episcopacy was, as Lindbeck describes it, "misused by being made superordinate and constitutive" instead of "a subordinate, instrumental, and fallible sign of apostolicity." The Lutherans simply went about the task of establishing an evangelical episcopate, often without using the historic title but always with the intent of discovering which kind of oversight, under the primacy of the gospel and within the arena of Christian freedom, is more appropriate. The fact is Lutherans have always been very clear in their minds about church structure. Difficulties have only arisen because some, probably influenced by external factors, have wanted to make specific ecclesiastical structures part of the gospel.

In some cases the historic title continued. In 1537 John Bugenhagen, who did not have episcopal consecration himself, created new bishops in Denmark. Around 1540 evangelical bishops were introduced in some of the German territories; Nicolas von Amsdorf is a notable case. In Sweden, whether or not the historic succession endured, the office of bishop was certainly reformed. Sven Kjöllerström is convinced that succession in the historic episcopate was definitely broken in the sixteenth century.[5] Whatever the merits of Kjöllerström's case, the pragmatic attitude of Swedish Lutherans is decisive. Early in this century the Church of England decided that the Swedish church had maintained the historic episcopate and invited Swedish bishops to assist in consecrating English bishops. In order to avoid misunderstandings, the Swedish Bishops' Assembly explained to the English in 1922 what the Swedish church understands by church structures:

> No particular organization of the Church and of its ministry is instituted *iure divino*. Our Church cannot recognize any essential difference, *de iure divino*, of aim and authority between the two or three Orders into which the ministry of grace may have been divided, *iure humano*, for the benefit and welfare of the Church.

And in 1936 the Archbishop of Finland used this Swedish statement as his own in writing to the Archbishop of Canterbury about the historic episcopate.[6]

BUT WHY NOT ADOPT THE HISTORIC EPISCOPATE AND SIMPLY UNDERSTAND IT IN A LUTHERAN WAY?

This move seems astute, although a bit like trying to eat one's cake and have it too. And is this not what the Swedes and Finns do? Are we not free as

Lutherans to adopt any type of church structure? Recent Lutheran studies on episcopacy often echo this theme.

The freedom of the gospel is at stake. We must be very clear in our minds about the game being played. Freedom in the Christian context is altogether different from "freedom as self-fulfillment" in the popular culture of our day. Christian freedom is the freedom we have as children of God to live by forgiveness and not by works of the law. Therefore we are free to work with other Christians to discover what is reasonable and appropriate in a particular situation. But if any requirement for unity is added to the proclamation of the free gift of salvation through Word and sacraments (CA 7, *BC* 32), a new law has been added to the gospel, and Christian freedom has been lost.

Are we then free to adopt the historic episcopate with our own theological understanding? That depends. Our Roman Catholic partners in dialogue would not accept such a reservation by Lutherans. Just as we can be very sure that Roman Catholics would reject any Lutheran move toward greater unity if Lutherans said they would take on the papacy but with a Lutheran understanding (for example, as *iure humano*), so also with the historic episcopate. The official Roman Catholic response to BEM insists that the threefold ministry is a "sacramental" structure and that the historic episcopate is not only a sign but a "guarantee."[7] The Orthodox would do the same. In their official response to *BEM* they insist that any perspective or dimension implying that the ministries described in M are not sacramental "is unacceptable."[8]

That leaves some Anglicans and the Consultation on Church Union (COCU)—not the Anglo-Catholics. For example, E. L. Mascall, an Anglo-Catholic, opposes requiring the historic episcopate without at the same time agreeing on the theology involved. He describes how not requiring a common theological understanding led to the breakdown of negotiations between Lutherans and the Church of South India.[9] But non-Anglo-Catholic Anglicans, holding a variety of theologies, have a more functional approach to the historic episcopate. In their view all the Lambeth Quadrilateral requires is that a person take on the historic episcopate in practice; the theology can vary widely, short of such absurdities as: the historic episcopate is opposed to the Christian faith, an illusion, intrinsically evil, and the like. There is confidence that thought will follow deed, that theology will follow in the train of adopting the historic episcopate in practice.

This approach is not unlike the proposal approved and commended to the churches by the Sixteenth Plenary of COCU, of which the Episcopal Church is a member. After stating that "bishops shall stand in continuity with the historic ministry of bishops as that ministry has been maintained through the ages" and that bishops will be ordained "in such a way that recognition of this ministry is invited from all parts of the universal Church,"[10] it concludes:

49) In doing so, the Church Uniting will not require any theory or doctrine of episcopacy or episcopal succession which goes beyond the consensus stated in this

document. It will recognize that it inherits, from episcopal and non-episcopal churches alike, a variety of traditions about the ministry of oversight, unity, and continuity. It will seek to appropriate these traditions creatively, and so to move toward an episcopate reformed and always open to further reformation in the light of the gospel: an episcopate which will probably be different from that now known in any of the covenanting bodies.

Since both "consensus" and "gospel" in this document are broadly construed, this proposal is unclear about what is included in an episcopate both "in continuity" and finding recognition "from all parts of the universal Church" (#48), yet at the same time appropriating "creatively" a variety of traditions, including the United Church of Christ and the International Council of Community Churches (#49). The theology is broad; all that is specifically required is that a church actually take on the historic episcopate.

But then are Lutherans not free to take on the historic episcopate with a Lutheran understanding at least with non-Anglo-Catholic Anglicans and COCU? What kind of freedom do the non-Anglo-Catholic Anglicans and COCU allow to those taking on the historic episcopate with their own understanding? Would Lutherans, at another point in history after due consideration for what was appropriate and needed, be equally free to lay the historic episcopate down with our own understanding? Would it be possible to take on the historic episcopate with our own understanding and yet recognize, as very occasional exceptions, the ministries of those who do not take on the historic episcopate, as a way of symbolizing the Christian freedom preserved within our newly found unity? Preliminary inquiries indicate that the answer is no in both cases. What then, Lutherans will ask, has happened to Christian freedom?

Here one may object that this whole line of reasoning overlooks the fact that many Anglicans understand the historic episcopate to be of the *bene esse* (well being) rather than the *esse* (being) of the church, hardly a requirement. First, Anglo-Catholics, precisely because they gravitate toward Rome, do hold that the historic episcopate is of the very *esse* of the church, and they object to the idea that as long as one actually takes on the historic episcopate, the theology required can be broad or indefinite.[11]

Second, *bene esse* is not the same as *adiaphoron*. The English Reformation did, to be sure, use the concept of *adiaphoron*, but in a different sense than the Lutheran Reformation.[12] The terms *bene esse* and *plene esse* (full being) do not have to do with Christian freedom or requirements added to the gospel, that is, the *adiaphora* questions, but about levels of unity in the church. If questions about Christian freedom and requirements added to the gospel come into play at all, it is only in the sense that, according to those holding that the historic episcopate is of the church's *bene esse* and *plene esse*, a given church does not require the historic episcopate in order to be part of God's saving work in the church precisely because the historic episcopate only belongs to the *bene esse* or *plene esse* of the church. But to lack the historic episcopate, according to those holding to it, is a defect when one recalls God's will for his church, namely, organic unity; thus the historic episcopate is a requirement for true unity because the pure preaching of the gospel and sacraments celebrated according to this gospel is not enough. It is evident that the Lutheran understanding of *adiaphoron*, according to which the gospel is the *esse* of true unity in the church (CA 7, *BC* 32) so that all else is a matter of Christian freedom *(adiaphora)* unless made a requirement for salvation, is a different kind of conceptuality from that implied by Anglican ideas of *bene esse* and *plene esse*.

Could Lutherans not then take on the historic episcopate with their own understanding and thus join with those for whom the historic episcopate is *bene esse*, such as non-Anglo-Catholic Anglicans and COCU? Probably yes, because the latitude of the theology held by those for whom the historic episcopate is *bene esse* is probably wide enough. Lutherans would have to negotiate some way, symbolic or otherwise, of demonstrating that the historic episcopate is not a legalistic requirement but an ordinance consistent with Christian freedom, because *for Lutherans an adiaphoron is only an adiaphoron when it is an adiaphoron for both sides*. We would also have to deal with the ironic fact that, as a sort of courtesy, those holding to the historic episcopate state that, when mutual reconciliation of ministries occurs with those lacking the historic episcopate, those with the historic episcopate also fill a lack although this means no more than that, up until that point, they have lacked those now taking on the historic episcopate.

Swedish Lutherans cannot really be used as an example proving that Lutherans can adopt the historic episcopate and simply understand it in a Lutheran way, because a Lutheran pastor without historic orders is not reordained when he or she becomes a pastor in the Lutheran Church of Sweden. At the other end of the spectrum, when an Anglican priest becomes a Roman Catholic priest, he is reordained, and the same is true when an Anglican priest becomes an Orthodox priest, in spite of the Orthodox principle of *oikonomia* (the church's stewardship of spiritual discernment about church unity).[13] Anglican priests who are women, of course, cannot enter either the Roman or Orthodox church as priests.

ARE BISHOPS NECESSARY FOR UNITY?

Are bishops necessary for the unity of the church? That depends on what is meant by "bishops," "necessary," "unity," and "church." Concerning bishops, *BEM* asserts: "Among these gifts a ministry of *episkopé* is necessary to express and safeguard the unity of the body" (M 23; cf. M 27). If by *episkopé* one means that there will be leadership and that leadership naturally includes authority, without specifying the nature and extent of that authority, who could object? Leadership with authority occurs in many ways. Necessary? Of course, to the extent that without authoritative leadership, unity is more difficult. But what is "unity"? Lutherans teach that the church, both one and visible, has as "its marks, the pure teaching of the Gospel and the sacraments" (Ap 7, 8.20, *BC* 171). Agreement on this is "enough" for unity (cf. CA 7; "it is enough"), an exclusionary principle indicating that other marks are not to be required for unity.

Such an explication of "bishops," "necessary," "unity," and "church," however, is unacceptable to some Lutherans. Bishops for them should be "real" bishops, by which they mean "sacramental structures," to use the current jargon, or at least they should be sacramentally understood "in our own way," that is, in their particular interpretation of an "evangelical episcopate." A signal that this view is being promoted is the word "consecration" when someone becomes a bishop—a growing usage in such circles.

"Real" bishops are "necessary," according to these particular Lutherans, because "real" bishops are *iure divino*, which is understood here either as New Testament prescription or as irreversible development. But who then decides which development is irreversible? Even the New Testament canon is variously understood; the Copts and Ethiopians have added to the twenty-seven books, yet who would exclude them from the church for that reason?[14] The canon, to be sure, is by far the most likely candidate for an irreversible development. In what possible sense, however, can other irreversible developments exist if the New Testament canon is *norma normans non normata?* Furthermore, it remains unclear how "irreversible developments," even such a development as the New Testament canon, could be elevated to the status of gospel and thus be other than *adiaphora*. The gospel was efficacious long before the canon.

Faced with such difficulties, the argument shifts to the fact that the historic episcopate is the majority view. But what then of the ordination of women, which is not practiced by even a strong minority of Christians? Yet who is prepared to argue that the ordination of women should be abandoned? The papacy is also the majority view, and again one hesitates. *BEM* judiciously avoided the whole subject. The Lutherans in the Lutheran—Roman Catholic Dialogue in the United States stated they would accept a papacy "so structured and interpreted that it clearly serves the gospel and the unity of the church of Christ, and that its exercise of power not subvert Christian freedom."[15] But can anyone point to such a papacy (and to such an evangelical historic episcopate) *in concreto?* Without working out a structure based on the primacy of the gospel and allowing for Christian freedom in practice, the vision of an ideal pope (the *papa angelicus*—and, to coin a term, the *episcopus angelicus*) remains an eschatological chimera[16] and should be labelled as such.

Have bishops in fact expressed and safeguarded the unity of the church (cf. *BEM*, M 29)? In the early church the bishop was one unifying factor, along with canon, creeds, councils, heresies, and persecutions. But canon, creeds, and councils have been more decisive sources of unity than bishops. Major tensions and disagreements among early bishops cannot be overlooked; it was not all sweetness and light. Bishops have been as great a source of disunity as of unity. The historic episcopate has not produced unity among those churches claiming the historic episcopate, such as Anglicans, Orthodox, and Roman Catholics. The jurisdictional struggles within Orthodoxy are well known. Episcopacy must therefore be seen as a fallible mark of church unity.

SHOULD BISHOPS SERVE FOR LIFE?

Why not have bishops for life? Could we? Of course we could because this is an *adiaphoron*. If bishops for life would be the most appropriate and effective way of carrying out the mission of the church, that is what should be done.

But some advocate bishops for life in a different sense. Their main thesis is that because bishops do what pastors do, although in a larger arena, they should be called to serve until they resign, retire, or die, like any pastor. Behind this thesis lies the presupposition that because ordination is not repeated (which is considered to be a basic indication of indelible character), ordination is sacramental in character and carries life tenure for the person holding pastoral office. According to this view, having a bishop serve for life is not an *adiaphoron*.

Their second thesis is that both pastors and bishops need lifetime tenure in order to carry out their mission; with tenure pastors and bishops do not have to concern themselves with pleasing others in order to continue, but can be free to proclaim the truth plainly, to be prophetic. If anyone is concerned about what happens when bishops are incompetent, the answer usually is: elect bishops with greater care and establish review committees in order to improve the quality of bishops.

Why then question having bishops for life? The root question is whether ordination is a sacrament. This is not the place to take up that whole question, yet it is worth noting that early Lutheran practice equated ordination and installation. Ordination thus was repeated in early Lutheran practice, particularly by Bugenhagen, although Luther did not, at least after 1535, continue this approach.[17] In spite of the use of the word "sacrament" in relation to ordination in the Apology 13.9–13 (*BC* 212–13), the text itself interprets this to mean the ministry of the gospel whose power comes solely from the external Word and not from ordination itself. As a major U. S. Lutheran study recently pointed out, the logic of the Lutheran position would call for repeating ordination even though this has not usually been Lutheran practice.[18] In fact, tenure in and of itself is a kind of power, and the question needs to be asked whether the power of tenure does not interfere with relying on the power of the Word.

Nor can it be claimed that ordination is analogous to baptism and therefore a nonrepeatable sacrament. To the contrary, precisely because, unlike ordination, baptism is the sacrament of new birth, it is nonrepeatable. The Lord's Supper and absolution, which along with baptism are the "genuine sacraments" (Ap 13.4, *BC* 211), are, on the other hand, repeatable. Even if marriage were a nonrepeatable sacrament for Lutherans, it would still not be an analogy proving ordination is nonrepeatable because in marriage both parties pledge their troth to each other for life, whereas the pastor is not committed to one congregation for life, although the congregation may be bound to give the pastor tenure.

Why then has it been, in the main, Lutheran practice not to repeat ordination? Does this indicate a residual memory of what ought to be, before the so-called emergency of the Reformation confused the situation? Probably not. Rather, most Lutherans have the perspective that ordination is not repeated because it is a calling like other callings, such as commissioning to military or missionary service or promotion to the status of teacher or professor, which are not repeated if there is a change in continuity, either of kind of work or of location. In fact, before modern industrial development changed the nature of work, it was possible to think of most work as a calling, based on one's expertise and place in life.[19]

That Lutherans think this way can be seen in how we have not hesitated to give pastors nontenured calls, and not only to those who are hospital and military chaplains or in staff ministries where all must resign when the senior pastor resigns. Nor have Lutherans hesitated to limit the length of term of office for bishop and even to limit the number of terms because of the obvious fact that incumbents are very difficult to unelect. In a similar fashion after centuries of experience many Roman Catholic orders limit terms for their leaders. Also, leaders from traditions with tenured bishops can be very candid about the problem of incompetent bishops. They will point out how it is politically unrealistic to think one can "simply elect better bishops" because in every political system it is the best politician who is elected, not necessarily the best bishop. Those advocating life tenure for bishops have not reflected on the problem of incompetent bishops and how this will be affected by recent legislation about the age of retirement or of how Lutherans would react to the idea of a presiding bishop with tenure. Most doubtful is the claim that bishops with tenure are more prophetic, for by far the greatest number of bishops in traditions giving life tenure serve their own establishments.

SHOULD BISHOPS BE TEACHING AUTHORITIES?

According to *BEM*, in the early centuries of the church the historic episcopate "was understood as serving, symbolizing and guarding the continuity of the apostolic faith and communion" (M 36). The church, to be sure, also used other ways in order to preserve the continuity of the apostolic faith, and "a" continuity in the apostolic faith has been preserved in churches without the historic episcopate (M 36–37). Even more striking is the statement that "there have been times when the truth of the Gospel could only be preserved through prophetic and charismatic leaders" (M 33).

This perspective is overlooked, however, by those who see the teaching authority of the bishop as the answer to present confusion about authority in the church. For them it is the bishop who particularly preserves and safeguards the apostolic faith, and in councils, together with other bishops, episcopal safeguarding is thought to be even more effective. Some would hold that bishops have been given a special charisma for teaching.

Of course bishops teach, not in the formal but in the general sense, and this is part of their leadership. But Lutherans have traditionally asked theological faculties to function as the *magisterium*, that is, the teaching office. The college of bishops has not been thought to have unusual teaching competence. Councils err, faculties err, and so do bishops. The bishop is a "fallible sign of apostolicity," as Lindbeck puts it.[20]

Indeed, bishops have been notably fallible. During the first generation of the Reformation no bishops stood on the side of the freedom of the gospel, with the exception of Georg von Polentz, Bishop of Samland, and Erhard von Queiss, Bishop of Pomerania, both from eastern Prussia. In the 1930s during Hitler's rule no Lutheran bishops stood up with the Confessing Church, with the possible exception of Bishop Theophil Wurm; on the Roman Catholic side things were no better, with Bishop Clemens August von Galen being parallel to Wurm. Only three out of eighty-three Roman Catholic bishops in Argentina opposed the terrorism of their recent military dictatorship.

Yet do not traditions with the historic episcopate have an advantage in safeguarding the truth of the gospel because at least the collegial dimension of the historic episcopate leads to continuity with the apostolic faith? It "is not apparent in Anglican experience," one Anglican expert points out:

> Here is a lamentable weakness—an apparent inability among bishops to agree upon what fundamentals should be agreed upon. How can the bishops be the guardians of a tradition which is itself unclear to them: if they are to be guardians of the faith, who is to be *their* guardian? . . . There is in no real sense a college of bishops in England.[21]

The question of a guardian for the guardians obviously raises the further question of the papacy, which has its own difficulties.

In contradistinction to all of this, Lutheran theology has held that the only teaching authority the bishop has is the authority of the gospel. Lutherans are irrevocably committed to the view that the authenticity of the gospel is the only guarantee of the legitimacy of structures in the church, rather than the converse.

WHO THEN ARE "REAL" BISHOPS?

Bishops have functioned variously, for example, as eighteenth-century lord bishops, civil magistrates, full-time pastors while part-time bishops, power brokers, chief executive officers, expert managers, masters of ceremonies, political representatives, and the like. Culture obviously shapes the role of bishops. Thus, as the church expands in the Third World, particularly in Africa, just as the authority figure of the tribal chief is part of the landscape, so it is natural to hold that the church should also have its chief, its bishop, and the same kind of deference should be given to the bishop as to the chief. The question is whether, as often in the past, the church is being led by the culture.

Is there anything absolutely essential to the office of bishop? Is, for example, the bishop to be the chief pastor and a pastor to pastors? At most the bishop can be a kind of symbolic pastor, a spiritual leader; opportunities for functioning in this way occur when the bishop is speaking to various groups, preaching and celebrating the Eucharist occasionally in each congregation, and writing. But the bishop is not "pastor" in the sense of doing all the proclaiming and celebrating in that jurisdiction; the local pastor according to Lutheran theology surely does not baptize or celebrate communion as the deputy of the bishop. The way the bishop functions as "pastor" will in fact be jurisdictional, that is, guiding and leading. Thus, although the bishop can be understood symbolically as a pastor who is like every other pastor except for having a larger jurisdiction, the leadership role creates a significant difference.

But is not the bishop at least "pastor to pastors"? A study in 1982 by the Southeastern Pennsylvania Synod of the LCA forces one to rethink this shibboleth. It is said to be "based on a false assumption" and "establishes an unreal expectation." The problem is that personal issues may have future professional ramifications and that both pastors and congregations want the bishop to be their pastor when the bishop agrees with them, but not when they are being criticized. The Southeastern Pennsylvania Synod recommends, therefore, extensive use of clustering and that each pastor, including the bishop, intentionally select a pastor for himself or herself.

Is not, finally, the bishop the only one who ordains? Not in the Lutheran tradition. "This right is a gift given exclusively to the church" (Tr 67, *BC* 331), not exclusively to the bishop. It may be that for purposes of good order ordination might be performed exclusively by the bishop, but as soon as this would be made a requirement, especially a kind of sacramental requirement implying among other things that the "fullness" of ministry lies in the bishop, the question of the gospel and Christian freedom described earlier would come into play.

Is the idea of an evangelical episcopate a contradiction in terms? It is clear, on the one hand, that the versions of the historic episcopate embraced by Anglicans, Roman Catholics, and the Orthodox are not compatible with the notion and practice of Christian freedom implied by the doctrine of justification by faith alone. The claim that a historic episcopate is necessary to the being of the church—whether to its being as such *(esse)*, to its well-being *(bene esse)*, or to its full being *(plene esse)*—effectively adds an element to the definition of the church foreign to the Lutheran Confessions and, indeed, makes of the historic episcopate a requirement of the kind specifically rejected by the Reformers and Confessors. In this matter Lutherans think the claims of gospel truth take precedence over the legitimate desire to manifest the visible unity of the church.

Lutheran theology and historical practice, on the other hand, make ample room for the function of oversight in the church. The theological and historical traditions of the Lutheran churches implicitly and explicitly recognize the need for leadership beyond the bounds of local congregations and grant the church a broadly construed freedom to provide for that leadership or *episkopé*. The Lutheran Confessions envision overseers of the church, evangelical bishops who are first and primarily evangelical pastors, who assume a role of wider leadership which may be defined differently by the people of the church in a variety of times and places.

The fundamental Lutheran argument, that the ungodly are justified by faith alone, implies, however, an even broader freedom than most Lutherans have yet appropriated. Authentic bishops, Lutheran theology suggests, will be men and women of God who lead the church in a way appropriate to the times and places in which they find themselves. They will need no other mandate than that already provided for them by the Scripture, the Confessions of their church, and the call of the Christians they are summoned to lead. That is what the Lutheran tradition means by "real bishops," and in this sense there can be a truly evangelical episcopate. Indeed, such an episcopate is desperately needed.

NOTES

1. See further, Joseph A. Burgess, "What Is a Bishop?" *Lutheran Quarterly* 1 (new series, 1987): 307–28.

2. Jaroslav Pelikan, *Spirit Versus Structure* (New York: Harper & Row, 1968), 37.

3. George Lindbeck, "Question No. 2, " in *Eucharist and Ministry*, Lutherans and Catholics in Dialogue, vol. 4, ed. Paul E. Empie and T. A. Murphy (Minneapolis: Augsburg, 1979), 58–59.

4. Robert Goeser, "Historic Episcopate and the Lutheran Confessions," *Lutheran Quarterly* 1 (new series, 1987): 214–32.

5. See Ivar Asheim and Victor R. Gold, eds., *Episcopacy in the Lutheran Church?* (Philadelphia: Fortress Press, 1970), 59–60, 117–20, 125–37, 239–40.

6. Ibid., 134.

7. "Roman Catholic Church," *Churches Respond to BEM*, Faith and Order Paper, no. 144, ed. Max Thurian (Geneva: World Council of Churches, 1988), 5:26, 33.

8. "Ecumenical Patriarchate of Constantinople," *Churches Respond to BEM*, Faith and Order Paper, no. 135, ed. Max Thurian (Geneva: World Council of Churches, 1987), 4:4.

9. E. L. Mascall, *The Recovery of Unity: A Theological Approach* (London: Longmans, Green & Co., 1958), 159–60.

10. *The COCU Consensus: In Quest of a Church of Christ Uniting*, ed. G. F. Moede (Baltimore: Consultation on Church Union, 1984), #48.

11. Mascall, *The Recovery of Unity*, 153–69.

12. B. J. Verkamp, *The Indifferent Mean: Adiaphoron in the English Reformation to 1544* (Athens, Ohio, and Detroit: Ohio and Wayne State University Presses, 1977).

13. Orthodox-Roman Catholic Bilateral Consultation, "The Principle of Economy: A Joint Statement," in *Building Unity*, Ecumenical Documents 4, ed. J. Burgess and J. Gros (New York and Mahwah, N.J.: Paulist Press, 1989), 334.

14. Werner G. Kümmel, *Introduction to the New Testament* (Nashville and New York: Abingdon Press, 1973), 503.

15. *Papal Primacy and the Universal Church,* Lutherans and Catholic in Dialogue, vol. 5, ed. Paul E. Empie and T. A. Murphy (Minneapolis: Augsburg Publishing House, 1974), 210: #28.

16. Peter Moore, "The Anglican Episcopate: Its Strengths and Limitations," in *Bishops: But What Kind?* ed. Peter Moore (London: SPCK, 1982), 123.

17. J. Heubach, "Ordination: III. Rechtsgeschichtlich und rechtlich," in *Religion in Geschichte und Gegenwart,* 3d ed. (Tübingen: J. C. B. Mohr, 1960), 4:1674.

18. *The Ministry of the Church: A Lutheran Understanding* (New York: Division of Theological Studies, Lutheran Council in the U.S.A., 1974), 6.

19. F. Lau, "Beruf. III. Christentum und Beruf, " in *Religion in Geschichte und Gegenwart* 1:1078–79.

20. Lindbeck, "Question No. 2," 58.

21. Moore, "The Anglican Episcopate," 132–33. Emphasis in text.

10

MICHAEL ROGNESS

"SERVING" IN THE BIBLE

The office of "deacon" is about as old as the church itself. Almost every church body today has deacons but with vastly different roles. Who and what is a "deacon"? The meaning of *diakonia/diakonein* in the New Testament is consistently "service"/"to serve." It usually refers to menial serving, most specifically serving tables, but takes on more general connotations according to its usage.

Jesus uses the term *diakonia*, "service," as fundamental to his own ministry, using the term both in its basic meaning as "serving tables" but then expanding it to mean service in general: "For which is the greater, one who sits at table, or one who serves? Is it not the one who sits at table? But I am among you as one who serves" (Luke 22:27; cf. John 13:13-15). Jesus tells his disciples that "the Son of man also came not to be served but to serve" (Mark 10:45; cf. Matt. 20:25-28; Luke 22:24-27).

It is clear from the Gospels that Jesus commends "service"/"servanthood" not as a separate office but as part of the ministry of all believers. We serve Jesus: "If any one serves me, he must follow me; and where I am, there shall my servant be also; if any one serves me, the Father will honor him" (John 12:26; cf. Luke 12:37). Being a servant of Jesus means we also serve others: "Whoever would be great among you must be your servant, and whoever would be first among you must be your slave; even as the Son of man came not to be served but to serve" (Matt. 20:26-28; cf. also Matt. 23:11; Mark 9:35; Luke 9:48).

Paul uses the word *diakonos* often: Christ as servant (Rom. 15:8; Gal. 2:17); Paul and other believers as servants (1 Cor. 3:5; 2 Cor. 3:6; 6:4; 11:15, 23; Col. 1:23, 25); Paul's fellow workers: Tychicus (Col. 4:7; Eph. 6:21), Epaphras (Col.

151

1:7), and Timothy (1 Thess. 3:2), although ancient manuscripts disagree on whether the word is *diakonos* or *synergos;* civil magistrates (Rom. 13:4); Phoebe (Rom. 16:1). The Latin Vulgate translates *diakonos* with *minister* in every one of the above instances, never as "diaconus," even Rom. 16:1, which refers to Phoebe. English translations appear almost arbitrary: the KJV uses "minister" almost all the time, the RSV uses "servant" more than "minister," and other translations use "agent," "helper," "deputy," and "fellow-worker." It is interesting to note that in the verses cited above no English version ever translates *diakonos* as "deacon," with the single exception of Rom. 16:1, although there even the KJV calls Phoebe "servant" rather than "minister" or "deacon" or the more common "deaconess" (a word that has no linguistic justification whatsoever, since no other offices are marked by gender).

THE SEVEN

The biblical source of the diaconate as an office is assumed to be Acts 6, when "the Hellenists" murmured against "the Hebrews" because the Hellenist widows were being neglected in the daily distribution *(diakonia)*.

> And the twelve summoned the body of the disciples and said, "It is not right that we should give up preaching the word of God to serve *(diakonein)* tables. Therefore, brethren, pick out from among you seven men of good repute, full of the Spirit and of wisdom, whom we may appoint to this duty. But we will devote ourselves to prayer and to the ministry *(diakonia)* of the word."

Chosen were Stephen, Philip, Prochorus, Nicanor, Timon, Parmenas and Nicolaus (Acts 6:2-6). Here again the verb means "to serve," used most often with serving tables. This passage includes that primary meaning, then extends the meaning to include also "serving *(diakonia)* of the word," which the RSV translates as "ministry of the word."

In the chapters that follow, any distinction between the role of the seven "servers" from that of the apostles soon becomes blurred. Indeed, immediately following the naming of the deacons, we read that Stephen "did great wonders and signs among the people," and his opponents "could not withstand the wisdom and the Spirit with which he spoke" (6:8-10). Witnesses were called who testified that Stephen "never ceases" to speak about Jesus. In response to the charges, Stephen delivered a lengthy sermon (chap. 7).

Furthermore, immediately after the death of Stephen, we read that Philip was among those who "went about preaching the word." He not only "proclaimed the Christ," but also performed signs of healing (8:4-8, 12). Following this, Philip explained the Scriptures to the Ethiopian eunuch and baptized him, and then "preached the gospel to all the towns till he came to Caesarea" (8:29–40). When Paul and his fellow travelers arrived in Caesarea they "entered the house of Philip the evangelist, who was one of the seven" (21:8). We have no record of Philip's work among the poor following his being named in Acts 6, but the clear record is that he did the same work as Christ called the apostles to do, namely, to preach, work miracles and baptize. That tells us that the definition of the original Seven was not rigidly fixed nor distinguished from the activity of the apostles themselves.

By the time Paul wrote his Letter to the Philippians, "deacon" seems to have become a recognized office. Paul opened his letter to Philippi by addressing the "saints in Christ Jesus who are at Philippi, with the bishops and deacons"— *episcopoi* and *diakonoi*—presumably as positions or offices in the church. That is the opinion of St. Jerome, who, after translating *diakonos* consistently as "minister," then switched to *diaconus*, a practice followed by all subsequent English translations. Even the KJV, which balked at calling Phoebe a "deacon" in Rom. 16:1, addressed the "deacons" in Philippi.

In Philippians Paul said no more about these offices, but in his first letter to Timothy, following his admonition for the bishop's office, Paul wrote again about deacons:

> Deacons likewise must be serious, not double-tongued, not addicted to much wine, not greedy for gain; they must hold the mystery of the faith with a clear conscience. And let them also be tested first; then if they prove themselves blameless let them serve as deacons. The women likewise must be serious, no slanderers, but temperate, faithful in all things. Let deacons be married only once, and let them manage their children and their households well; for those who serve well as deacons gain a good standing for themselves and also great confidence in the faith which is in Christ Jesus. (1 Tim. 3:8-13, RSV)

One interesting feature of this passage is the mention of women in v. 11. Were there women among the deacons in New Testament churches? If one translates *gunaikos* as "women," as it appears in the RSV and the Jerusalem Bible, it would seem to be the case. However, the KJV and others read "their wives," referring to the wives of the male deacons. The fact that the very next verse reads, in Greek, "Let the deacons be the husband of one wife," leans to the latter view, although the Jerusalem Bible leaves the question open: "Deacons must not have been married more than once." The original RSV reading, following the KJV, is "Let deacons be the husband of one wife . . . ," although subsequent RSV versions changed that verse to read, "Let deacons be married only once."

However, Paul himself named Phoebe as "a *diakonos* in the church at Cenchreae" (Rom. 16:1). Those who wish to retain the male limitation of the office argue that here Paul used the word *diakonos* in its more generic sense of "servant" rather than a term for a specific office of ministry. One can choose between "deacon" and "servant," but there is no justification for translating the word in its feminine form, "deaconess," as did the RSV.[1] In Titus 1:5-9 Paul listed qualifications of elders and bishops but not deacons. In none of his other letters are bishops, deacons, or elders mentioned.

Attempts to define the meaning of the term from contemporary secular sources have not proven helpful. The term *diakonos* is used generally as "servant," often suggesting menial labor or serving. One Jewish parallel often cited is the Jewish *hazzan,* the assistant to the ruler of the synagogue, but there is no indication from the Scriptures that this position was the pattern of the Christian deacon. The office of deacon, to serve the poor, is quite different than the *hazzan,* who is a sexton or beadle within the synagogue.

The New Testament leaves us with two impressions. First, the original Seven in Acts 6 is an office of *serving,* originally philanthropic and charitable work, although the work of the two we learn about, Stephen and Philip, is clearly evangelistic, indistinguishable from that of the apostles. Second, the qualifications for bishops and deacons listed in the Pauline literature are very similar, suggesting a close connection of the two offices.

THE DEACON IN CHURCH HISTORY

The Seven selected to serve in Acts 6 are never called "deacons," either in Acts or in the remainder of the New Testament. The word "deacon" does not occur at all in Acts. But since the Seven were appointed for the *diakonia* of tables, it was probably inevitable that their role or position would be given the title of "deacon," which means "servant" or "attendant." Irenaeus was the first to apply the title deacon to the Seven of Acts 6.[2] The *Shepherd of Hermas,* written about the beginning of the second century, still spoke of the care of widows and orphans as a deacon's responsibility,[3] but even at that time the office of deacon was taking on the role of assisting with public worship—preparing the altar, assisting with the Communion distribution, preaching occasionally (although the preaching function of deacons died out between the sixth and eighth centuries).

Ignatius and Polycarp in the early second century often name the offices of bishop, presbyter/priest, and deacon.[4] The *Didache* from the mid-second century listed the offices of bishop and deacon together, both elected by a congregation, and states that "their ministry to you is identical with that of the prophets and teachers."[5] By the time of Hippolytus's *Apostolic Tradition* from the early third century, deacons were institutionalized as the bishops' assistants. Presbyters were ordained by a bishop assisted by other presbyters, but deacons were ordained by a bishop alone (although persons for all three offices were chosen by election of the people).[6] The deacon's primary role was to serve the bishop in his liturgical and pastoral duties, particularly at Holy Communion, where the deacons received the offerings of the people and assisted in the distribution of the communion elements, including taking it to those who could not attend Communion. Added later was the task of reading the gospel. Preserving at least a part of the function of the original seven in Acts 6, they also visited the sick, poor, widows, orphans, prisoners, and brought them assistance from the church.

Women were deacons for the first several centuries of the church's life. In A.D. 110 the Younger Pliny's letter to the Emperor Trajan spoke of "young women who are *ministrae*," the Latin term for "servers" or deacons. The Council of Nicaea in A.D. 325 spoke of "deaconesses," noting that "as they have not been ordained, they must be classed merely among the laity."[7] However, a century later the Council of Chalcedon used the term "ordination" for deaconesses, stipulating however that "a woman is not to be ordained deaconess before she is forty."[8] The office of deaconess became widespread in the church, although their position was not the same as a male deacon. Between the sixth and eighth centuries, however, the inclusion of women as deacons or deaconesses died out, first in the West, then later also in the East.

The office of deacon was most important in the pre-Constantine church, when bishops were actually "senior pastors" of the central parish in a locality, the "hub congregation" surrounded by other smaller congregations. Since the bishop could not do all the liturgical functions in these growing parishes, deacons were needed to assist the bishops. By the early third century the office of "subdeacon" had even been founded, to assist the deacon.

With the establishment of the church in the Roman Empire in the fourth century, followed by a rapid growth in the number of parishes, bishops became diocesan overseers removed from the liturgical life of even the cathedral church. Congregations needed a presbyter/priest of their own, and in time the office of the presbyter/priest assumed the role as the pastor of a parish, with the bishop as overseer. Inevitably the diaconate as a separate office diminished in importance. During the Reformation era, Martin Luther favored the restoration of the diaconate to its original purpose, namely, to care for the poor and maintain church property.[9] John Calvin considered the diaconate as a distinct office for the care of the poor.[10]

TO THE PRESENT

Between the Reformation era and the present time the diaconate has developed into three directions. In the Roman Catholic, Orthodox, and Anglican churches the diaconate has become a steppingstone to the priesthood. A candidate for the priesthood is ordained a deacon in the course of his training for the priesthood. This is called the "transitional diaconate," because a person is a deacon only until ordination to the priesthood, then is no longer referred to as a deacon.

This pattern has changed in recent decades. Post–Vatican II Roman Catholics speak of the "restoration of the permanent diaconate," accelerated no doubt by the growing shortage of priests. Pope Paul VI issued a *motu proprio* on June 18, 1967, "Sacrem Diaconatus Ordinem," with guidelines for a restored diaconate. Most permanent Roman Catholic deacons are men who have full-time occupations in secular life, but who are ordained as deacons and authorized to assist in the life of a parish. The Sacraments of Penance and the Lord's Supper still require an ordained priest, with a bishop presiding at the Sacraments of Confirmation and Ordination. But a deacon may baptize, officiate at weddings, anoint the sick, officiate at funerals, preach and conduct worship, distributing the bread already consecrated by a priest. This is more a return to the diaconate of the Apostolic Age rather than of the Acts 6 model, that is, the deacon filling a liturgical function in the absence of a bishop or priest. The question is whether the restored diaconate in the Roman Catholic church will become indeed a separate order, or simply a means to fill priestly vacancies, or even a provision to enable married men to serve in priestly capacities.[11]

The modern day diaconate as an order of charitable service in the pattern of Acts 6 arose in Germany with the *Innere Mission* movement. In 1840 Johann Hinrich Wichern established the *Rauhes Haus* at Horn near Hamburg as a rescue home for neglected children. It quickly became a training place for people to work with the poor and sick. Those trained in turn established houses throughout Germany and other countries to minister to the sick, jailed, orphans, neglected children, and lately also to drug addicts. Wichern preferred the titles "brother"/ "brotherhood," but "deacon"/"diaconate" soon became universally used, and today there are over four thousand deacons in fifteen "brother houses" in Germany, plus others in Scandinavia.

In 1836 Pastor Theodor Fliedner founded an order of deaconesses at Kaiserswerth on the Rhine, near Duesseldorf, to serve sick and neglected children. He prepared a "Constitution for the Order of Deaconesses for the Rhenish Provinces," which was signed into effect that same year. This movement also spread rapidly, establishing institutions of deaconesses servicing all over the world, including the United States.[12] American Lutherans, particularly those of German descent, are familiar with the enormous service given by Lutheran deaconesses in this country. However their numbers are diminishing now that women are ordained and other lay ministries have been established. The term "ordination" has not been used for these offices of deacons and deaconesses. Rather, they are "commissioned" for diaconate ministry.

Many denominations designate lay leaders as "deacons." Those American Lutheran congregations that designate deacons continue the model not of Acts 6 but that of the early church: deacons assist in the worship and spiritual life of the congregation. In many cases a congregation's church council will include deacons and trustees. Deacons assist with the "spiritual" life of the parish, trustees with the "temporal" tasks, such as financial affairs and the maintenance of the property. This is of course a reversal of the deacon's original task, namely, to distribute food and care for the widows. Churches from other Reformation traditions have deacons, but their roles differ widely, from forms of service to liturgical functions, reflecting the ambiguity inherited from the early church.[13] The term "ordination" is not usually used for deacons.

CONCLUSIONS

Diakonia as service is of course the task of every Christian in every congregation. Although the specific scope of Acts 6 is the care of the church's own, that is, its widows, the broader vision of *diakonia* throughout the New Testament makes clear that Jesus' followers are to be concerned for the poor and needy. The establishment of the office of the Seven in Acts 6 was in response to a need, a need related to the preaching of the Word. The office was established because the apostles needed help, and the distinction was made between those who "serve the word," that is, those who preach, and those who serve tables, that is, care for the poor. The clear lesson of Acts 6 is that the primary task of the church is to proclaim the gospel, but that in the everyday life of a congregation additional people will be needed for other tasks.

The definition of the diaconate is not rigidly fixed, either in the New Testament or in the early church. It would be inconsistent with the New Testament pattern to adopt an office of deacon in imitation of some past form. If the need exists, as it does in the Roman Catholic church with its shortage of priests, then the diaconate as an office or order will be reinstated, as it was with the deaconess movement in the last century. What is important is that the ministry of *diakonia* is being carried out, not what titles are used.

One difficulty in restoring the diaconate as a distinct order is the diffusion of ministries in a congregation. These tasks are related to diaconal ministry— whether in charitable works of Acts 6 or liturgical functions of the apostolic and later diaconate—and most are done by part-time volunteers. Every congregation uses the talents of its people in many ways. When the need arose in the mid-1970s for congregations to sponsor resettlement families from Southeast Asia, committees were organized to do it. During the difficult economic times of the early 1980s, congregations banded together with others to form food shelves for the needy. Both were examples of diaconal ministry in response to a need, although ordinarily the title of deacon was not used for the people involved. Whether the title "deacon" is used or not, members of a congregation work together to enable and insure the preaching of the Word, as well to carry out the other tasks of a congregation. The intent of the diaconate is expressed in Paul's vision of a church where all persons use the gifts of the Spirit in various ways—prophets, teachers, miracle workers, healers, helpers, administrators, and so forth (1 Cor. 12:28). To bring that list up to date, organists, pianists, singers, youth workers, visitors, kitchen workers, and property overseers could be added. The ministry of *diakonia* is indeed alive and well, whether a church body or congregation uses the term "deacon" or not.

No one would dispute that a congregation carries out diaconal ministry. Indeed, the form and extent of that ministry is usually a lively topic of discussion in any congregation. The question of the diaconate as a distinct office or order is one of nomenclature. In every congregation there are people who serve in many ways. What shall all these people be called? Until now they have been called by descriptive terms—church council members, trustees, youth advisors, organists, teachers, to name a few.

Even in the process of its formation the ELCA is dealing with these questions. To provide a place for lay persons serving in the church, the ELCA Constitution has created the category of "Associates in Ministry" for some of these persons, but not to everyone. All persons contributing to the work of a parish are of course "associates in ministry" in the sense that their service contributes to the work of a parish. How shall the boundaries of this new title be determined? Some consider restoring the title "deacon," but there is yet no consensus on who should be included in the term. Furthermore, shall the church "install," "commission," "dedicate" or "ordain" laypersons serving in these positions? For clarity's sake should the church use the term "ordain" only for the setting apart to Word and sacrament ministry? Should it be used more generally?

In the discussion of the church's mission, the church cannot confine itself to a rigid "threefold office of ministry," that is, bishop, priest, and deacon, as sufficient to carry out the mission. The church's ministry is far broader and includes many more kinds of persons. If it were to restore the office of deacon, would it discard all descriptive position titles and call all people "deacons" who work with bishops and pastors? Would it give the title "deacon" only to full-time churchworkers, thus eliminating almost all members of a congregation who serve in various part-time positions? Should it designate some as deacons to serve the needy, hoping their example would be an incentive to all Christians to live in service to others?[14]

The discussion of ministry and office(s) of ministry can only be carried out by beginning with the mission of the church. Its primary mission is to proclaim God's grace in Word and sacrament, which is why the church designates "ordination" for that purpose. The lesson of Acts 6 is precisely the central importance of the proclamation of the gospel as the church's mission, a task that can only be carried out when many other people carry out other tasks of the church. As tasks need to be done in the church's mission, offices and positions are created to do them.

To be most faithful to the intent of the Seven in Acts 6 chosen to serve, the church ought not limit itself to any of the three common patterns of deacons described above—steppingstone to ministry, men's/women's order, or layperson helping with the exclusively spiritual nurture of the congregation. Rather, acknowledging that the church does many things in addition to Word and sacrament ministry, it will be an asset that these forms of service will vary with location, time, and circumstance, and that this service is organized and carried out not just by pastors, but by all the people in a congregation working together.

What is important is that Christians rejoice in "the varieties of gifts . . . the varieties of service . . . the same Spirit . . . the same Lord" with which the church has been blessed. In the discussion of offices and ministry in the church deliberations need to begin with this question: How shall the church's mission best be carried out?

NOTES

1. For a review of this issue, cf. *The Deaconess, A Service of Women in the World of Today*, WCC Studies, no. 4 (1966).

2. *Against Heresies*, in *The Ante-Nicene Fathers*, vol. 1, ed. Alexander Roberts and James Donaldson (New York: Charles Scribner's Sons, 1906–8), 1:434.

3. Ibid. 2:52.

4. *Early Christian Fathers*, ed. Cyril C. Richardson (Philadelphia: Westminster Press, 1953), Ignatius's Epistle to the Magnesians, 1:94f.; Epistle to the Trallians, 1:98f.; Epistle to the Philadelphians, 1:108–11; Polycarp's Epistle to the Philippians, 1:132f., esp. 133, where he describes the presbyter's work as "looking after the sick, not neglecting the widow or orphan or one that is poor," usually a description of a deacon's ministry, indicating that distinctions between offices were not rigid at that time.

5. Ibid. 1:178.

6. *The Apostolic Tradition of Hippolytus*, ed. Burton Scott Eston (Cambridge: Cambridge University Press; Ann Arbor, Michigan: Archon Books, 1962), 33, 38.

7. Canon 19, in *A History of Christian Councils*, Charles Hefele (Edinburgh: T. & T. Clark, 1894), 431f.

8. For a brief summary of the statements about women deacons in the decrees of the church councils, cf. H. J. Schroeder, O.P., *Disciplinary Decrees of the General Councils* (London: B. Herder, 1937), 107–14.

9. *LW* 28:296f.

10. *Institutes of the Christian Religion*, ed. John McNeill (Philadelphia: Westminster Press, 1960), 2:1061f.

11. For a survey of the status and role of deacons in the Roman Catholic church, cf. *Permanent Deacons in the United States, Guidelines on Their Formation and Ministry, U.S. Bishop's Committee on the Permanent Diaconate* (Washington, D.C.: Publications Office of the U.S. Catholic Conference, 1971).

12. Cf. the chapter by Paul Philippi in *The Deaconess*, 31f.

13. For example, cf. Donald F. Thomas, *The Deacon in the Changing Church* (Valley Forge, Pa.: Judson Press, 1969), a survey of the office of deacon from a Baptist perspective. Thomas speaks of "the usual, more liturgical responsibilities of the diaconate," but looks toward expanding the diaconate to "some of the ministries which are possible . . . where service and witness are of primary importance" (p. 53). He concludes: "Deacons may truly become servants of the church and the world as they enter into some of these new ministries" (ibid.).

For a survey of the role of deacons in various churches, cf. also *The Diaconate Now*, ed. Richard T. Nolan (Washington, D.C.: Corpus Books, 1968).

14. This is the proposal of James M. Barnett in *The Diaconate, A Full and Equal Order* (New York: Seabury Press, 1961). In his chapter, "The Deacon as Symbol," he argues for a reconstituted, separate diaconate order as a visible symbol of the church's task of service, in order that by example diaconal ministry of all church members might be enhanced. "The deacon above all epitomizes within his or her office the ministry Christ has given to his Church, the servant ministry to which we are all called and commissioned

in our baptism. . . . Deacons then are not ordained essentially in order that they may perform the distinctive functions of their order but to hold up *diakonia* as central to all Christian ministry" (141f.).

For further study, see the exhaustive bibliography, 209f. Cf. also a similar proposal in *The Ministry of Deacons*, WCC Studies, No. 2 (Geneva, 1965), 34.

11

Though the late 1960s were years of unprecedented social upheaval, Lutherans studied and debated women's ordination on the grounds of the Confessions and Scripture. Only at the end of the debates did the women's liberationists have much impact on the discussion. If the votes to ordain women had come after the feminist movement had gathered enough strength to threaten the establishment, women's ordination among Lutherans might have floundered. Even though arguments for the ordination of women were to some extent based on claims of equality or argued for on the basis of equal rights, and may ultimately have been the persuasive arguments to the delegates in both the ALC and LCA conventions, theologians of the two churches repeatedly resisted such reasons for the change. When conflict developed, it focused, in fact, on questions of biblical interpretation which were to send Missouri on its own course, and which had a decade before caused an uproar at both Augsburg Seminary and Luther Theological Seminary when the ALC was formed. How all this happened is worth considering now that the question of the doctrine of the ministry is once again under debate.

I

John Reumann gives the most detailed account to date of the various meetings, committees, and actions of the churches as they considered the question of women's ordination, although his account is, as he acknowledges, from the point of view of the LCA.[1] All of the Lutheran churches in the newly formed LCUSA, which included the ALC, LCA, LC-MS, and the Synod of Evangelical Churches, knew the question of women's ordination was coming during the 1960s simply because of the jaunty, liberal spirit of the times. One cannot overestimate the effect of Vatican II on the religious imaginations of the time. Lutheran theologians, in conversation with once implacable foes, were now able to think of

161

the doctrine of the ministry from the vantage point of the ecumenical movement. The old prejudices could be put aside in the rush toward unity.

Meanwhile, in their own churches old practices and traditions no longer seemed sacrosanct. Since 1938 when the church of Norway first authorized the ordination of women, the Lutheran churches of Europe had been increasingly willing to ordain women. This movement was opposed by, among others, German theologian Peter Brunner, who argued on the basis of Scripture and creation that women were not created to be pastors, that being a pastor was a deep violation of a woman's created nature.[2] This was, in turn, challenged by Krister Stendahl, the Swedish New Testament scholar, in a study, published in Sweden for the debate in 1958 over the ordination of women. Stendahl developed the position that the problem was hermeneutical: a matter of how to read the New Testament texts.

The American churches followed these developments closely. Luther Theological Seminary, with the approval of the ALC Board of Theological Education, had enrolled women who by the end of the decade would press for ordination. There were at the time growing numbers of women who had graduated or were enrolled at some of the seminaries of the church, though these were not the first women to attend Lutheran seminaries.[3] Some were known to have attended in the late 1890s.[4] But the question of women's ordination was not a matter for serious debate among Lutherans in America until the 1960s.

On June 30, 1964, an article appeared in the ALC's *Lutheran Standard* which asked: "Should women be allowed to occupy the pulpit or not?"[5] Reflecting on her recent trip to the LWF Assembly in Helsinki the year before, Anne Jordheim wrote that she had met many European woman pastors and was forced to wonder why there were no women pastors in the ALC. The article contained no specific reference to the New Testament strictures against women speaking in church. Hans Lilje, Bishop of Hannover, was said to be for the ordination of women, not "because of a shortage of pastors or a question of equality, but because the church is committed to preach the Word."[6] Jordheim concluded her article with a comment from one of the Finnish woman pastors she had come to know: "Sooner or later the seminaries of your church [the ALC] will have to launch their first female theologians. It is unavoidable. They are already forty-five years behind schedule."[7]

The next month, July 1964, someone wrote to *The Lutheran* (LCA) asking, "How does the Lutheran Church in America stand on the ordination of women?" The answer was brief: "The question has not come up in any broadly representative assembly of Lutherans in America, so no position has been taken. It's likely that there is very little sentiment in favor of ordination of women in the LCA."[8] Things were to change quickly.

In 1964, the ALC at its Second Biennial Convention had accepted a statement on the ministerial office. Though it had not mentioned the idea of ordaining women, it had opened the possibility with the language of its statement, which would be used six years later in the resolution to ordain women in the ALC.

> Since the needs of the church down through the centuries are subject to variation, we are led to Luther's conclusion, namely, that God has left the details of the ministerial office to the discretion of the church, to be developed according to its needs and according to the leading of the Holy Spirit.[9]

Through the next years *The Lutheran* and *The Lutheran Standard* included occasional news notes about other denominations ordaining women. Typical was a piece headed "Right of women to ordination gets wider discussion." The article stated that women were being ordained in Europe and in other American denominations. Saying that the Roman Catholic theologian Rev. George Tavard saw "no fundamental theological objection to the ordination of women,"[10] the writer added that soon an LCA commission on the ministry would "report on attitudes which American Lutherans can take to this possibility."[11]

In 1966, when Stendahl's book was translated into English, the LCA at its second convention considered a document on the ministry. Written by a committee of noted theologians and others, the report was eagerly anticipated by this new church.[12] When it came out just prior to the convention, the "Report of the Commission on the Comprehensive Study of the Doctrine of the Ministry" to the 1966 convention of the LCA was greeted with mixed emotions. The editors of the *Lutheran Quarterly* called for more clarity regarding ordination, although they did praise the document for being bold enough to think of enhancing and expanding lay offices such as "ministries in areas of civil rights, antipoverty campaigns, performing arts, labor-management relations, journalism, and the like."[13] Criticizing the proposal as fuzzy because it did not draw clearer distinctions between commissioning and ordaining, the editorial concluded by commending the commission's call for a study of episcopacy and the "advisability of ordaining women."[14]

Philip J. Hefner, then of Gettysburg Seminary, wrote a second editorial in the same issue of the *Quarterly*, praising the report and urging that the ministry of women be honored more by giving women "their full civil liberties in our midst (including adequate salaries, working conditions, terms of tenure, etc.)."[15] Eager to grant a fuller recognition to ministry by women, he was more hesitant on the ordination of women because of the ecumenical question.

> In the ecumenical perspective, we must weigh very seriously the effect that our ordination of women would have on other Christians. Would the ordination of women in our denominations be as irresponsible and offensive, ecumenically, as the promulgation of the Marian dogmas by the Roman church?[16]

When the "Report of the Commission on the Comprehensive Study of the Doctrine of the Ministry" was presented at the LCA's Third Biennial Convention in Kansas City, it "came under heavy fire and was sunk in deep water."[17] Critics appeared not to like the attempt to give full-time lay ministry status in the church: "Anyone selected by the church for full-time service might be commissioned, rather than merely employed."[18] The delegates rejected all such proposals. William Lazareth, then Dean of Philadelphia Seminary, attacked the report by arguing that baptism is the ordination to the universal priesthood of believers.

> We don't have to try to soup this up with a specious kind of commissioning. To make laymen second-class pastors rather than having the pastors assist laymen to be the baptized people of God seems to me a radical reversal of what the Reformation was about.[19]

The Convention, however, did like the recommendation of the Commission that the role of women in the ministry be studied. The "Report" had stated that "there is neither theological nor social consensus on this question" and concluded that a study was necessary.[20] To that end a resolution was crafted, after extensive debate, which mandated that the new commission chosen to continue the comprehensive study of the doctrine of the ministry also be charged with studying the ministry of women. After some debate, the final resolution stated simply that the president of the LCA, Franklin Clark Fry, appoint a commission of not more than fifteen persons for this purpose.

For some this was an inopportune decision that would complicate the church's ecumenical relations. President Fry had said it was not the best time to make the study. It would come, he noted,

> at the moment when we are entering into a new compact of friendship and cooperation with other Lutheran bodies and at the moment when we are actively engaged in ecumenical conversations with the great bulk of Christendom, the Roman Catholic and the Orthodox churches, which haven't the slightest intention of moving in this direction.[21]

Fry took care, however, to appoint three women to the commission, among them, Margaret Sittler Ermarth, who chaired the subcommittee (made up of members from the full committee) that was to be entrusted with research into the "whole problem of the role of women in the church."[22]

That same year the Board of Theological Education of the ALC reported to its 1966 Biennial Convention that it had permitted women to enroll in its theological seminaries to study for the B. D. degree, fully aware that the church did not ordain women. Not long after the conventions of the two church bodies, the ALC requested, at the November 17, 1966, Executive Committee meeting of LCUSA that the DTS pursue joint studies of ordination and ministry. In March 1967, the Board of Theological Education of the ALC took action to transmit the information to the Church Council that some of the women who were matriculated at Luther Theological Seminary in St. Paul were planning to request that they be certified for ordination. When the Council received this report in June 1967, it asked the DTS to study the question of the ordination of women, commissioning William Larsen, the ALC's Director of the Board of Theological Education, who was to become a strong supporter of the move, to prepare a paper on the ordination of women. In addition they invited Olaf Storaasli of the Luther Theological Seminary faculty to prepare a paper on the same question.

II

The biennial conventions of both the ALC and the LCA in 1968 seemed distracted by the war and violence of the times. Many of the resolutions in both conventions had to do with Vietnam, racism, and the war on poverty. In addition to those pressing issues, the LCA was caught up in the election of a new president to take the place of Franklin Fry, whose sudden death some weeks before had taken the church by surprise. The report by Edmund Steimle, chairman of the new commission on the ministry, to the 1968 Convention in Atlanta was only a preliminary report, given the short time between conventions.

Steimle informed the convention, however, that it was possible to highlight several things the commission had agreed upon: (1) their focus would be both upon traditional materials and modern sociological data; (2) the ministry had been entrusted to the whole church, but what that meant with respect to church order was not clear; (3) there were no "biblical or theological reasons for denying ordination to women."[23] What stopped the convention from approving the ordination of women, according to Reumann, was a plea from Professor T. A. Kantonen of Hamma Seminary, who persuaded the convention to delay action in hopes that other Lutheran bodies would concur with their very likely approval of women's ordination.[24]

During its Fourth General Convention, October 16–22, 1968, in Omaha, the ALC received reports that the Church Council was treating the question seriously.[25] Other issues seemed more pressing. One major decision of this convention was to declare fellowship with the LC-MS. Though the conflict between the moderates and conservatives in Missouri had not yet erupted, it was simmering. Questions of biblical interpretation, one of which the ordination of women was to become, were growing difficult. Fry's comments at the 1966 LCA convention, though not aimed at LC-MS, proved to be prophetic.

The week after the ALC convention of October 1968 the Luther Theological Seminary faculty issued a statement on the ordination of women which was precipitated by the request of some of their women students for a statement. The faculty's work, a brief but trenchant piece, concluded that there were four sets of objections against the ordination of women: biblical, theological, practical, and ecumenical. They noted, as others before them, that the most serious objection was the fact that the move to ordain women would further divide Christendom. But they concluded,

> In view of the considerations above, we can see no valid reason why women candidates for ordination who meet the standards normally required for admission to the ministry should not be recommended for ordination.[26]

They, too, were prescient in seeing that the most serious objection was the ecumenical. But not even their traditionally ambivalent feelings toward Missouri, nor their genuine and well deserved excitement over the new breakthroughs in the dialogues with Rome, pioneered in part by their own colleagues, prevented them from deciding in favor of women's ordination.

At the November 1968 meeting of the Executive Committee of LCUSA, a four-person Subcommittee on the Study on the Ordination of Women was appointed which was to examine prior studies, listen to consultants, and generate papers.[27] They agreed to a set of topics and presented papers addressing the issues on January 17–18, 1969. The topics were typically Lutheran, focusing on Scripture, the Confessions, and Lutheran history and tradition. The papers represent a cautious investigation of the question in the light of current scholarship, from the biblical to the sociological.[28] In addition to the papers, they heard reports from their special consultants. Ermarth gave a short account of the LCA studies on the role of women in the church; Richard Jungkuntz spoke of studies that the Commission on Theology and Church Relations of the LC-MS had recently adopted on women's suffrage. Kjell-Ove Nilsson, a scholar at Luther Theological Seminary visiting from Sweden, presented the subcommittee with information from the recent debate on the issue in Sweden. He was also asked to inform the subcommittee about the situation at Luther Seminary where two women in the senior class were seeking ordination. These women students were an ever-present pressure group on the ALC to decide.

This subcommittee concluded, in a "Statement of Findings" that was adopted by the Standing Committee of the DTS, on March 7–8, 1969, that in "the Biblical material and theological arguments we find the case both against and for the ordination of women inconclusive."[29]

The essential points of their findings were

1. that the biblical and theological evidence is not conclusive either for or against the ordination of women
2. that the sociological, psychological, and ecumenical considerations do not settle the question
3. that variety in practice on this question is legitimate within common Lutheran confessions
4. that the decision of the individual Lutheran church bodies should be made only after consultation with the other bodies and in sensitivity to the other Christian churches
5. that the question of the ordination of women involves the broader question of ordination itself, the office of the ministry, the ministry of the whole people of God[30]

166

When the Executive Committee of LCUSA met on April 10–11, 1969, apparently the topic was sufficiently vexing for the committee to postpone indefinitely any action on the findings, though it accepted recommendations that the presidents appoint representatives to a conference on the question and its implications for the churches. What was developing as the major difficulty was the hermeneutical question. Hopes for a final rapprochement with Missouri seemed elusive, even though Missouri, at its Denver convention that summer, voted by a small margin to declare fellowship with the ALC. This same convention granted women suffrage in the local congregations, with the warning that women should not exercise headship over men. Others had concluded, as Robert Bertram did on the Subcommittee appointed by LCUSA to prepare the "Statement of Findings," that once the church approved women's suffrage, the argument was over: women were speaking in church.[31]

In July 1969, in Denver, at the stormy convention of Missouri, which elected J. A. O. Preus as President of the LC-MS largely on the basis of his criticisms of those teaching the historical-critical approach to Scripture at Concordia Seminary, the church declared that

> those statements of Scripture which direct women to keep silent in the church and which prohibit them to teach and to exercise authority over men, we understand to mean that women ought not to hold the pastoral office or serve in any other capacity involving the distinctive functions of this office.[32]

With this, the issue of women's ordination became church-dividing. Preus pointed this out whenever he spoke about it to other churches. Though his statements were reported in the church press, they did not elicit much comment from the ALC and LCA. It is important to remember that at the time, this issue was receiving only minimal attention from both the ALC and LCA church magazines. Not even E. Clifford Nelson, editor and one of the authors of *The Lutherans in North America,* noted it as a major factor in the rupture between ALC and LC-MS.[33]

Because of the hermeneutical difficulties, each consultation made clear in its statement that the decision one church body made about women's ordination did not have to be church dividing because it was not a matter of the gospel. The difficulties were both intra–LC-MS and inter-Lutheran. Robert Bertram, a representative from the Missouri Synod who participated in the study, favored the ordination of women on the basis of his reading of the tradition and the Bible. However, the reports of the subcommittee had to pass through the Annual Meeting of the Council where an equal number of LC-MS, ALC, and LCA officials sat, among them, President J. A. O. Preus.

The consultation that the Executive Committee planned during its April meetings took place at Wartburg Theological Seminary, September 20–22, 1969. Three representatives from each church body met to study all of the materials from the study groups, as well as the "Statement of Findings."[34] One of the

participants, Roy Harrisville, of the Luther Theological Seminary faculty, refers
to this consultation and his preparation for it as a time in which he changed his
mind from being totally and absolutely opposed "to the idea of a female in the
pulpit" to being for it on the basis of his

> study of exegetical and dogmatic considerations. . . . I learned something about
> the Scriptural word with respect to women's ordination, and something from the
> confessions, whereas before I'd just simply entertained a prejudice against women
> in the pulpit, period.[35]

While the members of the consultation all agreed on many questions, once
again they could not settle the question of women's ordination. What they did
acknowledge was that the issue ought not to be divisive of Lutheran fellowship
"inasmuch as no compromise or violation of the Gospel is involved."[36] Martin
Scharlemann, another participant, later president of Concordia Seminary, argues
against women's ordination on the basis not so much of Scripture as of the
theology of the "orders of creation."[37] The "orders" were to be described two
years later by Scharlemann in his paper entitled "Orders of Creation and the
Principle of Ordination as it Pertains to Ministry." By orders he meant "those
social and political structures which are regulated by law in order to make life
in community both possible and enriching despite the conditions brought on
by man's fall." These structures that were given by God, even in the curse to
Eve that she would be subject to her husband, were another way for God to
continue creating. To attempt to apply principles from the kingdom of grace
(God's right hand) to the kingdom of law (God's left hand) would be to give a
"gospel answer to a law question."[38] Anarchy would follow such misguided
effort, Scharlemann concluded, much as Brunner had in 1959.

When the Standing Committee of LCUSA met again after the Dubuque
conference, it resolved to submit its original "Statement of Findings" to the
Executive Committee along with all of the background papers and an extensive
report on the September conference at Wartburg. The delicacy of the issue can
be read in the minutes which note that "divergent views do exist in the partic-
ipating bodies, but it [the Standing Committee] also emphasizes, as the September conference did, that no compromise or violation of the Gospel is involved
and that, therefore, divergent practice should not affect church fellowship."[39]

III

At issue every time was the hermeneutical question. What did the churches
think of the biblical admonitions that women should be silent in church because
women are to be submissive to men? From the first, the churches had agreed
that Scripture was not clear on the issue. By the Dubuque meeting the controversy was focused on the idea of "headship." Many of the respondents to a
questionnaire filled out after the Dubuque consultation agreed that "headship"

needed further study. No one, said Reumann, Chairman of the Dubuque consultation, had "argued against the ordination of women on the grounds that Jesus was male or that women are ontologically incapable of receiving the grace or charismata of God."[40] On the other hand, the argument from the "orders of creation" says much the same thing: by their very creation women are subordinate, and by their very nature not able to do the things a pastor is called to do.

When women began writing in the church press arguing for the ordination of women, they spoke almost exclusively of the biblical materials and theology that woman was not equal to man, perhaps because those were the arguments they always had to answer. Constance Parvey, one of the first women to be ordained in the LCA, dealt with the difficult scriptural texts and the history of the church's patriarchy, though she made little reference to the Confessions when she argued for the ordination of women.[41]

LaVonne Althouse had made a similar argument previously.[42] She said, as many others after her would, "We need, above all, to be willing to give up preconceptions of what is 'feminine' and what is 'masculine' so that God can give us to each other again in Christ."[43] Both of these women and many of their sisters chose to argue for the ordination of women because of their changing place in society, and the changing view of women in the society. The strategy was a common and understandable one, but it attacked deep-seated understandings of what it meant to be male and female. More and more the argument turned on what a woman was, rather than on what the pastor did.

IV

In 1969, at its Minneapolis Triennial Convention, the American Lutheran Church Women (ALCW) voted "to call a study conference or some other effective method of studying the role of women in the church with special emphasis on legislative participation and on ordination."[44] That work bore fruit. When it came time for the ALC to appoint a committee to study the ordination of women in order to make a recommendation of the Church Council, Frederick Schiotz, after a conversation with the ALCW Board, saw his way to appoint two women to the committee with three men.[45] He shrewdly appointed Margaret Wold, a leader from the ELC tradition, and Evelyn Streng, a strong representative of the old ALC. Their leadership proved crucial to the passing of the resolution approving women's ordination.

When the Executive Committee of LCUSA received the report of the Standing Committee and referred it to the Annual Meeting of LCUSA which was held in February of 1970, it asked the DTS to pursue more questions about ministry, that is, the universal priesthood of believers, the meaning of ordination, and the ordination of women—from the scriptural questions of headship and sexuality to cultural and anthropological questions.

All three presidents of the major Lutheran churches were present at the February 3, 1970, LCUSA meeting where the reports were disclosed and, in what Reumann describes as a "charismatic moment, . . . [everyone] seemed totally inclined to vote approval, but it had been decided to request only transmission of the DTS report to member churches for 'study and consideration.' "[46]

The studies were then "redacted" into a report that was made available to all the pastors and congregations of their respective churches. That study document—written by Raymond Tiemeyer—was ready for distribution in May 1970. Both Robert Marshall and Schiotz, presidents of the LCA and the ALC, sent the booklet to all the clergy of their respective churches. Dr. Preus, on examining the booklet, protested its cavalier treatment of the biblical texts. Though he did send the document "The Ordination of Women" to all Missouri clergymen, he included a letter saying he was dismayed that the "document handled the Biblical material rather flippantly."[47] Aside from his obvious disagreement with the historical-critical method used by the committee, his primary objection is to the tone of the report.[48] The booklet dealt mostly with what Scripture said, devoting three chapters to the biblical questions. One chapter surveyed women in Lutheran history and tradition, another the pragmatic consequences of ordaining women. There was very little in it about the doctrine of the ministry in the Lutheran Confessions.

About the same time, an ALC congregation voted unanimously to call a woman graduate of Luther Theological Seminary, but had not issued the call since the ALC Church Council would not authorize the ordination until the study process was completed.

V

As the conventions of the two church bodies neared, the two magazines of the churches began to carry more stories on the question, though it was not hotly disputed in the Letters to the Editor columns. *The Lutheran Standard* carried an article quoting Fred Meuser, Executive Secretary of the DTS, who, on noting that the various churches held divergent views on the issue, emphasized that "there was unanimous agreement among participants in the study that adoption of the practice or ordaining women by one or more of the several Lutheran bodies ought not to be divisive of church fellowship."[49] The article pointed to the study's conclusions about the inconclusive nature of the biblical materials and then announced that "three women graduated from Luther Seminary, St. Paul, and one or more may seek ordination."[50]

Another report in *The Lutheran Standard* two weeks later indicates once again Meuser's fear that the decision would hurt relations between Lutherans: "This does not mean that all Lutherans should be carbon copies of each other."[51]

About this time the LCW of the LCA adopted a position paper calling upon it to allow the ordination of women and "to implement these changes creatively and vigorously."[52] The LCW vigorously supported women's ordination and the development of materials that would be persuasive to the church. The most substantial work done by either church was Ermarth's *Adam's Fractured Rib,* a product of her study for the Subcommittee on the Role of Women in the Life of the Church. A compilation of the thinking about women in the church and society at the time, it quickly reviewed the role of women in the various church traditions—from Roman Catholic, Orthodox, Anglican, Baptist, Methodist, UCC, Church of the Brethren, and so on, and the various Lutheran traditions in Europe and America, concluding with four arguments against ordaining women:

1. Christ chose only men to be apostles;
2. God and Christ are masculine and thus a priest must be;
3. women by nature are unable to receive the indelible character conferred by ordination;
4. God has ordained for all time the subordination of women.[53]

Up until this time, though there were hints of it in the language of those who had worried about the ecumenical movement and the ordination of women, none of the statements for or against ordaining Lutheran women had used any of the first three reasons, though they had been mentioned and dismissed in Reumann's first paper.[54] Only the fourth reason, that women were created to be subordinate to men, was causing much difficulty for those promoting the ordination of women in the Lutheran churches. Ermarth concluded with an argument against "headship," which she refuted from sociological and psychological sources. The book relies, to some extent, on materials drawn from contemporary feminists for its support. It is surprising, for example, to see secular feminists quoted with such authority in such a book. The theological statements by the churches had repeatedly made clear that the ordination of women was not being done to extend rights to women, but rather on the basis of doctrine.

The April issue of *Scope,* the popular magazine of the ALCW, published three articles arguing for, against, and maybe on the issues of women's ordination. Dawn Proux argued yes on the basis of a call she had received from a congregation, that she should be ordained. Professor Herman Preus said no, contending against them on the basis of subordination and headship. Storaasli, who had participated in the study by writing a paper for the ALC Church Council, asked "Why Not?" Though he admitted to deeply felt objections at the thought of a woman in the pulpit, he could not find any theological strictures against them in the tradition. He reminded his readers of the theological content of the argument when he wrote "the human minister is commissioned by God to be the instrumental agent through whom he acts."[55] For Storaasli, as for Harrisville, the theological arguments overrode his cultural predilections not to ordain women.

On June 9, 1970, *The Lutheran Standard* printed a feature article by Wold on the ordination of women, which would be voted on at the upcoming biennial convention of the ALC. Wold was one of the best known women in the ALC and would soon become the ALCW Executive Secretary. Her article considered the place most women of the church were in: some against change, some for, some perplexed. She spoke for the typical ALC woman's "mixed feelings" about women's rights and feminism and her own struggle to be accepted. A Bible student herself, she handled those materials by focusing on the Galatians texts about equality and left it at that, glossing over the negative statements by referring briefly to previous studies, especially Stendahl's, which had determined that the scriptural witnesses were mixed. She concluded her article with a plea for conversation and discussion.[56]

In preparation for the conventions of both synods, each church paper published a preview of what issues were to be considered. Neither gave much play to the resolutions to ordain women, though *The Lutheran Standard* gave a few more details about the resolution's progress through the ALC Church Council where it had passed by a 75 percent margin.[57]

VI

It was for the LCA and its committee to write a more substantial piece of theology on the ministry and the ordination of women. Presented to the 1970 convention by a committee chaired by Steimle, and ably assisted by other theologians of note—Sidney Ahlstrom, H. George Anderson, and Martin Heinecken—the "Report of the Commission on the Comprehensive Doctrine of the Ministry" developed a confessionally sound way to speak of the doctrine of the ministry and thus the ordination of women.

The document divided the ordained ministry into two dimensions: the representative, and official or public.[58] The committee was careful to explain that it had chosen the word "representative" to guard "against the false notion that it is the clergy who constitute the Church," though they took pains to make it clear that they were not defining "representative" to mean one who "resembled" Christ.[59]

Appended to the Recommendations of the Commission was a position paper by the subcommittee on "The Role of Women in the Life of the Church." It found that there was nothing in the exercise of the " 'ordained ministry' as a functional office (the office of Word and Sacraments, that is, the official representative ministry—see the Preface to the Report of Commission) which would exclude a woman because of her sex."[60]

The subcommittee's document, drawn largely from Ermarth's book, then went on to discuss the history of women's work in the church, the sweeping revolution of women's liberation, the work of professional women in the church, the church's view of women's liberation, a short section on the ecumenical rediscovery of *diakonia*, concluding with a statement on the "problem of Ordination."[61] Secular feminism had clearly informed much of the work of the subcommittee.[62] There was only passing reference to the difficult passages of Scripture which so consumed the ALC and the LC-MS.

On June 29, 1970, about 10 P.M., the LCA in convention in Minneapolis, voted to change "man" in the bylaw that defined a minister of the church to "person." It passed by voice vote, though one woman asked that her negative vote be recorded. With that the first decision was made to ordain Lutheran women in the United States. There had been some attempts on the part of several delegates to defer the vote until two more years of study could be done, but after only one half-hour of debate the convention voted to ordain women. Dr. Anderson, who had led the presentation of the report, later said that advocates of the proposal were "dazzled" by the speed with which the convention acted.[63]

VII

In October when the ALC convention met, everyone was well aware of the action already taken by the LCA. Schiotz in his last speech as President of the ALC told the convention that since the committee that had been asked to prepare a resolution supporting the ordination of women had concluded that Scripture could neither "be used for support or denial of ordination for women," the decision fell into the category of those that "must be made on the basis of sanctified common sense."[64] The study committee of Bruno Schlachtenhaufen, Nelson, Streng, Johann Thorson, and Wold had prepared a resolution recommending the ordination of women, concurring with the "Statement of Findings" and referring back to a 1964 statement by the ALC on ministry:

> Since the ministerial office is not precisely defined in the New Testament, and since the duties of early officers were varied and interchangeable, and since the needs of the church down through the centuries are subject to variation, we are led to Luther's conclusion, namely, that God has left the details of the ministerial office to the discretion of the church, to be developed according to its needs and according to the leading of the Holy Spirit.[65]

Nothing was made of current feminist scholarship. Wold had been careful to avoid using such language in her article and her reluctance to be party to the radical feminism of the day kept the issue clean. After a brief debate, the resolution passed the October 1970 Biennial Convention of the ALC in San Antonio, 560 to 414 with one abstention. The victory was a narrow one and the decision would come up for further conversations in 1971 when the convention of the LC-MS adopted a resolution deferring enactment of "fellowship" until the ALC had responded to some concerns that Missouri had about the ALC, in particular its 1970 action to permit the ordination of women. In response to Missouri's request that ALC "reconsider" its action, Kent Knutson, General

President of the ALC, asked the three ALC theological faculties to respond to two questions:

1. Do you find that the Scriptures forbid the ordination or service of women in the ministry of Word and Sacrament?
2. Do you find in the Scriptures, orders of creation which enunciate a principle of women being subordinate to men which then pertains directly to the role women should serve in the ministry?[66]

Each of the seminaries prepared statements that concluded with a resounding no to both questions. The nature of the query forced them to deal directly with the Scripture and a vexing theological topic: the orders of creation. Joseph Burgess, pastor in Regent, North Dakota, was asked to prepare a paper entitled, "What Do the Scriptures Say about the Ministry of Women in the Church?" It began with the direct statement, "Ministry is servanthood."[67] Countering the argument of those promulgating "headship," the paper is a careful exegesis of the difficult verses in Scripture with a final appeal to the freedom of the gospel. The Evangelical Lutheran Theological Seminary in Columbus responded with a lengthy piece on the biblical material, but with a specific attack on the idea of the "orders of creation." Saying that the very term originated with nineteenth-century neo-Lutheranism in Europe, they did a thorough job of discrediting it as an idea that could deny women their calling to be pastors. Wartburg responded similarly, as did Luther. Duane Priebe of the Wartburg faculty prepared a detailed and complete analysis of the idea of *kephale* or headship in the Bible. Focusing on the nature of authority, he found that the authority in the Bible "lies in weakness . . . and resides wholly in the Gospel."[68]

VIII

Scripture is the source from which these Lutherans argued. Finally, perhaps ironically, it was Scripture they argued about. The original "Statement of Findings" had seen quite clearly into the future of Lutheran debates on the issue when it noted that one of the most vexing difficulties was "a hermeneutical question which lies not fully resolved among Lutherans on how one interprets and applies scripture."[69]

When the question came up again in 1971 the ALC, while clear on what the confessional answer would be, was forced to argue about what the Bible said about ordaining women, especially with older battles about inerrancy still fresh in the minds of the Luther Theological Seminary faculty in particular. The scriptural question was the question animating their discussion and work, so it is not surprising that the Luther faculty's answer to Missouri began with a very strong statement on the Bible:

We regard the entire Bible as the Word of God to be taken seriously as authority in all matters of faith and life. Yet there is no sentence or section which can be properly understood apart from its setting in a particular historical context. On

174

the other hand, there is no sentence or section which can be ignored or disregarded
as being no longer relevant. The task of biblical interpretation is to ask of the
entire Scripture the question of contemporary meaning in the light of historical
meaning.[70]

The question had been a hermeneutical question; now it was an ecumenical
one. The ALC's ecumenical committee was now the convener of the debate, as
both Fry and the Luther Theological Seminary faculty had foreseen.

In the end, the work of the seminary faculties made little difference. *The
Lutheran Standard* watched Missouri's 1971 convention with dismay and ALC
President Knutson wrote a concise and measured letter to the ALC after Missouri
voted to both continue fellowship with ALC but defer implementation of it until
ALC stopped ordaining women. Succinctly stating his position on the issue, he
concluded,

> one does not need to agree with the ordination of women in order to accept the
> position that the matter lies in the realm of administration in the church and this
> is a matter which should not in and of itself disrupt fellowship.[71]

The seminaries and study committees had provided a rich fare of biblical and
theological work helpful to anyone studying this question. They had warned of
the various difficulties that would come from it, saying the ecumenical difficulty
would be the most vexing. Their warnings were prophetic.

CONCLUSIONS

As the record shows, when the question of women's ordination was posed in
the 1960s, it seemed like an idea whose time had come, an inevitable consequence
of social progress. The Finnish pastors who had challenged Jordheim said as
much when they accused the ALC of being decades behind the times. Women
as well as men could proclaim the Word and God's justifying act in Jesus Christ.
To say this was to rely wholly on the Augsburg Confession for an answer to the
question.

When Lutherans in this country began to ask the question seriously, they
looked first to the Confessions, where they found no objection. They agreed,
however, that Scripture was mixed. So not surprisingly their work focused largely
on Scripture, even as the times were transforming the way men and women
thought about their social roles. Both the women's movement and the ecumenical
movement seemed part of a new consciousness that shunned old barriers and
conventions.

Some, such as Fry and Hefner, had inklings that the two movements were
on a collision course. When the Luther Theological Seminary's faculty issued
its statement, they were aware of the choice they were making and preferred
what they saw as the gospel truth to church unity.

Their predictions have come true. The ordination of women is now the cause
of disunity among Christians. Since the consecration of Barbara Harris, a black

woman, as a bishop in the Episcopalian church, some Anglicans have announced they are in "impaired communion" with the churches that ordain women. The Pope has written the Archbishop of Canterbury to voice his opposition to the ordination of women. Observers have said that Christian unity has been set back by decades if not centuries. Those in the ecumenical arena who are striving for "full communion," which implies the mutual recognition of ministries, have been stymied by this move.

One fact stands out in all of this discussion about women's ordination among Lutherans: Both ALC and LCA, when they came to the actual wording of their official documents urging the ordination of women, reached back into traditional Lutheran language about the ministry. As the LCA resolution had it: "There is nothing in the exercise of the 'ordained ministry' as a *functional*[72] office (the office of Word and Sacrament, that is, the official representative ministry) . . . which would exclude a woman because of her sex."[73] Theologians of the LCA considering the ordination of women from the point of view of function could change their minds about ordaining women, even if they were reluctant to do so.

On the other hand, it is important to recall the LCA document that recommended both a study of episcopacy and the ordination of women. Though episcopacy was largely ignored by the 1970 document, the ordination of women was not. However, since that time the feminist coalition in the LCA, and now the ELCA, has come under constant attack by those most interested in the ecumenical movement, particularly in ecumenical relations with Rome. In fact, the articles stressing the importance of Lutherans adopting episcopacy seem to regard it as the only way to stem the tide of what they think of as the feminist Protestantism now corrupting the ELCA. Is the ordination of women a small thing to give up for the sake of unity, as some are reported to have said, or is it something more than that now?[74] A leader of that group, Richard John Neuhaus, has hinted in his *Forum Newsletter* that women's ordination was decided too hastily and, though probably not rescindable, it posed an ecumenical problem since the remaining work between Catholics and Lutherans is centered on the mutual recognition of ministries. But he does suggest that if there is evidence in the gospel that women cannot be pastors, the ELCA should stop ordaining them.[75] The contradictions of the mid-sixties have hatched and are coming home to roost.

NOTES

1. John Reumann, *Ministries Examined: Laity, Clergy, Women and Bishops in a Time of Change* (Minneapolis: Augsburg Publishing House, 1987), 121.

2. Peter Brunner, "The Ministry and the Ministry of Women," *Lutheran World* 6 (1959): 248.

3. The study booklet by Tiemeyer claimed that in 1969, 109 out of 4,258 students enrolled in Lutheran seminaries were women. Only 17 were enrolled in B.D. programs,

7 at ALC seminaries, and 10 at LCA seminaries. None were enrolled in B.D. programs in Missouri seminaries. Tiemeyer, p. 45.

4. At the Hauge Synod's annual meeting at Our Savior's Lutheran Church in Lyon County, Iowa, October 9–11, 1894, there was considerable discussion about whether or not the deaconess home could train women candidates for mission with the United Church faculty that had just formed in Minneapolis. At that same meeting where the China Mission of the Hauge Synod also met, they decided to call Marietta Fugleskjel to be a missionary, asking her to take some classes at a theological seminary so that when she was finished she could be sent to the mission in China. *Kinamissionaeren* (November 1, 1894), 334. *Budbaeren* (December 8, 1894), 774. The next spring Daniel Nelson remarked in a letter to the *Kinamissionaeren* ([July 15, 1895], 223) that two women missionaries, Marie Christenson and I. Skaar, had both studied at the United seminary in Minneapolis.

5. Anne Jordheim, *The Lutheran Standard* 4 (30 June 1964): 14.

6. Ibid.

7. Ibid., 15.

8. "My Question Is . . .," *The Lutheran* 4 (29 July 1964): 46.

9. ALC, *1964 Reports and Actions*, 140.

10. *The Lutheran* 4 (11 May 1966): 29.

11. Ibid., 29.

12. Members of the commission included Charles Cooper (President of PLTS), Carl Braaten, Rodney O. Davis, Curtis Derrick, Walter H. P. Freitag, Herbert N. Gibney, Philip Hefner, Walter Kukkonen, H. Karl Ladwig, George Lindbeck, Jerome W. Nilssen, John Rilling, Jose David Rodriguez, Herbert W. Stroup, Wilson E. Touhsaent.

13. Editorial Comment, *The Lutheran Quarterly* 18 (1966): 99–100.

14. Ibid., 100.

15. "The Ministry of Women," *The Lutheran Quarterly* 18 (1966): 102.

16. Ibid. In a letter dated March 4, 1970, Hefner wrote to Margaret Sittler Ermarth to clarify the intent of his letter, saying that he was not, as some had made him out to be, against the ordination of women. See Margaret S. Ermarth *Adam's Fractured Rib* (Philadelphia: Fortress Press, 1970), 119.

17. *The Lutheran* 4 (20 July 1966): 25.

18. Ibid.

19. Ibid.

20. Ibid.

21. Ibid., 26.

22. Edmund A. Steimle, Chairman of the Commission on the Comprehensive Study of the Doctrine of the Ministry of the Lutheran Church in America, in the foreword to Ermarth's *Adam's Fractured Rib*. The new commission included Sydney Ahlstrom, H. George Anderson, Arnold E. Carlson, Margaret S. Ermarth, Marianka Fousek, Victor Gold, Jacob Heikkinen, Martin Heinecken, Albert H. Keck, Richard W. Lundin, Floyd Martinson, Sister Anna Melville, Ralph E. Peterson, Alfred H. Stone.

23. *1968 Minutes*, 755-56.

24. Reumann, *Ministries Examined*, 122. It would be more correct to say that Kantonen made this clear to the delegates. There is little evidence of a push to ordain women at this time. The report at the 1968 convention was of the nature of a progress report. The minutes report (756) that Dr. Steimle commented further that only an interim report was presented because there had been insufficient time to adequately prepare a final and definitive statement.

25. It had requested that the DTS study the question and had commissioned papers from William Larsen and later Olaf Storaasli of the Luther Theological Seminary on the issue.

26. *1970 Reports and Actions*, 327.

27. Members of the Subcommittee on the Study of Ordination of Women by the LCUSA were John Reumann, Chairman; Robert W. Bertram of Concordia Seminary; Stephen G. Mazak of Cudahy, Wisconsin; Fred Meuser of what is now Trinity Lutheran Seminary; and Paul D. Opsahl, the staff person from the Council. Their topics were, respectively, "What in the Scripture Speaks on the Ordination of Women?" "What Theological Reasons Are Being Given Pro and Con in the Ordination of Women?" "What in the Lutheran Confessions Speaks on the Ordination of Women?" "The Lutheran Tradition (Outside of the confessional writings) and the Ordination of Women?" "The Ordination of Women in the *Oikumene?*" Ronald Johnstone, a consultant, presented a paper on "Sociological Factors in the Ordination of Women," and Harold Haas (Concordia, Ft. Wayne) considered the "Psychological Factors in the Ordination of Women to the Pastoral Ministry."

28. ELCA Archives, *Protocol Document of LCUSA Minutes* (1970), Exhibit K, Exhibit A, 37.

29. "A Statement of Findings Relating to the Requested Study on the Subject of the Ordination of Women," in *The Ordination of Women*, ed. Raymond Tiemeyer (Minneapolis: Augsburg Publishing House, 1970), 52.

30. "Findings of March 1969," *Minutes of LCUSA* (February 1970), Exhibit G, p. 8.

31. Bertram, "What Theological Reasons are Being Given Pro and Con on The Ordination of Women?" *Protocol Copy of 1970 LCUSA Minutes*, Exhibit K, Exhibit A, p. 37.

32. *Denver Proceedings* (1969), Res. 2–17, p. 88.

33. Reumann contends that Professor Scharlemann's letter to President J. A. O. Preus of April 9, 1970, which is thought to be the precipitator of the investigation of Concordia Seminary specifically mentions the "orders of creation." Cf. *Exodus from Concordia: A Report on the 1974 Walkout* (St. Louis: Concordia Seminary Board of Control, 1977), 152.

34. The participants in this consultation were members of the subcommittee named above and the following: ALC, Roy Harrisville, William Larsen, Stanley D. Schneider; LCA, Margaret Ermarth, Martin J. Heinecken, Ralph Peterson; LC-MS, Fred Kramer, Martin H. Scharlemann, Edward H. Schroeder; Synod of Evangelical Lutheran Churches, Kenneth Ballas.

35. LNTS student paper, *The Concord* 7 (5 May 1978): 12.

36. *Report of the Division of Theological Studies*, LCUSA (February 3–4, 1970), Exhibit G, p. 8.

37. Reumann, *Ministries Examined*, 122.

38. Ibid., 1.

39. *Report of DTS*, Exhibit G, p. 9.

40. *Protocol Document*, Exhibit K, Exhibit A, p. 81.

41. "Ordain Her, Ordain Her Not . . . ?" *dialog* 9 (Summer 1969): 203-8.

42. "Ordain Women?" *American Lutheran* 49 (October 1966): 10–12, 21–22.

43. Ibid., 22.

44. *The Lutheran Standard* 10 (9 June 1970): 4.

45. DeAne Lagerquist, *From Our Mothers' Arms* (Minneapolis: Augsburg Publishing House, 1987), 153.

46. Reumann, *Ministries Examined*, 122.

47. James Pragman, *Traditions of Ministry* (St. Louis: Concordia Publishing House, 1983), 203 n. 36.

48. The beginning of the first chapter does seem flippant: "Woman was made only as an afterthought, and second-hand at that. She didn't even rate fresh dust—just a rib. Any man can spare a rib" (9). Those opposing the ordination of women would know from the first word that this study was out to persuade them to change their minds.

49. "Ordain Women? Yes and No, Study Finds," *The Lutheran Standard* 10 (17 February 1970): 22.

50. Ibid.

51. *The Lutheran Standard* 10 (3 March 1970): 20.

52. *The Lutheran Standard* 10 (14 April 1970): 20.

53. Ermarth, *Adam's Fractured Rib*, 124.

54. *Protocol Document*, Exhibit K, Exhibit A, pp. 10–114.

55. Storaasli, "Why Not?" *Scope* 10 (April 1970): 13.

56. *The Lutheran Standard* 10 (9 June 1970): 6.

57. *The Lutheran Standard* 10 (21 July 1970): 22.

58. *1970 Minutes*, 429-30.

59. Ibid., 429.

60. Ibid., 443.

61. Ibid., 450.

62. Ibid., 444 n. 2.

63. *The Lutheran* 8 (5 August 1970): 7.

64. "President's Report," *1970 Reports and Actions*, 141.

65. *1964 Reports and Actions*, 140.

66. Report of the Inter-Church Relations Committee of the ALC, *1972 Reports and Actions*, 460.

67. Ibid., 465.

68. Duane Priebe, Inter-Church Relations Committee's Report, *1972 Reports and Actions*, Exhibit C, p. 472.

69. Tiemeyer, *Ordination of Women*, 53.

70. "Statement by Luther Theological Seminary Faculty on the Ordination of Women," Inter-Church Relations Committee Report, *1972 Reports and Actions*, Exhibit E, 482. Two other ALC seminaries issued statements as well.

71. *Lutheran Standard* 11 (7 September 1971): 19.

72. Italics mine.

73. See note 58.

74. See *Exploring the Faith We Share: A Discussion Guide for Lutherans and Roman Catholics*, eds. Glenn C. Stone and Charles LaFontaine, S.A. (Paramus, N.J.: Paulist Press, 1980), 83. There is a section in the book on the theology of headship as a reason for not ordaining women, that is, the biblical reason; and then the statement that "there is also a small but well-spoken group of Lutherans who oppose women's ordination for a quite different reason. These Lutherans have a passion for eventually reuniting Western Christianity. For them, women's ordination poses still another obstacle for Lutheran-Roman Catholic dialogue."

75. *Forum Newsletter*, 17 (18 October 1988): 5.

12

ROLAND D. MARTINSON

Conversations with pastors whether in rural, urban, or suburban United States consistently reveal two common experiences of ordained ministry: overwhelming demands and ever-increasing expectations. Congregational task forces, councils, and committees; ministerial task forces and committees; judicatory assemblies, task forces, and committees; regional and churchwide responsibilities—all in their varying rhythms require more nights than some weeks and months provide.

OVERWHELMING DEMANDS

Those in the hospital need visits, as do those who are shut-in, dying, and bereaved. The chemically dependent, sexually abused, newly divorced, sexually addicted, physically abused, and depressed create constant flows of crises requiring immediate attention. Dysfunctional families, troubled marriages, and neurotic individuals create havoc in their own lives and that of the congregation. New members need care; so do the parents whose child is to be baptized. Those who are engaged require premarital preparation. Young parents need support; so do parents of teenagers, the handicapped, and mentally ill. Marriages need enriching; sorrow requires consolation; singles and seniors deserve attention. So do the unemployed, the middle-aged, newly married, and the childless. Soon, with evenings already committed to meetings, the days grow too short and double-scheduled nights far too long.

And then there is preaching! There are at least forty-eight Sunday sermons for most pastors. Then come Advent and Lenten services and Holy Week. Sermons must also be preached at confirmations, nursing homes, judicatory events, weddings, and funerals. Usually a pastor preaches seventy-five to ninety times a year to nearly the same hearers. Pastors are also expected to teach. At the least, they are usually responsible for confirmation, a Bible study, and the women's group leaders. In addition, any strong parish must have adult forums, new members' classes, parenting classes, baptism classes, first-communion class, evangelism and social ministry training as well as leadership, spirituality, and intergenerational retreats.

Congregational and judicatory reports require record-keeping, compiling, and framing. Budgets mean data-gathering, assembling, presenting, and balancing. There are conflicts between the trustees and the Christian education committees. Anonymous letters come from those who do not like the preaching or those who say the hymns are too hard to sing or the carpets the wrong color. Who is going to attend to long-range planning? The new church council members need orientation. How is all this to be accomplished with too few people and not enough money? Through leadership? There is more needed than a whole team could provide.

The litany could go on still. This beginning recitation simply points to the pressures upon pastors to produce. With the pressures come stress. A never-ending stream of demands eats away at the time for preparation, creating mediocrity and ineffectiveness. Renewed efforts and fresh resolve are difficult to marshall in the face of the resulting loss of worth and confidence. The pain and confusion gnaw at the pastor's spirit, cutting the congregation off from their clergy person's creativity and untapped gifts. Too often the heavy load destroys the pastor's being and personal relationships. Overwhelming demands and ever-increasing expectations constantly undermine ordained ministry. It is not a pretty picture, yet more often than not it is the real one in most pastors' weeks, years, or decades of ministry.

LOST IDENTITY

Most American clergy have arrived at this present state of affairs because they have consistently attended to a critical task—and with the best of intentions. Each generation of clergy is faced with the challenge of reenvisioning the work of ordained ministry in new and radically different contexts. A pastor by definition is one who thinks theologically about the flow of human relationships, events, and institutions so as to discern how best to minister the gospel. As with the Jesuits and missionary work, Martin Luther and the printing press, Methodist preachers and circuit riding, the propagation of the faith has often been in direct relation to the church's creative adaptation to culture. In so doing there is always great risk; risk that the authority and heart of ministry will give way to that which is tangential. At its best this distortion results in ineffective ministry; as its worst it compromises the gospel.

The reenvisioning of ordained ministry in the last two generations has diffused, conflicted, and distorted the office. As a result, many pastors have lost their identity. For Lutherans in the United States the primary language, symbols, and images describing the work of ordained ministry have come from the agrarian age. Pastors were the keepers of a religious world. Parishioners lived *coram deo*. Their critical question was "How do I find a gracious God?"

Agrarian, biblical terms described pastoral work. Pastors were shepherds feeding, guiding, and rescuing their flocks. They were to be among their people compassionately visiting and teaching. Pastors were priests representing God to the faithful and the faithful to God. As priests, pastors were set apart to handle holy transactions of guilt and grace. God needed spokespersons, so pastors set themselves over against the people as prophets confronting God's erring ones. Pastors prayed, studied, and preached. They were to lead a righteous life. God's authority was their authority. The new Israel, God's chosen people, the church, needed leadership so pastors were set above as kings expected to inspire, direct, and rule.

All of these agrarian, biblical descriptions came together in a single, unifying image: man of God. The rhythms of the pastor's life were those of nature. Parsonages or vicarages had "studies" where men prayed and prepared to preach and teach. Pastoral visiting related to life's passages and to accidents, illness, and death. They were men because women were not allowed ordination.

The first half of the twentieth century created a new world in which to minister. With the industrial revolution came new challenges and the need to envision new possibilities for ministry. Pastoral ministry brought new language, symbols, and images drawn from the city, corporate business, and industry. Pastors became the keepers of a religious department in a secular world. The religious question became: "How do I fit God into my world?" A radical shift in consciousness placed humans at the center of their own world. Humankind lived primarily *coram hominibus,* not *coram deo.* Yet this was, ironically, the age of great pulpits. Pastors were to be inspiring speakers with the pizzazz of Dale Carnegie selling God to humans, relating the sacred to the secular. Big churches were held in high regard, locally and nationally. Pastors became administrators concerned with organization, long-range planning, departments, and staffs. As religious specialists, pastors were to be educators, teaching religious values for at least the private sphere of existence. Developmentalism and religious education modeled in the church what learning specialists were doing in the schools.

Whatever else pastors did society expected them to inspire, to encourage, to provide from the spiritual dimension of life the strength and motivation to succeed in the larger societal sphere—the one that really mattered. Piety was tapped for what it could provide for the human enterprise. In these times the Rotary and Lions clubs had "sky pilots." The common, unifying image of ordained ministry was "pastoral director," described in H. Richard Niebuhr's work, *The Purpose of the Church and Its Ministry.*[1] There were fewer "studies" in parsonages; now most church buildings had education and administrative wings where pastors had "offices" and kept the hours and worked the rhythms of industrial America. For most pastors the transition from the images, expectations, and rhythms of an agrarian age was neither smooth nor ever complete, loading them with both layers of expectations, creating fatigue, confusion, and conflict.

The 1960s and 1970s brought the post-industrial age. The lure and promise of urban and industrial America were tarnished by urban blight, ghettoes, the decay of the rust belt, and the Vietnam War. Many clergy became protesters; most were seekers of God in a secular world. The critical new religious question was no longer: "How do I find a gracious God?" or "How do I fit God into a secular world?" but "How do I live in a world where there is no God?" People did not live *coram deo;* even life *coram hominibus* had become life in a world without God or in which God was hidden.

Now the imagery used to describe ordained ministry was drawn from psychology, sociology, and political science. Some pastors became people specialists, others focused on institutions. The people specialists listened, enabled, reconciled, and healed. Theirs was a ministry of presence. Caring ministries proliferated. Many pastors wrote books on small groups. Pastors called themselves counselors, crisis managers, chaplains, and community builders. Above all else these pastors were to be people persons. They read Seward Hiltner and Wayne Oates. Carl Rogers shaped their work as much as Karl Barth. They constructed round church buildings, put couches in their offices, and "saw" people for fifty minutes to an hour. Clinical pastoral education became a sine qua non.

The institutional specialists borrowed their tactics from macrosociology and political science. They were activists creating crises. The Berrigans and Martin Luther King were their heroes. They read Max Weber and Saul Alinski. These pastors were agents of change. Their pulpit was the barricade; their arena, the street. Inclusivity and raised-consciousness became tests of authenticity if not of "orthodoxy." A common, if not unifying, image of pastoral ministry emerged from these chaotic times. Whatever else a pastor was, she (for now there were women in growing numbers) or he was to be an enabler.

The changes created through reenvisioning ordained ministry in post-industrial America washed over the churches and their pastors who were already struggling with reconciling the images of agrarian and industrial eras. Most pastors now lived with three layers of expectations; their lives were driven by theories and constituencies with not only expanding and diverse but often disparate expectations. Fast-paced change and its courageous reenvisioning of ministry, without adequate integration, created more fatigue, confusion, and conflict for clergy.

The late seventies and eighties brought with them the global village and international economics. In this era pastors envisioned themselves either as survivors or as maximizers of options in a shrinking world. Many of their parishioners and others outside the church were now asking the religious question: "How do I live in a world destroying its future?" Most were asking: "How am I to be a 'have' in a world of 'haves' and 'have nots'?"

The language used to describe ordained ministry in this age is pluralistic, drawn from micro and macro systems, particularly those of communication, information, and economics. Pastors are to be visionaries expanding the consciousness of their people and opening their horizons to scenarios of the future. They are to be entrepreneurs able to marshall and manage the dynamics and resources necessary to bring a congregation's, a judicatory's, or a denomination's goals to fruition. As such they must be assertive, taking risks to move with that which captures the imagination of the constantly barraged consciousness of a culture expecting to be entertained. Pastors must be experts, in theology, of course, but more so in management by objective, team building, organizational development, computers, fund raising, leadership training, and desktop publishing. In a world of instant and mass communication pastors need to project a strong, positive image so that symbol-bearing, whether in worship as presider or on a task force as convener, becomes a studied art. As symbol-bearer one combines the proper mix of the hospitable, personal touch with the appropriate distance associated with authority and larger purpose. In order to fit all this into the days and years of ministry pastors must become proficient managers. Time is to be managed to the minute; stress so that it remains creative; people for maximum participation within minimum time frames; and within all the rest one must manage one's own career.

The rhythms of ministry are driven now by international economics which creates an ethos of materialism, individualism, and adversarialism that determine life expectations, pace, and economic fortunes in the city and on the farm alike. Pastors now have sophisticated tape players in their automobiles and complicated computer programs to keep them updated in intense, condensed bites as they rush from one appointment to the next. The overarching image of ordained ministry becomes one of a leader, the strong, decisive one who is out front aggressively taking her or his church through rough transitions into the future.

All the new images of ordained ministry driven by this era become a fourth layer of expectations. Pastors must be people of God; pastoral directors; enablers; as well as leaders with all the accompanying fragmentation. In the cacophony, both ministry and life become diffused, conflicted, and distorted. The ordained minister wonders, agonizes: Who am I? Am I everything? Am I anyone of significance? Am I anything others aren't? Do I have a place, a role in the scheme of history? Do I have any power and if so to do what?

APPEALS TO ARTIFICIAL AUTHORITIES

Pastors' cries for clear identities and the need for infusions of power have not gone unheeded. Their tension, their malaise, their pain have driven significant efforts to provide answers and resources. Research abounds. Institutes proliferate day by day. Convocations and task forces consider the profound multiplicity of ministry. Training programs in new ministries clamor for attendance. Associations bring together those of common ministerial expertise. Scholars shape their proposals. The avalanche of proposals and efforts provides much that is enlightening, clarifying the issues and moving the ministry of the gospel forward in diverse and pluralistic worlds. However, the rush of these proposals, their volume, their ready availability, their attractiveness have led the church to many solutions that exchange the gospel for false authorities with their accompanying secular and religious power. These appeals to artificial authorities each highlight significant issues and critical elements in gospel ministry, but result in making that which is a means into an end. Five of these artificial authorities are particularly evident: sacerdotalism, biblicism, professionalism, institutionalism, and subjectivism.

Sacerdotalism gives power to pastors through beliefs and rituals that emphasize the pastor's essential role as transactor between God and humankind. Clergy are to become keepers of the true symbols and rituals which mediate between the divine and the human. The rituals of times past and selected types of music are established as the proper expressions of the sacred. Clergy strive for expertise in the history, dress, paraments, and aesthetics that make liturgies authentic. Clergy are essentially different than other human beings. Through rituals handed down from the past clergy receive the exclusive permission, power, and character for handling the divine mysteries. In order to placard their role they are to dress differently both in society and in the worship services where they mediate between God and humankind. Pastoral identity is clear. Pastoral power is neatly defined. Pastors are clerics dispensing divine mysteries through sacred liturgies.

Of course, many of the concerns of sacerdotalism are vitally important to the ministry of the gospel. Leading worship faithfully and effectively is critical to assuring that the gospel is preached in its purity and the sacraments are rightly administered. Services poorly conceived and executed can turn worship into a museum piece or a charade or mere entertainment. But even at its best, worship and those who preside or assist or protect its history are not the gospel. Like anyone or anything else they have their value and power only as they point to the gospel and the God of life and mercies who comes to humankind. At its worst sacerdotalism turns the gospel into an exercise in aesthetics or priestcraft.

Biblicism gives power to pastors by declaring a particular translation and literal interpretation of Scripture to be divine speech that the pastor possesses and dispenses. Every word in the Bible becomes God's. These words of God mean exactly what the pastor says they mean. The pastor's power is derived from knowing the will and mind of God clearly and finally. The pastor's understandings of truth fed through the words of the Bible becomes divine truth. The weight of God, the force of the divine, flows through the pastor's speech. The trick is to memorize the words, learn the information, organize the content, and reduce all of Scripture into a unified whole with no tensions or contradictions. Thus armed with ultimate truth, the pastor has the answers to all of life's questions. Pastoral identity is clear. Pastoral power is neatly defined. Pastors are oracles dispensing divine answers through sacred language.

Of course, many of the tenets of biblicism are crucial to the ministry of the gospel. Scripture claims to be God's word. Scripture is the cradle wherein Jesus

Christ is carried from generation to generation. The life, death, and resurrection of Jesus Christ portraying the saving intentions and acts of God are the heart of the gospel. The Bible is our final norm in all matters of faith and life. But the Bible is not the gospel. In truth, the Bible is both a divine and human book. The Bible has its power not in each word interpreted by a particular pastor, but in that word's capacity to point to Jesus Christ as Lord and Savior of the world. At its best, biblicalism distorts the gospel; at its worst, it turns the gospel into a new law condemning humankind.

Professionalism gives power to pastors through imparting particular knowledge and skills that certify that the pastor is qualified to handle critical tasks. If pastors are to be respected professionals, sets of tasks unique to their work must be identified, researched, isolated, and quantified. In order to qualify as capable, the pastor must master the designated knowledge and skills, submit to a review by peers, and receive the appropriate titles, certificates, and privileges befitting one's level of competence . . . as member, candidate, diplomat, supervisor, and so forth.

A pastor might pick up several of these "union cards" in a multitude of guilds—including areas only tangentially related to the ministry of the gospel. A pastor might become an expert in work with individuals in crises, thereby picking up CPE or AAPC or ACPE credentials. A pastor might become an expert in organizational development, management by objective, or conflict resolution. A pastor must get the required C.E.U.s or a degree, preferably a doctorate, to include in his or her titles. A pastor might do the same in family-life education or marriage enrichment or church growth or political change, to name some examples. In these processes, the pastor's work is narrowed to a peculiar slice of individual or corporate human life and church activity. A new esoteric language is created by the inductees. Layers of educational, experiential, and political designations give status, meaning, and power to those who participate. Armed with knowledge, skill, a guild, status, and certificates, the pastor plies a variety of cures in neatly divided dimensions of the church and the world. Pastoral identity is clear. Pastoral power is neatly defined. Pastors are credentialed experts practicing their secular skills in sacred garb.

Of course, many of the intentions of professionalism are germane to the ministry of the gospel. The gospel has content and context. Pastors had best know both. Doing the work of the gospel in the church and the world requires enormous skill. Moreover, out of respect for the gospel, pastors can do no other than hold themselves to the highest of expectations. Pastors must be learned and skillful, faithful to their calling, doing the work of the gospel timely and well. Yet, even at its best, professionalism misplaces the ultimate authority and source of power in a pastor's ministry. The office of the ministry does not get its power from either human tribunals nor its occupant's knowledge and skill. The power of the office comes from God in Jesus Christ through the proclamation of the gospel and the administration of the sacraments. At its worst, professionalism turns the gospel into a set of skills rendering status and gain to their practitioners.

Institutionalism gives power to pastors through privileged positions in political structures. Layers of hierarchical bureaucracies create a political monolith called the church. With ascending and descending lines of authority flowing from times past through centralized contemporary political personages, power trickles down to each local pastor as twentieth-century feudal lord. A mixture of monarchical, corporate, and egalitarian political forms is pieced together to shore up the minister of the gospel with secular power. In order to participate and rise in this hierarchical, political power structure a pastor must mix Machiavellian and participatory leadership styles so as to wield power without appearing to be ambitious or controlling. Election or appointment to a position of responsibility is taken as a mandate to exercise one's will on behalf of or upon the whole. Questions of truth are decided by popular votes of committees or councils or assemblies or by who gets elected or handpicked. The task of a pastor is above all else skillfully to broker power, privilege, persuasion, and people. Pastoral identity here is clear. Pastoral power is neatly defined. Pastors are politicians wielding structural power in a religious institution.

Of course, the church is a human institution as well as God's new creation. If all is to be done in good order, organization, that is, structure, procedure, and leadership are necessary. Ways and means are vital in order to accomplish the work of the gospel. Authority must be exercised, decisions made, differences adjudicated. Pastors together with others in the body of Christ are key participants in the supervision of the life and mission of the whole Christian church on earth, the congregation on the next corner, and all that ties these together. There is much in institutionalism to commend it. Yet at its best, it turns the gospel into a religious hierarchy, more often than not substituting a theology of glory for a theology of the cross. At its worst, the gospel becomes an institution, the pastor a politician, theology politics.

Subjectivism gives pastors power through manipulation of human experience. People are to be touched, moved, and changed. Pastors must develop the techniques of influence in order to bring about desired results: excited individuals, growing Christians, enthusiastic members, dedicated leaders, compassionate caregivers, bold activists. Study of psychology and anthropology is necessary. One must know best how to approach the membership or the culture. One must get people's attention—not easy in an overstimulated world. One must capture a person's imagination—not easy in a technological era. One must appeal to a broad range of emotion—not easy in an anesthetized age. One must make a claim on the will—not easy in a "do my own thing" society. As a result pastors must know how to set the mood, take advantage of the moment, tell stories, raise consciousness, stir the conscience, fire resolve, evoke compassion, and on

188

and on. Pastors are to be diplomats, comics, storytellers, dramatists, directors, orators, and conversationalists. Pastoral identity is clear. Pastoral power is neatly defined. Pastors are artists shaping sacred scenarios in human consciousness and history.

Of course, subjectivism points to essential elements of the ministry of the gospel. The gospel is concrete, specific, and peculiar. It is "for me," "for you," for each human being in his or her own existence. The pastor as preacher, liturgist, or personal presence is drawn in each time and place into the encounter in which the Holy Spirit uses her or his words, presence, or actions to speak the gospel with nuanced, living clarity to people of a peculiar consciousness and context. Knowing that consciousness and context, imaging the gospel so it might well be heard as good news, is indeed one critical challenge facing the pastor. Yet, the power of the gospel is not in the pastor's power to touch, move, and change. The gospel is not a technique; nor is it sentiment nor entertainment nor positive thought nor just deeds.

Sacerdotalism, biblicism, professionalism, institutionalism, and subjectivism: each evidences critical supporting elements in the ministry of the gospel, yet each finally distorts the gospel by elevating the penultimate to the ultimate.

MINISTERS OF THE GOSPEL

At the heart of contemporary debate about ordained ministry stands a single question with its corollary. The question is this: "What is the gospel?" Its corollary is this: "What advances the gospel?" These questions and their answers define and empower ordained ministry.

What is the gospel? Is it not the message that the life, death, and resurrection of Jesus are God's decisive acts in history? Is it not the proclamation that in Christ we know God most clearly as the giver of life and truth? The gospel establishes the faith that God creates the universe and all it contains. The elements in all their combinations of inorganic and organic existence begin, continue, and end with God. God's gifts of consciousness, language, and meaning flow out of the past through the present and into the future. God establishes and sustains life and truth in all its mystery, splendor, and delicate harmony.

The gospel establishes another dimension of faith when God gives life and truth again and again and again in Jesus Christ. When human beings and institutions distort and destroy, God reorients and renews. When human beings and institutions alienate and oppress, God reconciles and frees. God's gift of life continues toward full and abundant existence as Jesus Christ calls persons into a community—the church—that is the heart of his continuing presence in the world. Members of this church are to experience in their corporate and personal lives the truth, love, and freedom God established in Jesus Christ. The church is to continue Jesus Christ's lifegiving work. Its members are to partic-ipate in advancing God's truth, love, and freedom in the world. Jesus Christ's life and mission lives on in them.

"In order to obtain such faith God instituted the office of the ministry, that is, provided the gospel and the sacraments" (CA 5, *BC* 31). "For through the word and the sacraments, as through instruments, the Holy Spirit is given; and the Holy Spirit produces faith where and when it pleases God, in those who hear the gospel" (CA 5, *BC* 31; Latin). In order that this "gospel is preached in its purity and the holy sacraments are administered according to the gospel . . . " (CA 7, *BC* 32). The church ordains, that is, duly calls (Ap 14, *BC* 214–15).

The work of the office of ordained ministry is to tend to the gospel, its content, power, form, and work. For the sake of this work, the Lutheran Confessions are insistent and thorough about duly calling, that is, ordaining, some who will see that the gospel's content, power, form, and work are accurately and boldly advanced within the life of the church and through the church in the world. Pastoral identity is clear. Pastoral power is properly defined and lodged. Pastors are ministers of the gospel: its purpose is their purpose; its power is their power. In assessing their office and evaluating their work, pastors, whatever their title, whatever their job description, always ask: What is the gospel? What advances the gospel? What gives life?

The office of ordained ministry has many faces. There is indeed common purpose and power. Yet that common purpose and power are advanced by multitudes of persons with varied gifts expressed within the diverse forms of the gospel. From the Old Testament we know of prophets, priests, and teachers of wisdom even challenging one another as they carried out God's mission with Israel. Each person was not everything. Moreover, priests were different from each other. So too were prophets and teachers of wisdom. Prophets, priests, and teachers of wisdom were all called and empowered by God to challenge, comfort, and instruct Israel. St. Paul's vision of God's gifts is similarly varied for the purpose of equipping the saints for the work of ministry for the building up of the body of Christ. There were at least apostles, prophets, evangelists, pastors, and teachers designated and gifted by the Spirit to work toward the above common goals in the church. As the early church lost its eyewitnesses of Christ and moved in ever widening circles in the world, the church found bishops, presbyters, and deacons critical to the work of tending the gospel and accomplishing its purposes. Bishops did not do everything; nor did presbyters or deacons.

The point and precedent are clear. Varieties of offices executed by peculiar people called by God were necessary to accomplish God's life-giving work in the world. Each "office" does not accomplish everything. Persons within a particular "office" will not carry out that office in exactly the same way even though there is a common core of tasks peculiar to that "office." Finally a combination of varied "offices" is needed to complement and challenge one another if God's saving purposes are to be accomplished fully and truthfully.

The implications for pastors are clarifying and empowering. The office of ordained ministry has a common core of tasks peculiar to that office. Persons of diverse gifts will exercise that office with considerable diversity as they discharge the common core of tasks peculiar to that office in specific times and places. Other "offices" will be needed in order to accomplish God's purposes fully and truthfully.

The office of ordained ministry, however, possesses a common core of tasks peculiar to its purposes. As a minister of the gospel the pastor is presider, preacher, teacher, overseer, presence, and pilgrim. These six roles grow out of the gospel, are empowered by the gospel, find precedents in tradition, and serve the reenvisioning of the office in each new time and place.

As presider of the worshiping community, the pastor brings theological expertise to the planning and execution of services which advance the gospel. Such questions as those of content, form, leadership, and effectiveness all require attention and care as a pastor leads her or his particular community in their interaction with God and each other around word and sacrament. To preside is not to be the only "performer" or leader in worship; it is to guide and lead a community in its varieties of worship as the church or Jesus Christ.

As preacher within and without the Christian community, the pastor proclaims the message of God's life-giving activity in Jesus Christ with clarity and specificity in peculiar times and places to particular people. Questions of content, language, form, and effectiveness all require attention and care as a pastor wrestles with text and context. To preach is not to repeat a formula in the jargon of the guild; it is an encounter in which God gives grace through words spoken in a shared consciousness of pastor and people.

Scripture, confessional statements, and living tradition provide information, giving substance and shape to the gospel. If the gospel is to do its work, that critical information must be available to its recipients in the languages and concepts of the texts and the context. So pastors are to be teachers knowledgeable of the tradition and skilled in the ways and means of conveying truth and evoking interaction with the gospel.

The gospel creates a common life in a corporate community. Whether international, national, regional, synodical, or congregational, the church seeks good order in its life and mission which flow from the gospel. Pastors are to see to the work of the gospel within varied and distinct institutional expressions of the church. Moreover, pastors are to be theologians at the intersections of organizational structure, process, and power, incessantly asking the question: "Does this serve the gospel?" Pastors are not the only ones in charge; together with those in charge, they are uniquely to do pastoral theology in the dynamics of organizational life. As such they participate in developing, sustaining, and redeveloping institutional life commensurate with the context, form, power, and work of the gospel.

The gospel brings life to the whole world. Its message cuts across every people, time, and place. It finally does its work, however, in each person, moment, and location. The gospel is "for you." Word and sacraments involve speaking and hearing, giving and receiving in particular languages, by peculiar persons in specific situations. So pastors go. They enter, take up residence, visit, join, listen, observe, accompany, administer, pray, hear confession, speak absolution, and counsel. Because the gospel is "for you," you in all your specific peculiarity, pastors are the personal presence that make the means of grace earthly, historical, and accessible.

The gospel is "for me." God desires to do God's life-giving work also in those who are called to be ministers of the gospel. Pastors have been baptized. They live by God's grace. To be a pastor is to need a pastor. Word and sacraments are to do their redeeming and sustaining work in the one who tends to them. To be a pastor is to worship, to study, to confess, to pray, to struggle, and to seek God's grace and wisdom as person, daughter or son, friend, citizen, perhaps husband or wife, father or mother, as well as ordained minister. To be a pastor is to be a pilgrim sustained by the gospel within the community the gospel creates. It is to cry to God with every other human being: "Lord, what gives life?"

Whatever else the context may demand; wherever else the gifts and personality of an individual may lead; the common, core tasks of ordained ministry are six: presiding, preaching, teaching, overseeing, bringing a personal presence, and being a pilgrim. Pastoral identity is focused. Pastoral power is carefully channeled. Both find expression in six crucial ways of being and doing.

The office of ordained ministry moves to the rhythms of gospel time. Certainly, pastors are grounded and exist in *chronos*. As measured clock time, *chronos* divides existence into units evenly meted out in the common flow of all creation. Like everyone else pastors have their full lifetime in which to be faithfully at work as ministers of the gospel. As such they must live with schedules, deadlines, and biological timetables. Yet *chronos* does not define the ministry of the gospel.

The gospel reshapes time into *kairos* and *telos*. As *kairos*, time divides and concentrates into the urgent and critical, the gospel announces the one thing needful: the kingdom of God is at hand, repent and believe! As *telos*, time moves toward and flows from a future assured in the death and resurrection of Jesus Christ. *Kairos* and *telos* transform the pace of ministry into a grace-filled set of priorities and flow of rhythms grounded in the confidence of God's decisive, history-determining work accomplished in Jesus Christ. Yes, there is urgency; yes, there are intense moments; yes, there is a goal. But the urgency is in a church faithfully announcing the gospel in season and out, a gospel that creates its own intensity and moves toward and from its own end.

So in the flow of measured time, pastors, confident of God's destiny for all history, faithfully carry out the tasks at the core of their office, aware that God's grace is sufficient for them as for those to whom they minister. The tensions are great, to be sure; but the gospel at the heart of the office finally transforms even the frenetic pace and the goals of our own making into a lifestyle shaped by grace.

The ordained ministry is the office of the ministry of the gospel, shared by people of many faces, who faithfully discharge a common core of tasks in rhythms governed by grace. The office's only authority is the gospel. It exists in the church for the sake of the gospel. Its work flows out of the gospel. Its pace is established by the gospel. To argue that pastors are ministers of the gospel is to place first things first; it identifies a pastor's true authority; it provides for flexibility and diversity in the penultimates; it defines "do-able" tasks. It shapes a humane, grace-filled calling.

NOTES

1. H. Richard Niebuhr, *The Purpose of the Church and Its Ministry* (New York: Harper & Brothers, 1956).

Ministry
and Vocation
for Clergy and Laity

13

MARC KOLDEN

If justification by faith apart from works is central to the church's under-standing of the Christian message, there are several implications for all Christians—clergy and lay, in their ministries and their callings. To put it succinctly, if works have nothing to do with justification, then all differences of status among Christians disappear. And, if works have nothing to do with justification, then (since they are commanded by God) they must have their focus somewhere else.

JUSTIFICATION, MINISTRY, AND VOCATION

Martin Luther saw these implications of his rediscovery of the gospel very early in the Reformation. Banishing works from the area of one's righteousness before God led him to enunciate the idea of the priesthood of all believers.[1] No longer could there be two levels of righteousness—one for ordinary Christians, another for those with special callings. All Christians were equally sinful and equally forgiven. All were equally priests in the New Testament sense—those who bear witness to the saving work of Christ and who intercede for their neighbors.

While later the idea of the priesthood of all believers became perverted in the direction of individual status (each one as her own priest, with direct access to God and no need for a clerical intermediary), for Luther this was an idea basic to Christian community, in which each one ministers to others by speaking the judging and comforting word of Christ.[2] Dietrich Bonhoeffer's *Life Together* is a modern example of Luther's understanding in this area, and the contemporary idea that every Christian is a minister or has a ministry also attempts to recapture this doctrine.

The other closely related implication that Luther also saw very early is that the reason that God justifies us by grace through faith and not by works is so that our works can be of some earthly good. God does not need our works; our neighbors do. We do not need to go elsewhere (that is, to a monastery) to serve God or to have a calling.[3] Rather, God calls us to serve right where we are: our "ordinary" locations and duties in the created world are our "callings" (vocations). Religious good works such as fasting and pilgrimages are useless if justification is by grace through faith, for these works help neither ourselves nor our neighbors. "Ordinary" earthly works (in our families, occupations, and nation) are the ways in which God's commands are to be carried out—always for the good of the neighbor.

That insight emptied monasteries and cloisters and gave a theological value to previously denigrated areas of life. Later, in its decadent form, the idea of vocation could link Christian faith to making money, on the one hand, or to staying in one's place in a static society, on the other.[4] But Luther's point was that Christ's salvation was to reclaim the creation and the Christian was to be a faithful and useful creature through whom God could continue to work creatively. Justification apart from works was to set the Christian free to do works of love for the neighbor, no longer bound to works of self-justification or "free" to ignore the neighbor.

The purpose of the office of public ministry is to proclaim the gospel of justification by faith in its purity so that every Christian may be a minister and have a calling. Then God's redeeming and creating work will get done. If we do not get these distinctions straight, all sorts of damage will be done. For example, if only God's redeeming work is the focus, we may become preoccupied with religion. Church activity, spirituality, other-worldliness, and a magnifying of the importance of persons with religious callings will be stressed. Daily life and the importance of God's law in its first (civil or political) use will be downgraded. If redemptive work is thought to be God's only work, religious-works righteousness will return even in the midst of an emphasis on forgiveness and salvation. (This has occurred at times in pietistic, neopentecostal, and liturgical movements.)

Or, if God's creative work is recognized but separated from the necessity of God's redeeming work, sin will be ignored and the norms of the age or the culture or the party or the family or the economy will rule: we will take them to be what God has created in an unqualified way. The claim, judgment, and intention of God that all of these forms are to serve the divine purpose will not be seen and they will be considered to be autonomous. This view will be its own condemnation, finally, because it will be life only under the law. (We see this in civil religion, the worship of progress, and our blind faith in institutions.)

The public ministry must proclaim the gospel in its purity so that each believer will be given a ministry and have a calling. If the ordained minister identifies "ministry" only with the role of the ordained, then the meaning of justification by faith has not been seen; such an emphasis on status is a blatant contradiction of justification by faith. And if the legitimacy and necessity of each Christian's calling in daily life are not proclaimed and explicated, the whole point of justification by faith and not by works has been missed; then, instead of free grace we will have what Bonhoeffer called "cheap grace," grace that does not free us from anything or for anything. Faith without works is not faith. Faith without vocation is mere belief.

Because pastors and theologians have given much more attention to the office of public ministry than to the ministry of all Christians and to Christian vocation, it is important in any study of ordained ministry defined in congruence with the doctrine of justification by faith to develop the implications for these latter areas. Doing so will help protect against the momentum toward clergy domination that inevitably develops in the church as a human institution and it will remind those who are clergy that they are instruments in God's reclamation project that involves not only the salvation proclaimed to all people but the temporal well-being of all creatures as well.

In a pastor's life there is considerable overlap between ministry and vocation, though there are also many differences. An ordained minister may also be a spouse, child, parent, citizen, volunteer, friend, church member, and the like. In these areas Christian vocation and the ministry common to all Christians may often be exercised by pastors in ways no different from those who have other occupations. Yet since the ordained person's public ministry is such a large part of her vocation, and since the Christian message is so central to that vocation, the common problem for many Christians of how to relate faith to their occupations may scarcely be noticed. Yet for most stations in life it is not so clear and the pastor must seek to draw out the implications of the gospel for other callings and not only her own. The pastoral vocation is odd. It is different from every other vocation in that it serves primarily the age to come while other vocations serve the needs of the present age. Clarifying the meaning of the ministry of all Christians and of the doctrine of vocation will highlight the oddness of the pastoral office and in so doing will show how it ought to support the ministries and vocations of all Christians.[5]

LAW AND GOSPEL

As both Luther and the Lutheran Confessions sought to explain the meaning of justification by faith apart from works, they insisted that a distinction must be made in the Word of God between law and gospel.[6] God's gracious Word comes to us either as law or as gospel and the difference is one of function: What does the Word do to us? How does it function? If the Word functions to demand something from us, to tell us what we must do, to protect us from harming ourselves or others, to make us conform to God's will or to our neighbor's need, then it is a Word of law. If the Word functions to forgive us for our failure to keep God's commands, if it sets us free from the powers of sin, death,

197

and the devil, if it promises us new life and gives us hope for the future—all on account of Jesus Christ—then it is a Word of gospel.

In the experience of Luther and of other Christians of his time, the message of Jesus had been heard almost exclusively as law—as a message telling people of a new way to make themselves acceptable to God by doing certain works. When Luther saw in the writings of the apostle Paul especially that the Christian message was rather a message of what God had already done in Jesus Christ to make us righteous, the power of the gospel as gift, promise, and freedom was rediscovered and the difference of this message from one of demand, exhortation, and accusation became evident. Luther insisted that while both messages were included in the Word of God, only the gospel was the saving Word, the church's true treasure. He said that preachers and teachers must make a distinction between law and gospel so that the gospel would be heard and preserved. Both law and gospel were held to be essential because God's Word functions in both ways, but they must be directed to their proper tasks: the law should not intrude into "heaven" (our standing before God) but should direct our lives in society for the benefit of our neighbors. The gospel should not be used to rule "on earth" but is the Word that saves us by giving us faith in what God has done and will do for our eternal salvation in Jesus Christ.

Yet if these two functions must be distinguished for the sake of preserving the unique and unexpected gospel, they must not be separated. Luther worked this out in several stages. He distinguished two functions or "uses" of the law. The first has to do with teaching, guidance, compulsion, and commands in daily life. This first use of the law was called the civil or political use, and it is similar to the common-sense notion of laws regulating life in society. For Luther law in its first use expressed the way things work in creation (as creation is designed by God): actions have consequences, adultery destroys marriages, stealing and killing destroy community, law-breaking has consequences both for the law-breakers and for their neighbors.

While some Lutherans have thought that the distinction between law and gospel requires them to praise the gospel and condemn the law, this is the case only when the law is preached as the way of salvation. In its proper place, "on earth" (to use Luther's term), the law is a most wonderful and necessary thing. The first use of the law is built right into creation and human beings are intended to live according to the law "on earth." Luther even speaks of people as being "justified by works" when it comes to being good and contributing members of society. In daily life it is important that we do the works commanded by the law and that we recognize and reward those who keep the law in this sense and that we condemn and punish those who do not. In this sense, Luther calls the law the "most important" thing on earth.[7]

There is also a second use of the law. It is not optional or occasional since it always accompanies the first use of the law because human beings are sinful.

198

Luther called this the "accusing use" of the law, and it has sometimes been called the "theological use" (as contrasted to the civil or political use). This is the law's function when, in commanding us to do something, it also reveals that we will not do it or have not done it or even in doing what is commanded we hate doing so and hate the one who commands us. If the law's purpose is to get our neighbor loved, but if we are sinners who would rather love only ourselves, then the voice of the law urging us to love our neighbors will at the same time reveal our lack of love for them and our inappropriate love only for ourselves; the law will accuse us. In its second use the law will reveal our sin, convict us, condemn us, and finally destroy us.

Only if the preaching of the gospel comes will there be a possibility of re-pentance and forgiveness and an end to the law's condemnation. This is why the gospel must be preached, why it is the church's true treasure, and why the gospel is held by Lutherans to be the only thing that matters in defining or identifying what is the true church or what form the office of ministry might take. The law is all around us—in the church's teaching and also in the structures, relationships, and demands of daily life. All people experience the law, although not all know it as God's law, but only the church has the gospel, only believers in Christ know the saving Word. The church must distinguish between law and gospel so that the saving Word will be proclaimed and God's Spirit will have means to make believers of us.

The distinction between law and gospel is not merely a theological fine point but a distinction rooted in the relation between God's creative and redemptive work. Most Christian communions have had to make some such distinction—whether in terms of nature and grace, providence and election, blessing and saving, two cities or two governances—in order to remind themselves of the complexity and comprehensiveness of God's work. Distinguishing but not sep-arating God's creative and redemptive work and relating law to creation and gospel to redemption is crucial when it comes to making proper sense of the mission of the church, its public ministry, the ministry of all Christians, and our callings in daily life.

If one sees God's creative work as basic and ongoing, and if one sees God's redemptive work in Christ to be in continuity with that creative work as its restoration and fulfillment, then it will be clear that salvation in Christ is for the sake of the world. Religion, church, and ministry will not be ends in themselves but means through which God reclaims the whole world. Service of God will be service in earthly things because the earth and its creatures are God's. Ministry will lead to vocation and vocation will complete ministry. The gospel will free us from the law's condemnation for service to the neighbor, whose good is the law's original intention.

THE MINISTRY OF ALL CHRISTIANS

In the New Testament the word that is translated often as "ministry" (*dia-konia*) is used in several ways.[8] Literally, of course, it means "service" and it can refer to many types of service, often unrelated to religious faith. Where *diakonia* is translated "ministry" in most English translations, two things almost always apply. First, the word "ministry" is modified by some additional phrase (for example, Acts 6:4—ministry of the word; 2 Cor. 3:6—ministers of a new covenant), so that *diakonia* does not mean ministry or service in some generic sense but is clearly defined by its qualifier. Second, when it is translated "ministry" it has to do with God's redeeming work, with the saving message of Jesus Christ. The paradigmatic usage is 2 Cor. 5:14-20, esp. v. 18: "All this is from God, who through Christ reconciled us to himself and gave us the *ministry of reconciliation*" (emphasis added). "Reconciliation" here refers specifically to that between people and God, as in v. 19: "God was in Christ reconciling the world to himself, not counting their trespasses against them, and entrusting to us the message of reconciliation."[9]

This way of speaking of Christian ministry as referring to "the ministry of reconciliation" is virtually a convention in American English, both in religious life and in theological language. This usage fits exactly with the understanding that the church's unique task is to bring its treasure, the gospel of Jesus Christ, to the whole world. The church's ministry has to do with promulgating the good news of salvation both by formal preaching and teaching and also by all words and actions inspired by Christ and thus bearing witness to him which are aimed at eliciting and nourishing faith.

The ministry of reconciliation between God and people is the "work of ministry" to which all the saints are called (Eph. 4:12). It is the "royal priesthood" into which all of us have been baptized for the very purpose of declaring the wonderful deeds of him who called us out of darkness into his marvelous light (1 Pet. 2:9). This ministry belongs to the whole church; the ministry is the one ministry of the church for which all members share responsibility. In biblical terms it is improper to use the words "the ministry" to refer to the ministry of the ordained alone.

The contemporary emphasis on the ministry of the laity has been a way of recovering the biblical understanding that every Christian is a minister. This recovery has been ecumenical and is summarized well in the report of the Second Assembly of the WCC in 1954: "As Christ came to minister, so must all Christians become *ministers of his saving purpose* according to the gift of the Spirit which each has received."[10] Christians of many communions have rightly affirmed that "everyone is a minister" and that "every Christian has a ministry." But not every single thing is ministry. Yet that is what has been suggested in many Christian circles of late: working, playing, voting, paying taxes, raising a family, protesting, mowing the lawn—all these things and many more are called ministry. Any sort of humane action, whether done by Christians or others, gets labeled ministry. All sorts of occupations and family responsibilities, things that keep the world going but have nothing to do explicitly with faith in Christ or with God's saving work, are likewise called ministry.[11]

These are nearly all good and commendable activities that Christians and all people might well be involved in, but calling them ministry is extremely misleading. The term becomes so inflated that it is almost meaningless. "Ministry" loses it biblical and traditional specificity in the effort to have everyone be a minister by making everything ministry. Who is kidding whom? And why? For some writers this usage is a way of wresting ministry away from clergy who have wrongly spoken of their own ministry as the only real ministry. For others it may be an unconscious form of Christian imperialism that suggests that good creaturely activity is not important until the church names it "ministry" and installs people into tasks that they were doing anyway, but now with a new label. Perhaps such talk is a way for religious professionals to maintain control: talk of "affirming" the ministry of the laity sounds extremely patronizing, in any case. The goal of calling so many things ministry is probably well-intentioned for the most part; it seeks to help all Christians live their whole lives with a sense of serving God, but using the word "ministry" to do that causes some real problems.

In a practical sense, if everything is called ministry it is likely that the church's unique ministry will become neglected by the majority of Christians and left to the few religious professionals. But we are all to be witnesses. The most important kinds of ministry may not be done in a formal way through the church's official ministry. As in the early church the message was carried by traders and refugees, teachers and tentmakers, so in our day polltakers tell us that friends, neighbors, and relatives rather than official ministers are the primary means by which people are drawn to the church and to faith in Christ. We need to take seriously that it will be all of God's people who carry on the most important communication of the gospel to the world at large—at home, at work, at school, at the sickbed, with the elderly, over lunch, in decisions, programs, and planning in arenas far from the institutional church. It is important to say both that every Christian is a minister and to insist that ministry has to do specifically with God's saving work if the unique treasure that is the church's chief reason for existing is to be brought to the whole world.

Theologically, the problem with using "ministry" in the generic or inflated sense is the failure to distinguish between God's creative and redemptive work *and to value both.* When we do make such a distinction it helps us speak of God's activity in all of life; then we can speak clearly and positively about God's ongoing creative, preserving, and governing work through the structures of creation itself. This work of God involves all people, whether they know it or not. When we know this, we can account for good in the world apart from Christ and the church. Also, we can then see the importance of calling people to faith so that they can clearly see their daily lives as being in the service of God. Distinguishing between God's creative and redemptive work helps define ministry precisely and biblically, and it will lead us to speak more accurately of our activity in daily life as our callings or our service instead of lumping all activity together under "ministry." Doing that is just confusing, and it risks leading us to think that our daily work is our witness or that our witness is our only important work. Either way, in such confusion some of God's work may not get done.[12]

THE CHRISTIAN'S CALLING IN THE WORLD

If every Christian is a minister, so also does every Christian have a calling. The doctrine of justification by faith apart from works makes it improper to reserve the term "calling" or "vocation" only for those who are thought to be totally devoted to religious works. In Luther's time, almost without exception only the full-time religious were said to have vocations. They were thought to be set apart from the sinful world in a "higher calling." Luther saw the contradiction in this and took the very same word, "vocation," and applied it to the ordinary activity in which every Christian was involved. To Christians who thought they were condemned to live completely mundane rather than spiritual lives, he brought good news:

> How is it possible that you are not called? You have always been in some state or station; you have always been a husband or a wife, a boy or a girl, or servant. Picture before you the humblest estate. Are you a husband, and you think you have not enough to do in that sphere to govern your wife, children, domestics, and property so that all may be obedient to God and you do no one any harm? Yea, if you had five heads and ten hands, even then you would be too weak for your task, so that you would never dare to think of making a pilgrimage or doing any kind of saintly work.[13]

It is important to note immediately that for Luther vocation was not the same as occupation; vocation included one's occupation but also all of the other creaturely activities with which one might be occupied. Vocation was life in the world lived in faith in the creating God. Here (in contrast to securing our salvation) it could properly be said that we cooperate with God. Luther said that God creates children through parents and raises them through parents and teachers. God milks cows through the farmer and gives daily bread through the farmer, the miller, and the baker. God rules the city and state through their officials and governs relations within creation through "natural law," which is God's will built right into the created order. Thus, when we do wrong we properly feel guilty; when we see someone suffering, we properly feel sympathy (if not, we are said to be inhuman). In every moment and activity of life, we have to do with the creating God, and our callings in most cases are imposed on us by our situation in life and our earlier choices. Even when we choose new situations (for example, marriage, a new job, a new place to live), God calls us in these new places.

For example, the doctrine of vocation would see that each person is called to be a faithful and loyal child (whatever that might mean in relation to different ages and situations with regard to one's parents); this gives a theological rationale to an ordinary biological and social situation. One understands this only in faith, but in faith one is to understand this. The close relation between law and creation is apparent here: the law in its first use is God's will as expressed in God's creating and ruling the creation. In this sense, the commandments, whether the Decalog, the Great Commandments, or the "Golden Rule," are to guide us in our callings.

The fact that we are to love our neighbors was not Luther's discovery; the church had always said that. What was new was the way he saw that such love was to be concrete, namely, *we are to love our neighbors in and through our callings.* The precise form of love will be defined by the calling: the child's demand for food from its parents; the sick person's need for care from the person assigned to that; the employing institution's need for work from its employees; the state's demand for taxes, voting, and obedience to laws from its citizens. As persons serve diligently and competently in their stations and offices, God will be able to bless people in a regular and effective way.

Of course, it is not usually so simple. Exactly how and if one responds to these demands will vary, both on account of the particularities and because every person and station is marred by human sin. The "law" of the land or of the market or of family relationships may be skewed in ways that actually pervert or prevent love of neighbor. Here, Luther insists, the gospel is always judge over the law: faith will have to help us discriminate between legitimate and illegitimate demands. The true good of our neighbor will have to be the test of every actual law. Christian freedom from the law in an ultimate sense means freedom for the neighbor; this will add flexibility and creativity to our stations and offices.[14]

The advantages of this "ethical reappraisal" (Grane) that Luther initiated with his doctrine of vocation are many. In Wingren's words, the doctrine of vocation expands the diaconate of an earlier period; Christians in their callings are a vast diaconate.[15] The idea of vocation does not lead people away from daily life but keeps them focused on creaturely matters, which God has called "good." Participation in the economy, education, health care, politics, providing housing, protecting human rights and human life, and the like are seen to be the major ways in which Christians serve God, in addition to each one's responsibility for the ministry of reconciliation. This understanding of vocation makes Christian obedience exceedingly concrete and specific and it puts the focus always on the good of the neighbor. Our stations and offices (or locations and responsibilities) help us see who our neighbors are and what they need. We cannot love every child, but we can love our child in very direct ways and work for the well-being of other children in a variety of ways. We cannot feed every hungry person ourselves, but we can help to feed those who are in our care, and we can do our part in one way if we are farmers, processors, or retailers, and in other ways as we are consumers and voters, and in still other ways through charity and lobbying. Our stations and offices will give us ways and means to act when the general command to love may seem too vague or leave us confused or paralyzed.[16]

Of course, there are actual or potential problems in understanding life in terms of vocation. At one level these are historical problems such as vocation becoming individualistic: my calling becomes a means of serving myself and my own, not my neighbors in the biblical sense. In our careerist and consumer society a self-centered understanding of vocation is a constant temptation. In a larger context, any view of Christian obedience that is shaped by the structures of society risks become "old" in the same way that structures tend to become self-perpetuating. Here our "old" self will fit right in, conforming to the world and its laws, and vocation will become a "dugout" (Paul Ramsey) to protect us from our neighbor ("I cannot help you; I have to do my job.") rather than a place in which to serve. Another problem historically has been the tendency among Lutherans, especially, to misuse Luther's reference to 1 Cor. 7:20— "Everyone should remain in the state in which he was called"—to reinforce class and role distinctions and prevent social change; this despite the fact that Luther's point in quoting this verse was simply to show that people did not have to go to a monastery to serve God but could serve wherever they were.[17]

A possible problem with vocation theologically is in its being linked primarily to law. That is, the very source of concreteness and specificity can also be a weakness if vocational demands are not given constant critical scrutiny. If actual law is not connected to the divine lawgiver and creator who is also the redeemer, and if creation is not understood in its dynamic biblical sense, then vocation according to the law may become static and oppressive. In modern secular society the idea of vocation will not be credible if attention is not paid also to rehabilitating the doctrine of creation, which underlies any theological notion of law.[18]

A final and extremely important issue related to vocation and law concerns their relation to the gospel and sanctification. One cannot control the law of God; it always functions to do what needs to be done. Among other things, the law always accuses, as the Reformers insisted. The Christian is *simul iustus et peccator* (simultaneously righteous and sinful). Our justification is our being forgiven on account of Christ through an external Word pronounced over us which changes our reality (our relationship to God), rather than our making ourselves holy (which we cannot do). Therefore we must understand that sin persists in each Christian until we draw our final breath. Luther said that the "old Adam" is not drowned in the rite of baptism but must be put to death daily. In other words, we need the law in its accusing use to convict us and crush us so that our sinful self will be put to death and the gospel may raise us to new life in Christ.

This putting the sinful self to death is our "sanctification."[19] Sanctification so understood is not the American idea of "every day in every way becoming better and better"; rather, it involves oneness with Christ in faith and dying to self. Many have viewed this daily dying metaphorically and made repentance into the psychological state of feeling sorry for our sins. Yet with so many sophisticated ways of dealing with guilt and low self-esteem, daily dying seems hardly necessary and sounds more like a morbid hangover from the Middle Ages. But Luther said something quite different: he thought of an actual death of the sinful self (not some metaphorical "death"). Such a death will come about under the law and the place that it will happen is where we live according to the law—in our callings! Not in religious exercises, not in prayer, not in any self-mortification, not in feeling sorry for our sins, but right in our roles and responsibilities where we work ourselves to death in loving our neighbors.[20]

These same locations and situations in which our new righteous self in faith is active in love, gladly doing what the law requires (that is, what the neighbor needs), are also the places in which the old sinful self, still loyal to Adam, is compelled to serve. For example, we ought to go to work joyfully, and in faith we do; but the law of survival also forces our old self, even against its will, to do so and thereby puts it to death a bit each day. We ought to love our spouse, if we are married, and we do; but at times the institution of marriage simply forces us to do so even when our old sinful self would prefer to wander off into some other relationship; thereby our old self is put to death a bit more.

In other words, there will be a cross in every calling: an instrument to put us to death. We do not need to invent or choose such crosses; they will be laid on us by our stations in life, whether in being arthritic or being caught in a frustrating job or in seeing only many years of schooling ahead. The cross will be laid on us—have no fear! we are sinful—in our callings. There, in the demands to love our neighbor, our old self will be crucified.[21] In the incredible wisdom of God's economy, the same good work that we do in our callings both gets our neighbor loved and sanctifies us. The solidarity of God's creative and redemptive work is nowhere more clear than here. The gospel's work itself will not be completed without vocation. The ministry of reconciliation leads to vocation and vocation completes ministry.

The church's mission must include both the unique ministry of the gospel and the teaching and practice of Christian vocation—by clergy and laity alike. The church's official ministers must know this and serve this comprehensive mission because all this is entailed in the doctrine of justification by faith apart from works.

NOTES

1. See especially Martin Luther, "The Freedom of a Christian" (1520), *LW* 31:333–77, esp. 353–56; also, "To the Christian Nobility" (1520), *LW* 44:123–217, esp. 127–29; "The Misuse of the Mass" (1521), *LW* 36:133–230, esp. 138–42; "Concerning the Ministry" (1523), *LW* 40:7–44, esp. 21–22; and Luther's several writings against Emser in *LW* 39: esp. xvi–xvii, 151–52, and 227–38.

2. See, for example, Paul Althaus, *The Theology of Martin Luther* (Philadelphia: Fortress Press, 1966), 313–14.

3. See especially Martin Luther, "The Judgment of Martin Luther on Monastic Vows" (1521), *LW* 44:251–400 and xi–xvi; "The Estate of Marriage" (1522), *LW* 45:11–49; "Whether Soldiers, Too, Can be Saved" (1526), *LW* 46:93–137; and "A Sermon on Keeping Children in School" (1530), *LW* 46:213–58. The most important interpretation of Luther's thinking on vocation is that by Gustaf Wingren, *Luther on Vocation* (Philadelphia: Muhlenberg Press, 1957); my understanding is shaped decisively by Wingren.

4. For brief but helpful discussion of the history of the idea of vocation, see Robert W. Green, ed., *Protestantism and Capitalism: The Weber Thesis and Its Critics* (Boston: Heath, 1959). See also John O. Nelson, ed., *Work and Vocation* (New York: Harper & Brothers, 1954), esp. chap. 2.

5. For support for the way I am describing the issues, see Wingren, *Luther on Vocation*, and especially his *Gospel and Church* (London: Oliver & Boyd, 1964). See also, Richard Neuhaus, *Freedom for Ministry* (New York: Harper & Row, 1979), and Herb Neve, ed., *Sources for Change* (Geneva: WCC, 1968), esp. 51–100.

6. The most complete source for Luther's understanding is in his "Lectures on Galatians" (1535), *LW* 26–27: esp. 26:122, 148, 309–10, 345. The confessional basis for interpreting justification by faith in terms of the law/gospel distinction is found in the Ap Art. 4, *BC* 107–68, and esp. 108–13. For additional interpretation, see Edmund Schlink, *Theology of the Lutheran Confessions* (Philadelphia: Fortress Press, 1961), chaps. 3—4; Leif Grane, *The Augsburg Confession: A Commentary* (Minneapolis: Augsburg Publishing House, 1987), 58–68 and passim; and Gerhard O. Forde, "The Christian Life," in Carl Braaten and Robert Jenson, eds., *Christian Dogmatics*, 2 vols. (Philadelphia: Fortress Press, 1984), 2:391–469.

7. Luther, "Lectures on Galatians," *LW* 26:5. See also Wingren, *Creation and Law* (Philadelphia: Muhlenberg Press, 1961) and *Credo* (Minneapolis: Augsburg Publishing House, 1981), esp. 58-79.

8. See, for example, the chapter in this volume by Roy A. Harrisville, "Ministry in the New Testament."

9. Diverse commentators agree that "ministry" is related directly and explicitly to the saving work of Christ; compare, for example, Rudolf Bultmann, *Theology of the New Testament* (New York: Charles Scribner's Sons, 1951), 1:304–7; *A Theological Wordbook of the New Testament*, s.v. "ministry"; Gustaf Aulen, *The Faith of the Christian Church* (Philadelphia: Muhlenberg Press, 1960), 361–66, esp. 364. Even H. R. Weber, who advocates the ministry of all Christians, agrees; see his *The Militant Ministry* (Philadelphia: LCA Board of Publication, 1963), chaps. 1—3.

10. W. A. Visser't Hooft, ed., The Report on the Laity, in *The Evanston Report: The Second Assembly of the World Council of Churches, 1954* (New York: Harper & Brothers, 1955), 161.

11. For examples on both sides of this debate, see Marc Kolden, "Cleaning Up Our Language About Ministry," *dialog* 25 (Winter 1986): 33–36, and Nelvin Vos, "Our Language About Ministry," *dialog* 25 (Fall 1986): 301–3. Vos objects to my use of ministry in connection only with God's saving work in Christ and suggests that I should take note of the many studies that he cites; but these are precisely the sorts of usage that I am calling into question.

12. Admittedly, in any given situation the distinction between ministry and vocation may be blurred, since reliable creative actions by a Christian may be perceived by some

as testimony to Christ or evangelical witness to distraught or lonely people may in fact help them in creative and not only redemptive ways. The distinction between God's creative and redemptive work is, after all, a human theological distinction about the work of God. The point is not that we can label God's work but that we can distinguish different purposes and goals in God's work (as these are portrayed in the biblical materials); making a distinction is to help us serve God's comprehensive work more faithfully. In practice, our ministry and our vocation will be all mixed together.

13. Luther, "Sermon on the Day of St. John the Evangelist" (John 21:19–24), in *The Precious and Sacred Writings of Martin Luther*, ed. John Lenker, 10 vols. (Minneapolis: Lutherans in All Lands Co., 1905), 10:242. Very similar sayings can be found elsewhere, for example, "Lectures on Genesis" (1539), *LW* 3: esp. 62, 128–30, 321–22.

14. Wingren, *Luther on Vocation*, esp. 143–61, 199–212, is helpful on this whole section.

15. Wingren, *Gospel and Church*, 158–72. The phrase from Grane, *The Augsburg Confession*, is from p. 162; see also 194–202.

16. Paul Ramsey, *Basic Christian Ethics* (Chicago: University of Chicago Press, 1950), elaborates on these ideas in a lengthy section on "vocational ethics."

17. See Luther, "Commentary on 1 Cor. 7" (1523), *LW* 28:3–56, esp. 39–47.

18. Many of Wingren's works underscore this point; also, Claus Westermann, *Creation* (Philadelphia: Fortress Press, 1974). Langdon Gilkey's work in *Reaping the Whirlwind* (New York: Seabury Press, 1976) and in his current research on God and nature is contributing important fundamental work to this effort.

19. See for example, Forde, "The Christian Life," or his *Justification by Faith: A Matter of Death and Life* (Philadelphia: Fortress Press, 1982), esp. chap. 3.

20. Wingren, *Luther on Vocation*, shows how this understanding runs all through Luther's work; see pp. 28–33, 48–73, 234–48. Vilmos Vajta, *Luther on Worship* (Philadelphia: Muhlenberg Press, 1958), 169 n. 23, points out Luther's advice to persons caught in the plague: "If you have a wife, child, brother, sister, or neighbor, stay and help. We owe a death to one another" (*WA*, TR 4:511).

21. The language of bearing the cross by staying in our calling and serving carries with it a risk: it may become a counsel of despair to and among the suffering and oppressed—that their victimization is their cross. To this we must object. God does not will evil; God does not will that people suffer or be oppressed. Legitimate crosses come in our seeking to do God's will by living out our callings. We must not allow the language of bearing the cross to be used against God's will.

AFTERWORD

*Perspectives
in
Perspective*

TODD NICHOL and MARC KOLDEN

Do these essays point to a single perspective on the ordained ministry? They do not. The chapters of this book both hint at and directly articulate significant different variations on a theme. Possible differences of opinion over the ordination of women are but one case in point. At the same time we think that these authors are consistent at crucial points, especially when their essays are considered in light of the fundamental question before them: How does the confession that the ungodly are justified by faith alone inform Lutheran thinking about the office of ordained ministry?

In venturing to assess these essays from the perspective established by this basic question, the editors again emphasize that we write in our own names only. In speaking about these articles and in making proposals of our own we do not presume to speak for our colleagues. As anyone who knows them or who reads their work presented here and elsewhere can testify, they are eminently capable of speaking for themselves.

The exegete and historians who write the articles in the first part of this book establish one of its themes at the outset. As a result of their commitment to critical methods, they resist the temptation to sweep the disparate facts and messy realities of history under the rug of an abstract ideal of Christian ministry. Nor do they subsume the testimony of the past into the vision of a consistent, progressive development achieving completed form in one or another century. Their research rather bears witness to a consistent sense of unity in purpose and an irreducible pluralism in forms of the ordained ministry among the Christians and Lutherans of the past. That is perhaps their most important contribution as individual essayists and collaborating scholars.

Departing from the position of Ernst Käsemann and others to lay to rest the ghost of an "early catholicism" in the New Testament, Roy Harrisville (chap. 1) argues that "ministry" in the New Testament denotes an activity dependent for its definition on the intent of God to save men and women from sin, death,

211

and the devil. He concludes that while ministry as service to the gospel is an indispensable part of the economy of God's dealings with humankind, its forms are variable. "Since," he says, "the New Testament forges no link between the saving event and a ministry construed as a permanent institution, it is clear that the saving event is the constant, whereas service to it is the variable." And again: "Utterance, belief, 'ministry' does not create its object. It is created by it." Thus a theme with variations to follow: consistent unity of divine purpose and historical pluralism in the service of that one purpose.

James Nestingen (chap. 2) follows Harrisville to argue—in the tradition of Hans von Campenhausen, Hans Küng, and other notable historians and theologians—that, while the ancient church sustained a dialectical tension between the claims of ecclesiastical power and spiritual authority, the early centuries also witnessed a decisive development in the doctrine and practice of ministry focused on the emergence of the episcopate.[1] As the bishops gathered to themselves and were given both power and authority in the church, their office became both hierarchical and bureaucratic in nature. Evidence of this development was the assignment to the bishop of the tasks of administering the Holy Communion, of formulating the authoritative teaching of the church, and of representing and even embodying the ministry and the church itself. The development of doctrines of personal succession and finally the emergence of the papacy are, he argues, the final stages in the evolution of the early church's understanding of ministry. This author further makes an intriguing connection between two parallel developments. Nestingen proposes that the evolution of the ministry in the early church is closely related to the rise of the eucharistic cultus and a preoccupation with the notion of sacrifice. This, he suggests, is the root of differences laid bare by the Protestant Reformation and once again apparent in intramural strife among contemporary Lutherans. Lutherans who think of the Holy Communion as the "Lord's Supper" will generally be put off by the early church's understanding of the ministry, while those who conceive of the Sacrament of the Altar as the "Eucharist" will be attracted by it.

Jane Strohl's essay (chap. 3) provides an ecumenical context for a close and more detailed study of Martin Luther and the Lutheran Confessions that follows. Despite the differences in doctrine dividing West and East, Roman Catholic from Protestant, and radical from conservative Protestant, Strohl argues that all of these Christians were united by a common core of conviction holding that "the ministry is established and maintained by divine action, whether the hand of God is seen in the impressing of an indelible mark, the clothing of the Word in human words of proclamation, or the imparting of spirit-filled prophecies and visions." Returning to the theme of tension between ecclesiastical power and spiritual authority, Strohl suggests that it is renewed during the dramatic events of the Protestant Reformation. Lutheran and Reformed Christians, she would have it, inevitably find themselves moving between the extremities of the

Roman Catholic and radical Protestant positions. Of the heirs of the magisterial Protestant Reformation, both Lutheran and Reformed, Strohl says: "They never divorced the call to ministry from the structure of the church. Yet their experience with the Roman hierarchy did not allow them to make a straightforward identification of authoritative ecclesiastical action and divine inspiration. God wills to work through the ministry, founded by God's Word for the gospel's sake. Yet at times God preserves the gospel in, with, and despite the ministry rather than through it."

While he agrees with Strohl that Luther and the early Lutherans found themselves on middle ground with respect to the ordained ministry, Robert Kolb (chap. 4) argues that Luther's reform resulted in a revolution rather than a compromise. Indeed, if both Kolb and Harrisville are accurate in their assessment of the sources under consideration, Luther's reform resulted in a notion of ministry characterized more by the unity of purpose and flexibility in form found in the New Testament than by the increasingly homogeneous, institutionalized models of the patristic and medieval periods. This consequence of Luther's reform sprang from its deepest sources and resulted in a sharply reformulated idea of the Christian ministry. The "ministry" was once again defined not primarily in terms of offices and officeholders, but in light of its actual work, or as—to use Peter Fraenkel's phrase—a "verbal noun." As the editors of the critical edition of the Lutheran Confessions put it: "Luther did not understand the office of ministry in clerical terms."[2] Finally, for Luther and the early Lutherans, it amounted to this: the Word of God spoken in sermon and administered in sacraments requires speakers and administrators. This, of course, is reflected in the famously spare definition of the ministry found in Article 5 of the CA, which speaks not of institution or status or personnel, but of the activity of God in the Word: "God instituted the office of the ministry, that is, provided the Gospel and the sacraments. Through these, as through means, he gives the Holy Spirit, who works faith, when and where he pleases, in those who hear the Gospel" (CA 5, *BC* 31).

Readers of Kolb's chapter versed in the history of the interpretation of Luther and the Lutheran Confessions will note its emphasis on the call to the public ministry and the indispensability of that ministry in the life of the church but its comparative lack of interest in questions of clerical status, polity, structure, and ecclesiastical power. Consuming interest in these topics, Kolb's essay implies, are more a function of the history of territorial Lutheranism, a result of modern denominationalism, and a product of the confusions of modern scholarship than a necessary expression of the dynamics of Lutheran theology. A theology of the ordained ministry informed by Luther and the Lutheran Confessions, Kolb argues, will insist on the primacy of God's Word as the agent of God's work and will consider human work to proclaim and administer that Word under the rubric of service and not of power. It is this that most definitely marks

Luther's departure from the developing tradition of the early church and the Middle Ages. It is this that makes Lutherans adamant foes of the ecclesiastical pretensions and theological hyperbole that often attach themselves to ministry, priesthood, and episcopacy. And finally it is this that makes Lutherans so insistently economical in what they are willing to say about ministry in contemporary ecumenical conversation.

In his study of Lutheran Scholasticism and Pietism (chap. 5), James Pragman indicates that these heirs of the Lutheran Reformation maintained its traditions regarding the public ministry while developing and accenting them in new ways. The scholastic genius for distinction, for example, placed a number of explanatory devices around the essential confessional definition of ministry: two of them are the notation of difference between immediate and mediate calls, and the parsing of the distinction between the absolute and relative necessity of the ministry to the church. While the successors of the Lutheran scholastics have not always continued to use these distinctions—and cannot without the Aristotelian categories that support them—they ignore these devices at the peril of historical illiteracy and vague theology. The scholastic proposal, Pragman's essay suggests, may not command the agreement of contemporary Lutherans but it does summon them to rigor and clarity in their theology of the ministry. Further it suggests the value of sharp theological distinctions as well as of the scholastic commitment to the teaching and preaching of right doctrine. As he demonstrates that scholasticism was and is anything but "dead," Pragman also indicates that classical Lutheran Pietism was hardly anticlerical. Like Luther, the Pietists pursued their program in the interest of more effective pastoral practice. Maintaining in its theological essence the confessional and scholastic understanding of the ministry, they also emphasized the importance of lay activity and prized mutual endeavor among pastors and laity. Both movements, Pragman holds, stress the primacy of the Word of God while each puts the accent differently: the scholastics on the ministerial duty to maintain the continuity of divine truth in the church and the Pietists on the task of edifying and activating the people of the church in zeal for the gospel. Students of later Lutheran history will easily recognize here the origin of impulses frequently reappearing in later periods.

The essay of Walter Sundberg (chap. 6) argues that fundamental changes in the Lutheran doctrine of ordained ministry were not undertaken until the nineteenth century—upon which the twentieth has been in many ways little more than a commentary. Sundberg argues that Lutheran rethinking of the question of ministry was spurred by dramatic events in the political history of the German states, particularly Prussia, in the nineteenth century. In that crucial moment in the evolution of modernity, Lutheran territorial authorities comfortable in their inherited privileges were profoundly threatened by the spectre of democracy born of the French Revolution and its bloody aftermath. In this highly charged context, Sundberg argues, it was the Reformed theologian Friedrich Schleiermacher who eloquently represented the continuation of the authentic Reformation teaching concerning the ordained ministry. In so doing, Schleiermacher put himself at great personal risk by opposing formidable political forces. On the other hand, important Lutheran theologians of the day, including F. J. Stahl and Wilhelm Löhe, approached the question of ministry on the basis of a politicized hermeneutic conceived in the interests of preserving traditional European hierarchies in church and state. The result was the emergence of the "evangelical catholic" position on ministry among Lutherans. Stahl, Löhe, and like-minded theologians were at the same time challenged by other prominent Lutherans, among them J. W. F. Höfling, who advocated a transference theory of the ministry attuned to the emergence of the modern democratic context. More nuanced alternatives were sponsored by theologians associated with the University of Erlangen. These complexities were often ignored, however, when a typology pitting *Stand* against *Amt*, divine institution against ecclesiastical convention, ontology against function, authority against majority, was used to portray alternative Lutheran understandings of the ministry. That the simplicity of this typology continues to commend itself to those who would tidy Lutheran history and polarize contemporary debate over the ministry by means of caricature is a testimony to the grip of the nineteenth century on theological imaginations in the twentieth. Sundberg's discussion also raises the disturbing question of the extratheological basis out of which the evangelical catholic position emerged and in which it is often discussed in the present. Discerning readers will be left to ponder why it is, for example, that contemporary advocates of the evangelical catholic position are often found supporting conservative social and political positions and taxing advocates of other views on the ministry for ethical laxity. Finally Sundberg's essay leaves open the question of whether contemporary Lutheran preoccupation with Orthodox, Anglican, and Roman Catholic forms of the ministry simply indicates a fundamental confusion among Lutherans about their own history and the ecumenical implications of their tradition.

In his study of selected developments in the history of American Lutheranism (chap. 7), Todd Nichol demonstrates that in the United States Lutherans by and large avoided the European controversy discussed by Sundberg. American Lutherans instead elaborated a doctrine of ministry directly linked to the tradition of the Reformation as it had been mediated by the seventeenth and eighteenth centuries. These pioneers were also acutely sensitive to the new context in which they found themselves. The result, Nichol indicates, was the emergence of a considerable consensus on the doctrine of ministry—at once faithful to the norms of the Lutheran tradition and appropriate to the modern American context—which held that the public ministry of the church is divinely instituted; there is one such office; the appointed tasks of the ministers of the church are the preaching of the Word and the administration of the sacraments; the call to the public ministry normally originates in the Christian congregation; ordination to the ministry of the church is a ratification of the call including the laying on of hands and intercessory prayer for the new pastor; the office of oversight is a practically necessary ordinance the arrangement of which is left to the discretion of the church.

In the essay opening the second part of this volume (chap. 8), Gerhard Forde develops an understanding of the ordained ministry in terms of fundamental Lutheran convictions. Beginning with God's election of believers to salvation, the theological obverse of the doctrine of justification by faith alone, Forde demonstrates that the task of ministers is to make known God's electing grace. The office of the public ministry is thus established as God acts to save the ungodly through the preached Word and the sacraments. The ground of the ministry is not, therefore, in an institutional or sacerdotal legitimation. The Word of God spoken in the sermon and administered in the sacraments demands and creates the office. The consequent assignment of the church is simply to see to the responsible service of preaching and the administration of the sacraments. While granting that the office of the ordained ministry is threatened by Christianity's increasing relegation to the private sphere, Forde argues that the proper Christian solution is not to seek to elevate the ministry in the esteem of church and world, but to stress the call to public office in the present order. The result is a high doctrine of the ministry that does not, however, resort to hierarchy or mythology to sustain its altitude.

The principal contention of Joseph Burgess in his discussion of episcopacy (chap. 9) is that no structural elements are necessary to the life of the church beyond the gospel alone. Such structures, although important and practically necessary in different ways at various times and places, exist only to assist the church in its mission to the world and are not divinely instituted. Burgess maintains that neither longevity nor the support of a majority of Christians can override the claims of the freedom granted by the gospel. The Lutheran Confessions, he shows, permit only a carefully circumscribed acceptance of the ministry of bishops. He regards as fatuous the notion that Lutherans could adopt one or another version of the historic episcopate which could satisfy the demands of Roman Catholics, the Orthodox, or Anglo-Catholics. Once again, for Burgess, evangelical freedom is the crucial issue. Lutherans, Burgess maintains, are obliged to retain their freedom to alter or abolish conventions of oversight in the interests of effective ministry. Burgess's extensive discussion of the problems associated with the various historic episcopates (for example, life tenure, lack of unity among episcopal communions, false teaching) illuminates in detail the dangers that attend the absolutizing of one form of ecclesiastical oversight. The undue attention to form characteristic of most arguments on behalf of the historic episcopate, he proposes, indicates precisely how easy it is to displace the gospel as source and norm of both church and ministry.

Michael Rogness (chap. 10) points out that in the New Testament service and servanthood *(diakonia)* are spoken of as the responsibility of all Christians. In the Acts of the Apostles and the Epistles of the New Testament the emphasis, he argues, consistently falls as heavily on service as on office. Subsequent history reveals deacons performing a number of tasks in different circumstances. Their office changed according to the demands of the context in which the church found itself. Rogness concludes that the office of deacon has never been rigidly fixed and should not be. Its strength has been in its flexibility and its ability to meet changing circumstances. Restricting works of service to only one order within the church would, he argues, be a step backward for modern Christians. Since diaconal service is the responsibility of all Christians, "we ought not limit ourselves to any of the common patterns of deacons. . . . Rather, we need to acknowledge that the church does many things in addition to Word and Sacrament ministry, and that this service is organized and carried out not just by pastors, but by all the people in a congregation working together."

The story of how American Lutheran women came to be ordained as told by Gracia Grindal (chap. 11) is yet another demonstration of the flexibility with respect to form and tradition that accompanies a theology centered on justification by faith alone. Among American Lutherans, she argues, it was not primarily the feminist movement that led toward the decision to ordain women; it was, rather, the availability of trained women that caused these churches to ask what would prevent them from serving in the ministry. Not surprisingly, therefore, matters of biblical hermeneutics were more hotly debated than questions of gender and human equality, since persons on both sides of the issue thought primarily in terms of the church's call to office rather than of ordination as a "right" owed or earned. Importantly, Grindal notes that American Lutheran proponents of the ordination of women did not consider such an innovation a threat to the unity of the church, since for them the question of the ordering of ministry was held to be something for the church to settle rather than a divinely prescribed matter. Yet, because some Lutherans and many other Christians disagree on this point, Grindal points out, this matter is a vexing one for contemporary ecumenists. It is an ominous development, she thinks, that those who support an historic episcopate for Lutherans also often state or imply that they ought to stop ordaining women. In Grindal's pointed phrase, to ordain women in this context is to prefer the gospel truth to churchly unity.

From the perspective of a pastoral theologian, Roland Martinson (chap. 12) speaks against a reliance on counterfeit warrants for the ministry. Not denying either the validity of the concerns that often prompt this move nor the possible value of some of the authorities cited, Martinson cautions against confusing the authority of the gospel with the structures of the present age. He warns those who do confuse them that, while their pastoral identity seems clear and their ecclesiastical power appears to be neatly defined, this will finally result in the forfeiture of true authority. A deeper problem gives rise to the tendency to rely on artificial authorities: in each instance, the person of the pastor displaces the gospel as the locus of authority. The office of the ministry, in these cases, is construed in terms of power rather than of service; the gospel then becomes a law binding people to ministers in an illegitimate way. In place of artificial authorities, Martinson insists, ministers must serve the gospel, not stand over it; they must tend to the service of the Word of God rather than use the ministry for their own purposes. To do this would express the authentic pastoral identity of the minister of the Word, and then the authority of the ministry would be that of the preached Word and sacraments, no more and no less. This would consequently lead to the evolution of a multiplicity of forms because the church will always ask "What advances the gospel?" Venturing a response to this question, Martinson suggests that the advance of the gospel will always require of its ministers that they be preachers, presiders, teachers, overseers, companions, and pilgrims. If they are these things to their people, they will be tending to their proper business.

Marc Kolden (chap. 13) seeks to sort out relations both between clergy and laity as well as between the concepts of ministry and vocation—cognizant both of the anticlericalism often involved in the debate about ordained ministry and of the confusion generated by the application of the word "ministry" to all Christians. The doctrine of justification by faith alone, he argues, rules out all differences in status among Christians and leads to the recognition that all believers are ministers and priests of the church. But this does not exhaust Christian responsibility in the world, since "ministry" refers specifically to obedient service to God's work of reconciliation in Christ. However, Christians are also involved in service to God's created world in their callings in daily life. If such a distinction is not sustained, the whole range of Christian responsibility may not be seen, and either the unique ministry of the gospel will be neglected or the particular calling of each Christian in the world will be minimized. If such a distinction is not maintained, the false inflation of claims on behalf of the ordained ministry can lead to neglect of the callings of lay members of the church. Likewise, if thinking is awry on this point, the office of the public ministry can be denigrated and the work of the laity overemphasized. Kolden insists that it is important that pastors know and teach these ideas so that those who are ordained will not see themselves or be seen as somehow more holy than those in the lay estate and so that both ministers and laypeople will recall that dutiful service in worldly callings is essential for individual Christians and to the mission of the church as a whole.

COMMON GROUND

In considering the ordained ministry from different perspectives, always with justification by faith alone at the center, the theologians who write here all in one way or another emphasize the Lutheran tradition of commitment to flexibility in form and practice for the sake of consistent service to the gospel. On the one hand, this consensus maintains that such unity of purpose and flexibility in practice is necessary to insure the proclamation of the gospel in given times and places. On the other, this agreement is also characteristically Lutheran in the importance it assigns to Christian freedom.

These authors are clearly committed to the catholic and evangelical heritage of the Lutheran churches. Yet, for all of them, this commitment to a confessional tradition is subordinate to another: they give their first loyalty to the gospel of Jesus Christ alone. As evangelical Lutherans, they display an undeviating loyalty to the doctrine of justification by faith alone as a true summary of what is at the center of that gospel. This is the ground of their conviction that all churchly form and expression is meant to serve a purpose: that in the church form follows function, that ministry follows mission and serves it, that preachers are called and ordained to proclaim the gospel.

That is not to say, however, that these theologians teach a mere functionalism. All of these authors insist that the office of the ministry is divinely instituted and an indispensable part of the economy of the church. They emphasize that, while Lutherans at their best have consistently abolished or relativized hierarchical distinctions within the ranks of the ministry and the church as a whole, they have also perennially taught that God has given the church a ministry— that is, provided it with the Word and the sacraments—and that from the ranks of the church servants of that ministry have always been called by divine command.

These essayists are also consistent in their objection to a rationale for ecclesiastical hierarchy they think specious, and this, too, is a consequence of their understanding of justification. They consistently reject arguments for the divine institution not only of hierarchal polities but of ecclesiastical oversight and governance of any kind. A historical Lutheran antipathy to clerical hierarchy is, indeed, particularly evident in these essays and is all the more striking in light of the theological and cultural conservatism so often characteristic of Lutherans. To put it plainly, some if not all of these authors argue or imply that there are urgent theological reasons, as well as obvious historical grounds, for Christians to be very cautious about the establishment of ecclesiastical hierarchy. A tendency to works-righteousness, they indicate, is innate to hierarchical systems claiming divine or traditional authorization. Whether in their historical objections to the supremacy of bishops, or in their refusal to give fundamental religious meaning to the distinction between clerical and lay members of the church, or in their often fierce revolts against a bureaucratic spirit in the contemporary churches, Lutherans bear their revolutionary traditions faithfully when they argue that structural provisions in the church and for the ministry must be judged in terms only of their usefulness in the service of the gospel.

This may be said still another way. These theologians are unwilling to identify God's ends with human means. They insist that God's authority cannot be identified with the church or the ministry but only with the authority of the Word spoken by the Holy Spirit. No credentials—sacramental, bureaucratic, or other—can serve to authorize the ministry except in a denominational, penultimate sense. Credentials, to put it bluntly, are of this present age, while God's authority in the gospel is of the age to come. No Lutheran was more definite about this than the mentor of the American Lutheranism of the eastern seaboard, Henry Melchior Muhlenberg: "Experience shows that neither Episcopal, nor Ministerial or Presbyteral Ordination doth infuse any natural or supernatural Gifts or Qualities, otherwise we should not find so many counterfeited Ministers, refined Hypocrites, and grievous Wolves in the Christian Church on Earth, instead of true and faithful Shepherds."[3]

The same caveat that applies to the church as a whole, indeed, stands over the ministry with special pertinence. While the church is the body of Christ, Lutherans maintain, its structure and governance are not prescribed by God in the Scripture. For this reason Lutherans do not ascribe divine institution to any single polity or to any ecclesiastical tradition, including their own. In these matters they contend that Christians are granted a freedom qualified only by their commitment to mission in the world for Christ's sake. Pursuant to this mission, it is the task of the church to see to it that its people and ministers provide the means of grace to those who need them. In this task the people of the church are free to fashion and adapt, retain and reject such forms as their mission requires. It is the conviction that this is so that prompts them to apply to the ministry in particular what Robert Jenson has rightly said of the church in general:

> The Reformers did not deny that the church will be—and rightly so—institutionalized, but they did deny that the church itself is an institution. To formulate the difference somewhat crassly: medieval thinking said that God created an organization, the church; the Lutheran Reformation said that God gathers people and that this gathering, the church, creates an organization to carry out its mission. This does not make the organization unimportant. On the contrary, it makes the organization of the church the field of the believer's free historical judgment and responsibility, and so makes it precisely as important as we are.[4]

SOME PROPOSALS ON THE MINISTRY

1. Lutherans put the doctrine of the ministry in its proper perspective, place it in appropriate theological position, and give it an authentic definition when they acknowledge the primacy of the Word of God and the theological priority of the doctrine of justification by faith alone.

For Lutherans the Word of God is the radiant center of Christian experience and the norm for faith and life. To acknowledge this, to reflect on the question of the ordained ministry in the light of the Word of God and its work, is to consider the public ministry of the church in its most appropriate perspective. To do this is also to make crucial distinctions and definitions often forgotten in discussions of the called and ordained ministry.

Three of these definitions and distinctions are particularly important to Lutherans. First is the revolutionary definition of the ministry prompted by the confessors' insistent emphasis on the Word of God. The ministry in its strictest sense is precisely the Word of God. Although the exegesis of CA 5 is disputed, the drafts preliminary to it and the basis of the final articles on doctrine make perfectly clear the intent of the confessors. The Schwabach Articles on 1529 make the confessional argument in precise terms: "To obtain this faith, or bestow it upon us men, God has instituted the ministry, or the oral word, viz. the Gospel, by which he causes this faith and its power, use, and fruit to be proclaimed, and through the same, as a means, bestows faith by his Holy Spirit, as and where he will; other than this there is no means, mode or way to receive faith. For thoughts outside of or before the oral word, however holy and good they appear, are nevertheless nothing but lies and error."[5] Preaching and the sacraments themselves, according to a strictly historical reading of the final text of the CA, are the ministry. They are essential, vital, indispensable, divinely ordained elements in the life of the church. Second, and again strictly construed, it is only as a consequence of this prior necessity, only because a spoken word requires speakers and visible words require utterance, that there is necessarily an ecclesiastical office of the ministry. Thus, in vocabulary reminiscent of that used by the Lutheran Scholastics, it may be said that an ecclesiastical office of the ministry is a relative or dependent or consequent necessity in the life of the church rather than an absolute or independent necessity. Third, the questions of how this office is to be filled and who shall serve in it are matters separable from the questions of the definition of the ministry and ecclesiastical office.

If on the one hand, all three of these definitions and distinctions obtain, then a good many subsidiary questions can be put in proper, consequent order. If, on the other hand, these fundamental rubrics are subverted or ignored, then a whirlwind of confusion and controversy of the kind inherited by Lutheran churches in the United States at present can be predicted to continue. The deepest source of this confusion and controversy is in a misunderstanding of the basic dialectic governing discussion of the ordained ministry. Historically, it seems, Lutheran difficulties with the ministry originate in the conviction that the ministry defines itself over against the church. This is the origin of a persistent preoccupation with questions of the place of the ordained ministry in the definition of the church, debates over the origins of the ministry, of *Amt* versus *Stand*, and of church political constructs of every other sort. A misunderstanding of the relation of church and ministry finally produces a fatal fear of conflict between ecclesiastical power and spiritual authority.

An acknowledgment of the primacy of the Word of God and of the theological priority of the doctrine of justification by faith involves a recognition that the ministry (like the church as a whole) stands under the Word of God and is defined by it. In its essential nature the ecclesiastical office of the ministry is defined only by the service of the Word of God. In turn, faithful and effective service of the Word may legitimate contingent claims on behalf of ecclesiastical office, polity, structure, hierarchy, or personal position in the church. All such claims, however, are indeed contingent and to be evaluated in terms of authentic service. No such claims can pretend to enduring validity in the life of the church.

In more precise theological and practical terms, Lutheran traditions of ministry speak clearly and economically about the public ministry of the church. Properly defined, the ministry itself—that is, the spoken Word—is a divinely ordained, constituent element of the church. For its service there is necessary in the church an office of the public ministry to which individual Christian ministers are called and ordained. The nature of this office is defined by its service in the preaching of the gospel and the administration of the sacraments. In other matters, the historical forms of this office are left to the discretion of the church and may be altered as the juxtaposition of mission and context require. By confessional warrant, Lutherans consider the call of a congregation or the church at large necessary and sufficient for induction into this office. To this call an ordination, understood as public affirmation of the call accompanied by prayer and the laying on of hands, may be added. Some Lutherans, with the qualified assent of the confessors, ascribe a sacramental significance to this act, although most Lutherans reject this position and all are obliged to observe the precise limits attached to the confessional latitude on this point.[6]

2. The office of oversight among Lutherans can take a variety of forms in the service of its proper tasks, the propagation of the gospel and the upbuilding of the church.

The function of oversight among the congregations and assemblies of the church is not divinely instituted but a product of the historical experience of the church, a practical necessity. Because it is this and no more, the work of oversight may be served in a variety of ways. That they have often assigned this task to one minister in a specific jurisdiction, that the political regime of the U.S.A. is notable in its predilection for a strong single executive, and that large sectors of the Christian church have been governed by the monoepiscopate does not oblige Lutherans to adopt or retain the polities they now enjoy or to continue the offices of president and bishop as they now exist. The task of oversight is a practical necessity; its forms are a matter of freedom.

Not only the theology, but also the history of the Christian churches around the globe, suggest a number of options left largely unexplored by American Lutherans in their consideration of the office of oversight. At least three and probably all four of the earliest overseers of the emerging Lutheran movement—those who undertook the famous visitations of the Saxon congregations—were, for example, lay members of the church.[7] There is no theological reason to indicate that the prospective bishops, presidents, or superintendents of the Lutheran churches in the United States cannot be from among its lay membership. Nor is there any theological reason to restrict the office of oversight to a single individual. A variety of collegial forms have appeared in the past and could be employed again. The oversight of the church could easily, for example, be exercised by a council composed of both lay and clerical members or exclusively of one or another of these groups. These possibilities could be explored at both the national and local levels. The Roman Catholic church, to cite one example from another tradition, does not have a single national head in the United States. The Presbyterian Church in the U.S.A., to mention another, is overseen by a series of consistorial bodies presided over at the national level by a Moderator and Stated Clerk, both of whom may be either lay or ordained. These and other possibilities are all open to Lutherans as they form and reform their churches. To mention only one more particular possibility it is not theologically unthinkable, nor would it be as practically impossible as many might claim, for the various regional judicatories of individual Lutheran churches to order, govern, and oversee themselves in a variety of ways. Circumstances in Austin, Minnesota, and Austin, Texas, are different, and forms of service might vary accordingly.

While all these possibilities stand open before Lutherans, only one is foreclosed. That is to argue that any particular form of the office of oversight is essential to the life of the church (whether of its actual being or *esse*, or of its well-being or *bene esse*, or of its full being or *plene esse*) or intrinsic to its unity. These are claims usually associated with contending versions of the historic episcopate. They are sometimes expressed in traditional form and sometimes in more demythologized, practical forms developed as a result of the contemporary ecumenical movement. To these proposals, Lutheran theology answers that it is potentially hospitable to episcopacy but in a form stripped of the argument for its necessity to the church and radically subject to the Word of God. This means that Lutherans will not attribute to the overseers of the church functions that belong exclusively to the Word of God including, for example, magisterial authority or the signification of the unity of the church. Nor will they assign to their overseers functions that are properly exercised by all of the people and pastors of the church including, for example, the proclamation of the Word and the ordaining of pastors. Swedish theologian Gustaf Wingren speaks in the language of the Lutheran tradition when he says that if Lutherans accommodate themselves to claims for episcopal status and authority in these matters traditionally advanced by Anglicans, Roman Catholic, and Orthodox theologians, "the Reformation will have been quite washed away."[8]

Positively, Lutheran theology affirms the function of oversight and defends the freedom of the church to pursue it in a variety of forms. This conviction was given classical expression by the bishops of the Church of Sweden in 1922:

> Our Church has not attached decisive weight either to the doctrine of ministry in general or to what is usually called the Apostolical Succession of Bishops and the questions thereby implied. The deeper reason for this is derived from our fundamental conceptions. . . . No particular organization of the Church and of its ministry is instituted *iure divino*, not even the order and discipline and state of things recorded in the New Testament, because the Holy Scriptures, the *norma normans* of the faith of the Church, are no law, but vindicate for the New Covenant, the great principle of Christian freedom.[9]

3. Lutherans are free to devise a multiplicity of offices in the church to complement the work of all the faithful and that of those who are called and ordained to the ministry of the Word.

The essential Lutheran argument concerning the definition and practice of ministry suggests that the church is free to devise and discard not only forms of the public ministry of the Word, but to create and reform or abandon any other offices that the proper service of the Word and the world requires. Since by nature neither the public office of the ministry of the Word nor any other offices establish gradations of rank among the members of the church, matters touching particular duties, the honor paid to occupants of such offices, financial recompense, and canonical status are left to the discretion of the church. On the other hand, this proposal would preclude any argument for a diaconate or other office that maintains or implies that such an office is a necessary element in the economy of the church or that it represents an indispensable aspect of the one office of the ministry.

4. In its commitment to faith and freedom, unity of purpose and flexibility in form, the Lutheran tradition can offer new hope for constructive progress to the ecumenical movement.

The contemporary ecumenical movement has run aground on the matter of ministry. A number of well wrought, ecumenically courageous initiatives have come to nought on the question. Perhaps the best known of these is the *BEM* proposal of the Faith and Order Commission of the WCC. It proposes a carefully nuanced modern version of the threefold ministry as the norm for all the Christian churches of the world. Particularly with regard to the ministry, however, its reception has been mixed. The Roman Catholic and Lutheran churches in particular have been sharp in their criticism of the document's proposals for the ordering of bishops, presbyters, and deacons.

It can be argued that among Lutherans and Protestants in general, the fundamentally retrospective character of their proposals has sealed the fate of *BEM* and other similar initiatives. It has become increasingly apparent that the path toward the unity of the churches does not point backward through history to a model of ministry and episcopacy that emerged out of a crisis in the ancient church and was elegantly refined in theological terms, if grossly corrupted in practice during the Middle Ages, but rather points forward toward a new sense of mission and an inventive engagement of the Christian tradition with modern culture.

The current impasse in the ecumenical movement presents Lutherans with an unsurpassed opportunity to initiate progress in both mission and ecumenism. It is a moment for Lutherans to abandon their pattern of reacting and responding to proposals on the ministry and instead to create and initiate new ventures in ecumenical progress. It is the genius of Lutheran theology, if it has not always been the practice of the Lutheran churches, to insist in ecumenical conversation on the gospel alone, to bear witness to it faithfully, and to regard all other things as negotiable or *adiaphora*. To put this another way, it is the fundamental mark of the Lutheran theological tradition to distinguish between what is essential to the church and what is inessential. That is not to say that inessential things are insignificant, but only to put them in their proper place.

This suggests that Lutherans might now step boldly forward in the ecumenical arena and bear witness to their priorities, declaring throughout the *oikumene* that it is as dangerous for the churches to say too much about the ministry as it is for them to say too little. Lutherans might make of the present impasse an occasion to invite all Christians to give public assent to that which is most important, the gospel of God's justification of the ungodly by faith alone, and to make all other things secondary. As one step toward this end, the Lutheran churches of the world could quite properly, on the basis of their theology, unilaterally announce their recognition of the ministry of all churches that confess the catholic faith. For Lutherans this would be no more than to act on the conviction that their theology authorizes them to recognize the ministry—the Word of God wherever it is in action—as something of divine doing rather than of human fabrication. This is neither a call for the organic union of the churches nor an attempt to resolve differences in denominational order by ignoring them. It is merely to recognize that where the Word of God has been uttered and the sacraments administered according to the promises of God, there the church has been gathered and a ministry has been at work. Lutherans regard the forms of the office as matters of human convention. Responses to this proposal would no doubt measure the degree to which the churches of the world are truly both evangelical and catholic. It would also be, among other things, to test the conviction that certain forms of the historic episcopate can be understood in evangelical fashion, that is, that they can reflect a conception and practice compatible with the cardinal tenet of evangelical faith and consistent with authentic Christian freedom.

Ecumenical progress is not likely to occur on the basis of proposals to refashion one or another inherited model of the ministry. A genuine breakthrough will more probably occur when Lutherans—or others who join them in taking up task of the reformation of the church—venture to place the gospel and the gospel alone at the center of ecumenical discussion and action. When that happens the ministry, Lutherans confess, will be understood as the work of God in spoken word and administered sacraments. The office of the public ministry will then take a variety of forms in given times and places, and servants will be called to it and other offices in the church to exercise their gifts in a multitude of ways. More importantly, when that happens the church of God will find itself about its proper mission, the propagation of the gospel of the justification of the ungodly by faith alone.

NOTES

1. In addition to von Campenhausen, see as an example, Hans Küng, *The Church*, trans. Ray and Rosaleen Ockenden (New York: Sheed & Ward, 1967).

2. *Die Bekenntnisschriften der evangelisch-lutherischen Kirche Herausgegeben im Gedenkjahr der Augsburgischen Konfession 1530*, 6th ed. (Göttingen: Vandenhoeck & Ruprecht, 1967), 58 n. 1.

3. *The Journals of Henry Melchior Muhlenberg*, eds. Theodore G. Tappert and John W. Doberstein (Philadelphia: Muhlenberg Press, 1942–58), 3:256.

4. Eric W. Gritsch and Robert W. Jenson, *Lutheranism* (Philadelphia: Fortress Press, 1976), 135–36.

5. "The Foundation of the Doctrinal Articles," in *The Book of Concord: or the Symbolical Books of the Evangelical Lutheran Church with Historical, Introduction, Notes, Appendixes and Indexes*, ed. Henry E. Jacobs, 2 vols. (Philadelphia: General Council Publication Board, 1908), 2:71–72.

6. If, for example, ordination is a sacrament in this contained and uniquely Lutheran sense, so also are prayer and marriage, Melanchthon points out. See Ap 13, *BC* 211–14.

7. See "Instructions for the Visitors of Parish Pastors in Electoral Saxony," in *LW* 40:272.

8. *The Living Word: A Theological Study of Preaching and the Church*, trans. Victor C. Pogue (Philadelphia: Muhlenberg Press, 1960), 102 n. 3.

9. This statement may be consulted in "Documents on Church and Altar Fellowship in the Scandinavian Churches," in Vilmos Vajta, ed., *Church in Fellowship: Pulpit and Altar Fellowship Among Lutherans* (Minneapolis: Augsburg Publishing House, 1963), 182–83.